Using REBT With Common Psychological Problems

Joseph Yankura, PhD, is a psychologist in private practice in Merrick, New York. He is also a school psychologist in Long Beach, New York, and an adjunct clinical supervisor for the doctoral program in clinical psychology at the C. W. Post campus of Long Island University. He has coauthored five books with Windy Dryden, including *Daring to Be Myself: A Case Study in Rational-Emotive Therapy*, *Counselling Individuals: A Rational-Emotive Handbook* (2nd ed.), and *Developing Rational-Emotive Behavioral Counselling*. His current interests lie in developing disorder-specific REBT treatment manuals, and in refining cognitive-behavioral treatments for anxiety disorders.

Windy Dryden, PhD, is Professor of Counseling at Goldsmiths College, University of London. He edits 12 book series in the areas of counseling and psychotherapy, and has published over 100 books (including *The Practice of REBT*, coauthored with Albert Ellis). His major interests are in developing the theory and practice of REBT, and in eclecticism and integration in psychotherapy.

Using REBT With Common Psychological Problems

A Therapist's Casebook

Joseph Yankura, PhD
Windy Dryden, PhD
Editors

Springer Publishing Company

Springer Publishing Company, Inc.
536 Broadway
New York, NY 10012-3955

Cover design by *Margaret Dunin*
Acquisition Editor: *Bill Tucker*
Production Editor: *Pamela Lankas*

97 98 99 00 01/5 4 3 2 1

Library of Congress Cataloging-in-Publication Data

Yankura, Joseph.
    Using REBT with common psychological problems: a therapist's casebook / Joseph Yankura, Windy Dryden.
        p.   cm.
    Includes bibliographical references and index.
    ISBN 0-8261-9800-7
    1. Rational-emotive psychotherapy—Case studies.   I. Dryden, Windy.   II. Title.
RC489.R3Y34   1997
616.89'14—dc21   97–14148
                                                                   CIP

Printed in the United States of America

Contents

v

Contributors

Raymond DiGiuseppe, PhD, is Professor of Psychology at St. John's University in New York City, and Director of Professional Education at the Institute for Rational-Emotive Therapy. He has published over 60 journal articles and book chapters, and has coauthored 5 books (including *A Practitioner's Guide to Rational-Emotive Therapy*). His present work is focused on the assessment and treatment of anger problems, and the treatment of externalizing disorders in children and adolescents.

Albert Ellis, PhD, is the creator and primary exponent of rational-emotive behavior therapy. He is President of the Institute for Rational-Emotive Therapy in New York City, and has authored more than 700 articles and over 50 books. His recent books include *Reason and Emotion in Psychotherapy, Revised and Updated* and *Better, Deeper, and More Enduring Brief Therapy.*

Paul A. Hauck, PhD, is a psychologist in private practice in Rock Island, IL. He has authored numerous self-help books, which are noteworthy for their accessibility to the layperson. His titles include *Overcoming Depression, Overcoming Worry and Fear,* and *The Three Faces of Love.*

Patricia McKeegan, PhD, is Assistant Professor of Psychology at the State University of New York, College at Old Westbury. She is also an Adjunct Professor and Clinical Supervisor in the Clinical Psychology Doctoral Program at Long Island University, C. W. Post Campus. She maintains a private practice in Merrick, NY, and has lectured extensively on Attention Deficit Hyperactivity Disorder to both professionals and parents.

Jennifer B. Naidich, MA, is a doctoral candidate in the Clinical/School Psychology program at Hofstra University. She is a staff psychotherapist at the Institute for Rational-Emotive Therapy, and a school psychologist at the Whitestone School for Child Development in New York City.

Mark D. Terjesen, MA, is a doctoral candidate in the Clinical/School Psychology program at Hofstra University. He is a staff psychotherapist at the Institute for Rational-Emotive Therapy, and a school psychologist at the Milestone School in Brooklyn. He is involved in research on assessment and treatment of anger in children and adolescents, and has conducted anger-management workshops based on REBT and behavioral techniques.

Ricks Warren, PhD, is Director of the Anxiety Disorders Clinic and Associate Director of the Pacific Institute for Rational-Emotive Therapy of Lake Oswego, OR. He is also Adjunct Professor at the School of Professional Psychology at Pacific University in Forest Grove, OR. He is coauthor (with George Zgourides, Psy.D.) of *Anxiety Disorders: A Rational-Emotive Perspective.*

CHAPTER 1

Introduction

Joseph Yankura and Windy Dryden

ALBERT ELLIS developed rational emotive behavior therapy (REBT)[1] in the mid-1950s, after becoming dissatisfied with the results he was obtaining with patients in his psychoanalytic practice. He became convinced that psychoanalysis and psychoanalytic psychotherapy were woefully inefficient means for helping patients with the problems that led them to seek treatment, and found that these individuals attained better outcomes when he actively taught them to monitor and modify the dysfunctional cognitions underpinning their disturbance (Yankura & Dryden, 1994). He published preliminary findings on his new method of treatment in a paper entitled "New approaches to psychotherapy techniques" (Ellis, 1955), and

---

[1] Rational emotive behavior therapy (REBT) has undergone several name changes since its initial formulation by Ellis in the mid-1950s. Ellis originally tagged his creation "rational therapy" (RT) in order to highlight its philosophic and cognitive aspects. This name, however, contributed to misunderstandings, as a good number of mental health professionals began to identify RT with 18th-century rationalism and also accused Ellis of ignoring the importance of emotions in human functioning. As such, Ellis renamed his treatment approach "rational-emotive therapy." He changed the name again in 1993 to "rational emotive behavior therapy" in order to underscore the behavioral components of the therapy.

subsequently embarked on a long and fruitful career as REBT's primary theoretician, practitioner, and promoter.

Although Ellis and REBT initially encountered stiff resistance from the established psychotherapeutic community, REBT now stands as one of the most widely practiced forms of cognitive-behavior therapy. Ellis is, in fact, sometimes referred to as the "grandfather of cognitive-behavior therapy." His professional work was formally recognized by the American Psychological Association when he received its Award for Distinguished Professional Contributions to Knowledge in 1985 (*American Psychologist*, 1986).

To date, thousands of mental health practitioners have received training in REBT, and numerous REBT centers and institutes have been established in the United States and abroad. In addition, over the course of the last four decades, a great many books on the theory, practice, and self-help applications of REBT have been published. None of these volumes, however, have comprehensively illustrated (through actual case descriptions) REBT's application to a variety of clinical disorders and special populations.[2] We decided to remedy this situation by producing two casebooks: The first volume (which, of course, you are now reading) deals with common clinical disorders, whereas the second volume deals with special applications of REBT. We believe that these volumes represent a worthwhile contribution to the existing REBT literature, and we hope that they will demonstrate REBT's wide applicability in a form that will be both informative and highly palatable for the reader. Students in training may find it helpful to see REBT "in action," as it is actually implemented by a number of different therapists working with a variety of clients. Readers who are more seasoned practitioners may find the two casebooks useful as a source of ideas for refining their own REBT practice.

It should be noted at this point that the casebooks are not intended to provide a basic introduction to the theory and practice of REBT. Readers wishing for such an introduction are referred to *The Practice of Rational Emotive Behavior Therapy* (Ellis & Dryden, 1997). This book provides a foundation in REBT concepts and techniques, and describes sequenced steps for applying REBT to individuals, groups, and couples.

---

[2] One book, *Growth Through Reason: Verbatim Cases in Rational-Emotive Therapy* (Ellis, 1971), provides seven cases illustrated with a substantial amount of transcript material. The case material presented, however, is not organized according to actual clinical diagnoses or special applications.

Let us now provide you with a chapter-by-chapter preview of the present volume's content. In chapter 2, Ricks Warren describes REBT's application to generalized anxiety disorder (GAD), one of the most common of the anxiety disorders. After reviewing general background material and an REBT conceptualization of GAD, he presents the case of Donna, a married mother of two children in her mid-30s. His therapy with Donna follows the framework offered in the Worry Control Treatment described by Craske, Barlow, and O'Leary (1992), but incorporates emphases and techniques that are distinct to REBT. He quickly identifies approval anxiety as being central to much of Donna's worrying, and also shows her how her shame about her anxiety and worry constitutes a secondary problem. Warren's case example nicely illustrates how REBT can be effectively melded with alternative cognitive-behavioral approaches.

Chapter 3 illustrates REBT's application to depression. Paul Hauck and Patricia McKeegan contrast the cognitive therapy approach to this problem (Beck, Rush, Shaw, & Emery, 1979) with the REBT model, and then show how the latter was effectively used in Hauck's work with Clara, a 52-year-old woman depressed about problems she was experiencing in her third marriage. Hauck's (1973) tripartite REBT model of depressogenic cognitive processes provides a relatively simple (yet effective) means for diagnosing and treating depressed individuals. We have, in fact, found this model quite useful in our own work with clients.

There has been a recent increase in the general public's awareness of and interest in attention deficit/hyperactivity disorder (AD/HD). It is our impression that this heightened awareness has resulted in an increase in the number of children referred to mental health practitioners for this problem. In chapter 4, Patricia McKeegan details her work with Michael, a boy whose AD/HD was first diagnosed in the early years of elementary school. McKeegan's therapy contacts with Michael spanned the midchildhood through midadolescent stages of development, and thus provide an excellent depiction of the manner in which REBT can be tailored to help a child with AD/HD meet the varied challenges of the developmental period. McKeegan begins by providing the eight-year-old Michael with a basic emotional education, and proceeds to teach him to utilize rational self-talk. By 16 years of age, Michael is able to dispute his operative irrational beliefs and has become a much better self-regulator of his thoughts, feelings, and behaviors.

In chapter 5, Joseph Yankura describes the rational emotive behavioral treatment of panic disorder with agoraphobia (PD-A). His chapter provides brief review of current pharmacologic and cognitive-behavioral interventions for this disorder, and emphasizes the advantages of the latter over the former. It next describes the general cognitive-behavioral approach to conceptualization and treatment of PD-A, which is contrasted with the REBT approach. Yankura then presents the case of Angela, a young woman who experienced her first panic attack while an undergraduate in college. Interestingly, Angela had received general cognitive-behavioral treatment prior to beginning REBT, but had derived limited benefits from it. By the end of her treatment with REBT, she had made significant progress with her presenting complaints. Yankura's chapter ends with a call for well-designed studies to test whether REBT's unique aspects augment treatment outcomes for PD-A clients.

Chapter 6, by Mark Terjesen, Raymond DiGiuseppe, and Jennifer Naidich, describes and illustrates the REBT approach to conceptualizing and treating problems with anger and hostility. They report in their introduction that anger problems have received relatively scant attention in the empirical literature, and note that several writers have proposed that specific anger diagnostic categories be added to future editions of the American Psychiatric Association's *Diagnostic and Statistical Manual of Mental Disorders* (DiGiuseppe, Tafrate, & Eckhardt, 1994). Their case description presents Peggy, a young woman seen in treatment by the first and third authors. Peggy experienced significant and recurrent anger problems in her relationship with her boyfriend, and received both individual and couple's therapy. While one of the outcomes of her treatment stands in contrast to relationship goals she expressed at the outset of her therapy, Peggy appears to have made good progress with respect to anger control and assertiveness.

Albert Ellis provides the rational emotive behavioral perspective on treating obsessive-compulsive disorder (OCD) in chapter 7. He gives a comprehensive overview of REBT treatment methods for this debilitating problem, and particularly describes how he applied a number of these methods in his treatment of John, a 32-year-old teacher with OCD. Ellis acknowledges the difficulties that therapists may encounter in trying to help clients who have OCD, but notes that if they themselves have unconditional self-acceptance and high frustration tolerance, they may find working with OCD clients to be a rewarding experience.

In the concluding chapter of this volume, we review a number of features of REBT that make it unique among cognitive-behavioral approaches to psychotherapy. We note that REBT still needs to be submitted to rigorous, systematic empirical tests with respect to its effectiveness with specific clinical disorders, and issue a call for REBT disorder-specific treatment manuals. The production of such manuals would be an important step in facilitating the sort of research that would demonstrate the clinical disorders for which REBT (relative to other psychotherapies) may be the treatment of choice.

We hope that the reader is able to learn from and enjoy this compendium of case studies, and that the second casebook volume, on special applications of REBT, will also be found to be worthwhile reading.

REFERENCES

Awards for Distinguished Professional Contributions: 1985. [Albert Ellis]. *American Psychologist, 41,* 380–397.

Beck, A. T., Rush, A., Shaw, B. F., & Emery, G. (1979). *Cognitive therapy of depression.* New York: Guilford.

Craske, M. G., Barlow, D. H., & O'Leary, T. A. (1992). *Mastery of your anxiety and worry.* Albany, NY: Graywind Publications.

DiGiuseppe, R., Tafrate, R., & Eckhardt, C. (1994). Critical issues in the treatment of anger. *Cognitive and Behavioral Practice, 1,* 111–132.

Ellis, A. (1955). New approaches to psychotherapy techniques. *Journal of Clinical Psychology Monograph Supplement, 11,* 1–53.

Ellis, A. (1971). *Growth through reason: Verbatim cases in rational-emotive therapy.* Palo Alto, CA: Science and Behavior Books.

Ellis, A., & Dryden, W. (1997). *The practice of rational emotive behavior therapy.* New York: Springer Publishing Co.

Hauck, P. A. (1973). *Overcoming depression.* Philadelphia: Westminster Press.

Yankura, J., & Dryden, W. (1994). *Albert Ellis.* London: Sage.

CHAPTER 2

REBT and Generalized Anxiety Disorder

Ricks Warren

IF YOUR CLIENT characterizes him or herself as a worrier, answers "yes" to the question, "Do you worry excessively about minor things?" and reports spending over 50% of his or her waking hours worrying, the odds are good that your client is suffering from generalized anxiety disorder (GAD; Brown, O'Leary, & Barlow, 1993).

Interestingly, professional views of GAD have shifted from a DSM-III (American Psychiatric Association, 1980) residual "wastebasket" anxiety-disorder category (Rapee, 1991b), to be assigned only when criteria for another anxiety disorder had not been met, to being "the basic anxiety disorder" in DSM-IV (American Psychiatric Association, 1994). Associated with this most recent view of GAD is the conceptualization of worry, that is, anxious apprehension, as the fundamental process in all anxiety disorders (Barlow, 1988):

> Anxious apprehension is defined as a future-oriented mood state in which one becomes ready or prepared to cope with upcoming negative events. Anxious apprehension is associated with a state of high negative affect and chronic overarousal, a sense of uncontrollability, and an attentional focus on threat-related stimuli (e.g., high self-focused attention or self-preoccupation and hypervigilance). Whereas the process of anxious apprehension is considered

to be present in all anxiety disorders, the content (focus) of anxious apprehension varies from disorder to disorder. (Brown et al., 1993, p. 139)

Thus, as examples, panic-disorder clients worry about future panic attacks, socially phobic clients worry about disapproval and embarrassment, and clients with obsessive-compulsive disorder (OCD) worry about contamination or being responsible for harm.

Recent research on the nature of normal versus pathological worry has contributed greatly to our understanding of GAD. Although both GAD clients and nonanxious controls worry about similar matters, for example, family, money, work, and illness (Sanderson & Barlow, 1990), clients with GAD worry more often and about more things, view their worries as less realistic and, perhaps most importantly, experience their worry as uncontrollable.

PREVALENCE, ONSET, AND AGE AT PRESENTATION

Typically, GAD clients report a gradual development of their condition, either dating back to their mid-teens or having been present as long as they can remember (Rapee, 1991a). Accordingly, some authorities have suggested that persons with GAD may view their worry as part of their personality (i.e., ego syntonic), given its long history (Brown et al., 1993), and others have recently conceptualized GAD as a form of personality disorder (Sanderson & Wetzler, 1991).

In contrast to a relatively high prevalence in the general population, only about 10% of clients presenting to anxiety clinics receive a primary diagnosis of GAD (Barlow, 1988). GAD clients typically seek treatment in their late 30's, on the average, around 25 years later than the onset of their condition (Rapee, 1991a).

Though survey results vary, the prevalence of GAD in the general population appears to be about 4% (Barlow, 1988), making GAD one of the most common anxiety disorders. In addition, evidence suggests that GAD is the most frequently assigned additional diagnosis for clients with another principal anxiety disorder diagnosis (Sanderson, DiNardo, Rapee, & Barlow, 1990, cited in Brown & Barlow, 1992).

The presence of generalized anxiety per se is common, not only throughout the anxiety and affective disorders, but is also considered an important aspect of all psychopathology (Sanderson & Wetzler, 1991), and a common problem in the general population

(Shepard, Cooper, Brown, & Halton, 1966, cited in Barlow, 1988). In fact, generalized anxiety has been estimated to be present in 40–50% of patients seeking primary health care (e.g. Dunn, 1983, cited in Barlow, 1988).

COMORBIDITY

The majority of clients with a principal diagnosis of GAD receive comorbid diagnoses, most often social or specific phobias. In addition, one study found that 50% of GAD clients received an additional Axis II personality disorder, most frequently avoidant, dependent, and not otherwise specified (NOS) (Sanderson & Beck, 1990, cited in Sanderson & Wetzler, 1991). Other studies have reported personality disorder comorbidity rates ranging from 32% to 50% (Sanderson, Beck, & McGinn, 1994; Sanderson, Wetzler, Beck, & Betz, 1994; Shadick & Borkovec, 1991).

THEORETICAL MODELS

Barlow's (1988) model of the development and maintenance of GAD is fundamentally related to the concept of anxious apprehension described above. To briefly summarize: Owing to both biological and psychological vulnerabilities, individuals respond with intense neurobiological reactions to certain negative stressful life events. Hypothesized childhood experiences, in which significant events were perceived as unpredictable and/or uncontrollable, sensitize individuals to perceiving current life events as unpredictable and/or uncontrollable. One's perceived inability to cope with these events, as well as the worry process itself, leads to further heightened arousal. Hypervigilance and associated narrowing of attention on the focus of one's worries further increases arousal and may eventually impair performance in the various life spheres (e.g. work, interpersonal relations).

Borkovec and his colleagues (e.g., Borkovec, 1985; Borkovec, Shadick, & Hopkins, 1991) emphasize the cognitive avoidance function that worry may play. "The most exciting possibility emerging from recent research is that worry may be directly, immediately, and negatively reinforced by the avoidance of imagery, and therefore . . . of peripheral physiological activation. GAD clients fear negative somatic arousal and affect" (Borkovec et al., 1991, p. 44). Thus, according to Borkovec and his colleagues, worry may serve a purpose, which is to avoid imagining feared events and the resulting arousal. Though the discomfort associated with worry is unpleasant, the discomfort associated with imagery, and the arousal it generates, may be perceived as even more aversive. Borkovec et al. (1991) further suggest that worry becomes uncontrollable because of the immediate negative reinforcement by its suppression of somatic anxiety. Consistent with this view is research demonstrating that GAD clients respond to psychological stress with autonomic inflexibility, that is, decreased variability in autonomic responses such as heart rate. Apparently GAD is associated with the shutting down of affect while worrisome imagery activates it. Further, muscle tension discriminates between GAD and most other anxiety disorder clients and normal controls. Interestingly, DSM-IV (APA, 1994) physical-symptom criteria reflect this pattern of responding. Thus, in contrast to the other anxiety disorders where autonomic arousal is a salient feature, GAD is uniquely characterized by muscle tension.

In addition, this avoidance of fear imagery prevents full accessing and modification of fear structures in long-term memory, contributing to the maintenance of GAD. Also, worry involves brief, interrupted exposures to fear-related stimuli, which may result in incubation, that is, increase in fear, whereas more continuous exposure (via imagery) would result in habituation and decreases in fear.

Rapee (1991a, 1991b) has reviewed research investigating information processing models of GAD centering around constructs involving perception of personal threat and low perceived control over threat. Rapee (1991a, 1991b) reminds us that generalized anxiety is a personality trait present in all individuals to some degree. Similar to Barlow (1988), Rapee hypothesizes that early experiences with uncontrollability may interact with general or trait anxiety in the development of GAD. In terms of maintenance of GAD, Rapee (1991b) has reviewed evidence from studies demonstrating biases in information processing. Perceptions of threat (e.g., Beck, Emery, & Greenberg, 1985, cited in Rapee, 1991a, 1991b) and perceptions of control (e.g., Lazarus, 1966, cited in Rapee, 1991b) have been the major areas of study.

As an example of work in this area, Butler and Mathews (1983) found that anxiety patients, compared with depressives and normals, were more likely to interpret ambiguous information as threatening, overestimated the probability of personally experiencing threatening events, and rated the negative events as more costly.

Though earlier life experiences involving perception of unpredictability and uncontrollability of aversive events seem plausible as developmental vulnerability factors for the later development of GAD, little relevant evidence for these events has been obtained. However, work in this area is currently under way. For example, Roemer, Borkovec, Posa, and Lyonfields (1991) presented evidence that college students meeting GAD criteria (compared with their nonanxious counterparts) recall relationships with primary care givers characterized by rejection and fear of abandonment. These findings appear consistent with Borkovec et al.'s (1991) hypothesis that "chronic worriers may have a history of aversive events associated with other people, especially events having to do with emotional expression, the potential loss of love or approval" (p. 47).

TREATMENT

The majority of studies evaluating cognitive-behavior therapy (CBT) for GAD have found various forms of CBT (usually relaxation, cognitive therapy, anxiety management training, or various combinations of these procedures) to be more effective than no treatment. In addition, improvement is typically maintained at follow-up, and anxiolytic medication usage usually decreases significantly. Unfortunately, the magnitude of gains has been modest, and findings of clear-cut superiority of one form of CBT over another have been rare. See Brown et al. (1993) for a more detailed review of relevant studies reporting the above findings.

Experts in the field of GAD and its treatment propose that the modest improvements and lack of superiority of one CBT treatment over another resulted from the fact, until recently, treatments were not precisely tailored to the fundamental aspect of GAD, that is, uncontrollable worry (Borkovec & Costello, 1993; Brown et al., 1993). The most effective CBT treatments developed thus far appear to be anxiety management (Butler, Cullington, Hibbert, Klimes, & Gelder, 1987; Butler, Fennell, Robson, & Gelder, 1991) and applied relaxation and coping desensitization (Borkovec & Costello, 1993). The effectiveness of these CBT treatments suggests the importance of treatment including, in addition to familiar cognitive and relaxation skills, exposure to avoided activities, increasing self-confidence and enjoyable activities, and combating demoralization (Butler & Booth, 1991).

A new treatment protocol for GAD has been recently developed by Barlow and his colleagues. Although only initial outcome data are yet available, this treatment package appears quite promising, as it incorporates procedures targeting each of the core features of GAD (relaxation, cognitive restructuring, worry exposure, and worry behavior prevention). See Brown et al. (1993) for a detailed description of treatment; Zinbarg, Craske, and Barlow (1993) for a therapist's guide; and Craske, Barlow and O'Leary (1992) for a client manual.

DIAGNOSIS AND ASSESSMENT

Table 2.1 presents DSM-IV criteria for GAD. Several changes from the DSM-III-R (American Psychiatric Association, 1987) are consistent with the description and conceptualization of GAD presented above. The requirement of two or more spheres of worry has been changed to the requirement that worry be excessive, focused on a number of events or activities, and be perceived as difficult to control. In addition, rather than having to experience 6 of 18 physical symptoms, (e.g., restlessness, dry mouth) as in DSM-III-R (APA, 1987), clients must only report three of six physical symptoms to meet DSM-IV (APA, 1994) criteria. These six items are from the Motor Tension and Vigilance and Scanning clusters of DSM-III (APA, 1980) with the autonomic hyperactivity symptoms having been eliminated. These physical symptom changes are a direct result of empirical findings on symptoms that best discriminate GAD patients from patients with other anxiety disorders. As noted above, these symptoms are consistent with recent theoretical reviews of the function of worry in GAD (Borkovec et al., 1991).

Historically, the diagnostic reliability of GAD has been lower relative to the other anxiety disorders. Brown et al. (1993) discuss likely factors that may have contributed to this lower reliability and offer suggestions to enhance the clinician's diagnosis of GAD.

1. In looking for the presence of physical symptoms, determine whether the reported symptom is associated with worry or a coexisting condition such as panic disorder. For example, does difficulty

Table 2.1 Diagnostic Criteria for 300.02 Generalized Anxiety Disorder
(*DSM-IV*)

A.   Excessive anxiety and worry (apprehensive expectation), occurring more days than not for at least six months, about a number of events or activities (such as work or school performance).
B.   The person finds it difficult to control the worry.
C.   The anxiety and worry are associated with three (or more) of the following six symptoms (with at least some of the symptoms present for more days than not for the past 6 months). *Note*: Only one item is required in children.

   1. Restlessness or feeling keyed up or on edge;
   2. Being easily fatigued;
   3. Difficulty concentrating or mind going blank;
   4. Irritability;
   5. Muscle tension;
   6. Sleep disturbance (difficulty falling or staying asleep, or restless unsatisfying sleep).

D.   The focus of the anxiety and worry is not confined to features of an Axis I disorder, for example, the anxiety or worry is not about having a panic attack (as in panic disorder), being embarrassed in public (as in social phobia), being contaminated (as in obsessive-compulsive disorder), being away from home or close relatives (as in separation anxiety disorder), gaining weight (as in anorexia nervosa), having multiple physical complaints (as in somatization disorder), or having a serious illness (as in hypochondriasis), and the anxiety and worry do not occur exclusively during posttraumatic stress disorder.
E.   The anxiety, worry, or physical symptoms cause clinically significant distress or impairment in social, occupational, or other important areas of functioning.
F.   The disturbance is not due to the direct physiological effects of a substance (e.g., a drug of abuse, a medication) or a general medical condition (e.g., hyperthyroidism) and does not occur exclusively during a mood disorder, a psychotic disorder, or a pervasive developmental disorder.

From American Psychiatric Association: *Diagnostic and Statistical Manual of Mental Disorders, Fourth Edition.* Washington, DC: American Psychiatric Association, 1994, pp. 435–436. Reprinted with permission.

concentrating occur during worry about potential loss of job or only occur during panic attacks?

2. Ascertain whether the client worries about minor events. As noted above, this type of worry is highly associated with GAD in comparison to other anxiety disorders.

3. In determining whether the client's worries are excessive and uncontrollable, Brown et al. (1993, p. 152) recommend asking the following five questions:

- Do you find it very difficult to stop worrying or, if you need to focus on something else, are you able to successfully put the worry out of your mind?
- Do you find that, if you are attempting to focus on something like reading, working, or watching television, these worries often pop into your mind making it difficult to concentrate on these tasks?
- Do you worry about things that you recognize other people do not worry about?
- When things are going well, do you still find things to be worried and anxious about?
- Does your worry rarely result in your reaching a solution for the problem that you are worrying about?

4. Assess for comorbid conditions, as they may exert a significant influence on treatment outcome (Brown & Barlow, 1992). For example, Barlow et al. (1992) found that depression was associated with a less favorable response to CBT.

5. Conduct a brief medical history and encourage clients to schedule a physical exam if it has been over 2 years since the client's most recent check-up.

6. Evaluate for drug and alcohol intake, as use of or withdrawal from certain substances may produce GAD-like symptoms.

In the most recent well-controlled GAD treatment studies (e.g., Borkovec & Costello, 1993), the Anxiety Disorders Interview Schedule–Revised (ADIS-R; DiNardo & Barlow, 1988) has been the structured clinical interview used to diagnose GAD. It is recommended that clinicians administer at least portions of the ADIS-R to assist in anxiety disorder differential diagnosis.

A number of questionnaires that may be quite useful for clinicians have been used in assessment of GAD. A particularly helpful inventory is the 16-item Penn State Worry Questionnaire (PSWQ) developed by Borkovec and his colleagues (Meyer, Miller, Metzger, & Borkovec, 1990). The PSWQ is a reliable and valid measure of the trait of worry that discriminates between clients with GAD and those with other anxiety disorders. The State-Trait Anxiety Inventory–Trait Anxiety subscale (STAI; Spielberger, Gorsuch, & Lushene, 1970) is a widely used measure of degree of trait anxiety. Similarly, the Eysenck Personality Questionnaire–Neuroticism Scale (EPQ-N; Eysenck & Eysenck, 1975) is a good measure of the trait of neuroticism or emotionality, which is highly correlated with anxiety. The Beck Anxiety Inventory is particularly useful in differentiating clinical anxiety and depression (BAI; Beck, Epstein, Brown, & Steer, 1988), and the Beck Depression Inventory (BDI; Beck, Ward, Mendelsohn, Mock, & Erbaugh, 1961) is frequently used to assess level of depression.

Two other, less well-known questionnaires are recommended by Barlow and his colleagues (Brown et al., 1993) in the assessment of GAD patients. The Reactions to Relaxation and Arousal Question-naire (RRAQ; Heide & Borkovec, 1983) measures fear of relaxation, and the Depression, Anxiety and Stress Scale (DASS; Lovibond & Lovibond, 1992) measures the presence of tension. The stress (tension) subscale of the DASS has proved useful in differentiating GAD clients from clients with other anxiety disorders (except for OCD), and has significantly correlated with the PSWQ (Brown et al., 1993).

Finally, self-monitoring devices, such as the Weekly Record of Anxiety and Depression (see Brown et al., 1993, for an illustration of this form) are useful for assessment and ongoing monitoring of treatment interventions. In addition to monitoring daily levels of anxiety, depression, and pleasantness on a 0–8-point scale, clients can also report the percentage of the day (0–100%) they spent worrying.

RATIONAL EMOTIVE BEHAVIOR THERAPY CONCEPTUALIZATION OF GAD

As indicated earlier, anxious clients are characterized by cognitive bias, that is, compared with nonanxious persons, clients with anxiety disorders are more likely to (a) interpret ambiguous information as threatening, (b) overestimate the probability of the occurrence of potentially dangerous events, and (c) rate the feared events as more aversive or costly (Butler & Mathews, 1983). Ellis (1980) hypoth-esizes that this cognitive bias results from more basic underlying "musturbatory" ideologies. Awfulizing and negative rating of self and others are viewed by Ellis as derivatives of the primary musts. These evaluative beliefs are typically brought to bear on life events related to performance, approval, and discomfort. Ego and discomfort dis-turbances are the emotional consequences (Warren & Zgourides, 1991).

In the case of GAD, REBT theory would hypothesize that GAD clients worry about family or money matters, for example, because they believe certain problems "must not occur, and it is terrible and unbearable if they do" (Ellis, 1987), and that the "inability to cope with such problems and beliefs is evidence of lowered self-worth" (Warren & Zgourides, 1991, p. 174).

Interestingly, Borkovec et al. (1991) have offered theoretical speculations related to issues of approval and self-worth that are consistent with aspects of the proposed REBT model as developed below. For example:

> The combination of social fear in worry, fear and avoidance of somatic anxiety, and the social origins of thought suggests that chronic worriers may have a history of aversive events associated with other people, especially events having to do with emotional expression, the potential loss of love or approval. (p. 47)

In addition, Borkovec et al. (1991) note that "degree of worry correlates most highly with social evaluative fears (e.g., fears of criticism, fear of making mistakes)" (p. 47). These authors also note that such social-evaluative fears "guarantee that many life circumstances can pose threats to the adequacy of one's anticipated performances, circumstances, and self-concept" (p. 47). In a related vein, in the Penn State GAD Project (cited in Borkovec et al., 1991), the miscellaneous category of worries most frequently contained topics related to self-worth.

Finally Shadick, Roemer, Hopkins, and Borkovec (1991) have suggested that it might be profitable not only to categorize worry into global-content spheres (e.g. finances), but also to investigate common themes that may underlie various worries.

> A client may report being worried about "Finances," but whether this worry is a function of fears of insufficient funds, or fears of anticipated spouse anger over mismanagement of funds, or both, would not be revealed without further, systematic interviewing.... Further research might usefully employ catastrophizing questions. ("What is worrisome about that? ..., and if that happened, what would be worrisome about that?") in an effort to identify the specific underlying fears of any general worry topic. (p. 3)

REBT readers will recognize this approach as inference chaining (Dryden & Yankura, 1993), and as what Burns (1980) has termed the *vertical arrow technique.*

Before leaving the REBT conceptualization of GAD, it should also be noted that, consistent with Barlow (1988) and Eysenck's (1967) concept of neuroticism, REBT theory hypothesizes that biological factors (i.e., a labile, overactive autonomic nervous system) are vulnerability factors in the development of GAD (and other anxiety disorders). REBT would further hypothesize that

> such biologically vulnerable individuals more easily develop irrational beliefs that are activated by stressful life events and then brought to bear on life's problems. Irrational beliefs and thinking styles subsequently create emotional distress (e.g., anxiety, depression) that interfere with rather than facilitate problem-solving. As this process continues, the GAD client further worries about worrying and its debilitative effects, which may also lead to feelings of being out of control and unable to cope, as well as damage to one's physical health. (Warren & Zgourides, 1991, p. 174)

Warren and Zgourides (1991) also hypothesized that GAD clients may hold various misconceptions about worrying which may be important in the initiation and maintenance of the worry process. The following are examples of such misconceptions:

1. If there is a possibility something dangerous might happen, I should worry. It's the responsible thing to do.
2. Worrying may ward off danger.
3. It's better to be prepared and hypervigilant for danger than to suffer the discomfort of being hit by surprise.

Initial research supports the presence of similar worry-related beliefs. For example, Roemer et al. (1991) provided evidence that worriers, compared with nonworriers, more often believe that worry may make bad things less likely to happen. Roemer et al. (1991) also found that worriers tend to believe that worry is a way to distract self from more unpleasant emotions, and that worry facilitates problem solving.

Consistent with Borkovec's theory that worry may facilitate the avoidance of aversive somatic states, REBT would postulate that discomfort anxiety (DA) would underlie this avoidance process. This may be similar to Warren and Zgourides (1991) proposal that the avoidance of intrusive thoughts and images associated with traumatic events may be due to attempts to avoid the discomfort inflicted by these cognitive events, and thereby contribute to the development and/or maintenance of posttraumatic stress disorder (PTSD). Further, the finding that it is common for GAD clients to avoid situations or activities that relate to their worry (e.g., a person who worries about finances may avoid balancing the checkbook) would also be considered as related to DA.

REBT ASSESSMENT

I recommend that REBT practitioners use many of the same assessment devices reviewed above. As Brown et al. (1993) recommend, portions of the ADIS-R (DiNardo & Barlow, 1988) provide useful questions for establishing the GAD diagnosis. The PSWQ (Meyer et al., 1990) is also useful diagnostically and as an outcome measure. The BDI (Beck et al., 1961) is useful in assessing level of depression and as another outcome measure. The General Attitude and Belief Scale (Bernard, 1990), a comprehensive scale, and the Belief Scale (Malouf & Schutte, 1986), a briefer scale, are useful measures of irrational beliefs potentially related to GAD problems.

PREVIOUS REBT TREATMENT STUDIES

I am not aware of controlled studies testing REBT with DSM-III (APA, 1980) or DSM-III-R (APA, 1987) diagnosed GAD. Several studies have evaluated the effect of REBT on generalized anxiety, however. REBT reduced trait anxiety in community mental health clinic clients (Lipsky, Kassinove, & Miller, 1980), and rational-restructuring was superior to self-control desensitization and progressive relaxation in reducing chronic worry in community volunteers (Robinson, 1989).

CASE ILLUSTRATION

Donna, a 36-year-old married mother of two children (an 8-year-old boy and a 6-year-old girl) was referred to the Anxiety Disorders Clinic by her primary-care physician. After learning about her complaints of anxiety, Donna's physician had discussed with her the option of trying a benzodiazepine on a short-term basis, but Donna worried that she might "get hooked on the pills," as had her friend Jill. Donna reported that she and her husband had moved to Oregon about 8 months ago, because of her husband's job relocation. Donna indicated that she had received brief marital counseling 2 years earlier, and that the marriage was currently stable. Donna was currently working part-time, developing her medical transcription business.

The following REBT treatment follows closely the worry-control treatment developed by Craske et al. (1992). I recommend that REBT practitioners familiarize themselves with this protocol, as it appears to be among the most effective of the recently developed CBT treatments for GAD.

Session 1

During the first session, I obtained the above information, then went on to clarify the client's reason for seeking treatment, and conducted the clinical interview to establish the diagnosis.

T: Well, Donna, if I recall correctly, you said on the phone that your physician referred you to me because you were anxious all the time. What I would like to do today is to find out a lot more about your anxiety and then try to end the session by giving you my opinions about your situation. If we have time I'll go over the kinds of things I would recommend for treatment. How does that sound?

C: Fine, I guess. I don't know why I'm so anxious. I've always been somewhat anxious, but it seems like it's getting worse. I feel like I'm losing it.

T: Sounds like you're really feeling overwhelmed, maybe a bit scared that you won't be able to cope if things don't get better.

C: Right, I feel sort of out of control. It's really hard to concentrate, and my sleeping is getting worse.

T: So your concentration and sleeping aren't good. Let me ask you about some other physical symptoms that often go along with anxiety.

(At this point, I had planned to move toward asking about what kinds of things Donna was anxious about, but since she mentioned some physical symptoms, I decided to pursue those for a while.)

C: The main thing is that I feel tight, or tense. My neck and shoulders hurt all the time. It seems like I can never relax. I feel agitated a lot. By the end of the day I'm exhausted.

T: What about your heart beating really fast, or feeling a sudden surge of fear?

C: Do you mean anxiety attacks? I've had a few of those a long time ago, but not recently.

As Donna is reporting the kinds of physical symptoms characteristic of GAD clients, my hypothesis is that this may turn out to be her diagnosis. I also want to check out the presence of depression, and then start checking out worry.

T: Donna, what about depression? Have you ever considered yourself depressed?

C: Well, I'm probably depressed now, but not like I was 2 years ago when my marriage looked like it was on the rocks. I could hardly get out of bed then. But now my mood isn't so good, and I don't seem to enjoy things as much as I think I should, but I wouldn't say I'm depressed.

T: Okay, we're nearing the end of the session. I'll give you some questionnaires to fill out. One will be a depression inventory. We'll see how that looks. But for now, I'd like to find out more about your anxiety. Can you tell me what you're anxious about? Does it stay at about the same level all the time, or does it vary depending on the situation?

C: Well, I'm sort of anxious most of the time, but it gets worse when I have to deal with different things.

T: Often times when people feel anxious a lot of the time, it's because they worry a lot. Would you consider yourself a worrier?

C: Definitely. I've always been a worrier. My mother tells me that when I was a child I worried about something bad happening to her. I remember crying in grade school when I couldn't get my homework just perfect. I'm also somewhat of a perfectionist, I guess.

T: Donna, let me ask you this—what percent of your waking hours would you say you spend worrying?

C: Gosh, 100%! No, let me think . . . I'd say, maybe 70%. It's really getting out of hand.

T: No wonder you find it hard to concentrate. It's probably hard to turn your mind off to get to sleep, too?

C: Right. At night in bed, I seem to rehash all my worries of the day. When I wake up in the middle of the night, I really worry! Everything seems more terrible then, and sometimes I worry about the dumbest things!

T: Like what? What worries seem dumb?

Here, I'm looking for whether Donna worries about "minor matters," another potential piece of evidence to support a GAD diagnosis.

C: Well, I worry about whether I said something that hurt someone's feelings. I worry about what if I'm late to an appointment the next day.

T: It seems like it's always worse at night.

C: Right, but I worry about these same kinds of things during the day.

T: What else do you worry about during the day?

C: (Starts to cry.) I'm really worried my husband will get laid off after we moved all this way from the east coast. There's been talk of downsizing. They never told us that when he took the job.

This line of inquiry continued, and revealed additional worries related to (a) her son's not getting along with other kids at achool, (b) failing at her medical transcription business, and (c) whether her lawn looked good enough for their neighborhood. While social evaluative concerns appeared significant, Donna did not appear to meet full criteria for social phobia. She did, however, appear to meet criteria for dysthymia.

As the session neared the end, I wanted to stop in time to give Donna feedback on my diagnostic impressions, discuss treatment recommendations, and explain the first homework assignment.

T: Donna, before we run out of time, let me give you my impressions about your anxiety. It sounds to me like you may have an anxiety disorder called generalized anxiety disorder, or GAD. Basically, this is the "worry wart" disorder. The main problem with GAD is excessive worry that's hard to control. The physical symptoms seem to result from worrying so much. But it's kind of a vicious cycle. When you feel tense and agitated, that's fertile ground for worry. I think your depression is related. When your mind is focused on the potential of so many negative things happening, it's pretty hard to be in a good mood or to focus on enjoyable activities.

C: Wow, I'm a mess, aren't I? I'm really a basket case.

T: You probably feel like one. Would you like to hear some ideas about what I think would be helpful to get control of your worry and feel less anxious?

C: Anything that will help.

T: Well, I would estimate that we would need to get together around 12 to 15 sessions, maybe less, maybe more. There are several things that I think would help. One, I can teach you some relaxation skills to help control your muscle tension and restlessness. That could even help with your sleep. Two, we'll work on how to actually control your worrying thoughts; and three, we'll figure out ways to change your behavior so that you don't avoid things as much, and can go at things less perfectionistically. That's just a nutshell summary. We'll go into more as we go along.

Donna agreed to give counseling a try, though she expressed some fear that therapy seemed like one more big thing that she would have to do. At the same time, she reported feeling relieved that we had broken her anxiety down into component parts, that I understood her situation, and that there was a plan to make things better.

Donna was given the PSWQ, BDI, STAI, BDI, and the Weekly Record of Anxiety and Depression for daily self-monitoring of her anxiety, depression, pleasant feelings, and percentage of the day spent worrying.

Session 2

I started this session by asking Donna if she had any reaction to our first session that she wanted to discuss, and if she had any questions about treatment. Next, she gave me her questionnaires and we went over her self-monitoring forms. She was quite compliant in keeping her data, and I reinforced her accordingly, emphasizing the importance of her being an active participant in her therapy, both in and outside of sessions.

Donna obtained a PSWQ score of 65, a BDI score of 19, and a STAI score of 58. These scores are in the range of scores typically obtained by GAD clients, suggesting significant problems with chronic worry, moderate depression, and high general anxiety (80th percentile).

C: I guess I should tell you, I really have mixed feelings about therapy. I feel hopeful that you can help me deal with my worries, but this week I really became aware of how much I worry. I guess I've been feeling sort of inadequate, or bad about myself—I should be able to knock it off. My husband keeps telling me not to worry, and I just can't control it. When I'm around him and other people that seem so together, I feel shame, I guess, that I have an anxiety disorder.

T: Donna, unfortunately what you're describing is very common. In a sense, you have a problem of worrying, and then a secondary problem about your worry and anxiety—feeling down on yourself—the shame about having the original worry and anxiety problem.

C: I told you I was a mess!

T: We call this two problems for the price of one.

C: Great.

T: What I would suggest we do today is talk some more about the model of worry and anxiety that we'll be operating from, and then start looking at some ways to help you be more accepting of yourself with your worry and anxiety while we work to overcome it.

My hypothesis at this point is that some more education about GAD will help Donna begin to see hope for gaining control over her worry and anxiety. Also, I am hoping it will facilitate her ability to view what may currently seem like a global sense of dysphoria as a number of specific problems for which solutions can be obtained. This "divide-and-conquer" approach may thus foster an increased sense of self-efficacy, in that she can solve one problem at a time. I am also predicting that, by working initially on the secondary problem of shame and lack of self-acceptance, she will be learning ways of getting at irrational beliefs that probably underlie her worrying, that is, musts, awfulizing, and self-downing about performance and approval issues. As Yankura and Dryden (1990) have stated:

> After clients are somewhat freed from the extra stress produced by negative self-evaluations, they are able to stop questioning their worth and competence. This, in turn, allows them to more fully face their primary problems and more effectively dispute their irrational beliefs. (p. 32)

T: How about if we review the nature of worry and anxiety now? What I would like you to do is to close your eyes for a moment and begin to worry about, let's say, being late for an appointment. As you focus on the worry, what do you feel in your body?

C: I feel my shoulders and neck tightening. I'm also beginning to feel anxious and kind of down.

T: Let's suppose you imagine that you're on your way to your appointment as you worry about being late. What's your driving like?

C: I'm starting to go too fast, getting too close to the car in front of me. I'm worried that the doctor will think badly of me if I'm late.

T: Okay, Donna, go ahead and open your eyes.

C: That wasn't much fun. That's the story of my life.

T: All too familiar, huh? Well, what I wanted us to look at is the nature of worry and anxiety, and to break it down into several components. First, we had the worry thoughts, right? Then your body tensed up and you imagined yourself hurrying to prevent being late. So there we have the thoughts, physical symptoms, and related behaviors. All of this, in a sense, makes up the emotion of anxiety. Does that make sense?

C: I guess. I never really analyzed how it's all connected.

T: In my experience, if we can break down the worry process as
     we just did, we can teach you ways to address each of these
     components. For example, we can challenge the idea that you
     will be late and how awful it would be if you were. We can use
     relaxation skills to reduce the muscle tension and help you to
     deliberately slow down your behavior and not hurry to pre-
     vent the lateness. It turns out that changing any one aspect of
     the process helps change the others, but to give you the most
     power, we'll help you deal with all three components. Now,
     does that make sense?

C: I think so.

T: The other concept that's important here is that worry and
     anxiety are related to perceiving situations as dangerous, ei-
     ther physically or psychologically. When we view an event as
     dangerous, we become vigilant, looking for signs of danger,
     and our body prepares for action.

C: What's dangerous about being late?

T: Well, think about it. You said before that you worried the
     doctor would think badly of you if you were late. Could this
     be the danger? In other words, a threat to your sense of
     self-worth.

C: Maybe. I see what you mean. I never thought of it as danger,
     but I do worry about other people's approval.

T: Right. We usually think of danger as relating to physical dan-
     ger, but our bodies react in the same way when we perceive
     emotional danger. Your body tenses up and your focus nar-
     rows while your behavior speeds up to help protect you from
     the "danger." This, of course, is adaptive when you're in a
     truly dangerous situation, but in your case, you are geared up
     for a possible event that, by itself, is not really dangerous to
     your physical well-being.

C: I guess that's why I'm tired so often. I'm constantly in a state
     of emergency. Everything seems so dangerous, as you put it.

T: Exactly! How about trying to put into your own words what
     I've been trying to explain.

Here, since I'm rather didactic, I want to get Donna more involved in processing the information I've presented, as well as check out whether she grasps the concepts presented. After doing this, I move on to the issue of dealing with her shame about having problems with worry and anxiety.

T: In the time that's left, let's start talking about how you put yourself down about having worry and anxiety problems. First of all, do you see any benefit of downing yourself for being anxious? Does it help motivate you to work on your problem?

C: Not really. I just get bogged down further and feel worse. I've been told my standards are too high, that I'm my own worst enemy.

T: Well, since there doesn't seem to be any benefit in the shame and putting yourself down, would you like to work on being more accepting of yourself?

C: Sure. Can people change the way they feel about themselves?

T: Actually, yes, by changing their thinking. For example, when you feel shame about your anxiety problem, what thoughts do you have about yourself?

C: Well, I feel inferior to people who aren't anxious, people that are more easy-going. And I feel like I should be more normal like they are.

T: Okay, so basically it sounds like you're telling yourself two things: One, I shouldn't have an anxiety problem, and two, since I do, I'm less of a person, inferior to other less anxious people.

C: You got it.

T: So, it's actually these thoughts that cause the shame and feelings of inferiority. Somebody else might think, gee, I wish I didn't have these problems, but I do. That does not make me an inferior person, just a human being. Nobody's perfect.

C: Yeah, but I don't think that way.

T: I know, but if you did think that way and really believed those thoughts, do you think you would feel the shame?

C: I guess not.

T: Well, we'll work on learning to think that way so you'll get better at accepting yourself. My guess, too, is that then we'll actually help you worry less if some of your worries are tied up with things that threaten your sense of self-worth.

This session covered a lot of ground, and was largely didactic. As such, I decided that in future sessions I would try to use more socratic questioning as I helped Donna explore her basic beliefs that drive her worry and anxiety. For homework, I gave Donna a copy of *You Can Change How You Feel* (Kranzler, 1975). I asked her to read it and to write out an ABCDE sequence related to feeling ashamed and inferior due to her having an anxiety disorder.

Session 3

This session was spent reviewing Donna's reaction to *You Can Change How You Feel* and going over her ABCDE exercise. She found the book useful, though she wondered if she could actually change her old, engrained ways of thinking.

The remainder of the session was spent making a progressive muscle relaxation tape for Donna. I explained to her the rationale that learning a relaxation skill often helps clients to be able to more successfully change their worried thinking, and that it might give her a tool to increase her sense of control.

Donna's homework assignment was to practice with the tape once a day.

Session 4

Following a review of Donna's relaxation practice, I suggested that we spend the majority of the session exploring one of Donna's main worries. Donna chose the worry that her husband would spend their money unwisely.

T: Okay, Donna, let's look at this worry about what would be the worst thing about your husband spending too much money. What would that mean to you?

C: Well, we might have to sell our house.

T: And if that happened, what would you do?

C: Well, I don't know. I've never thought it through.

T: Well, let's think it through now. What would you do if you had to sell your house?

C: Well, I guess we would have to find a smaller house in a neighborhood not as nice as ours.

T: Are you worried about how it would affect your kids?

C: Well, sure. I would hate for them to have to move again, change schools, and Michael [Donna's 8-year-old son] already has trouble making friends.

T: So, one bad thing about moving to a smaller home would be the effect on the kids. Sounds like you're not really worried you'll be out on the street, homeless.

C: No, I don't know why, but I don't worry about that.

T: Okay, what else would be really bad about having to move to a smaller house?

C: (*Pauses and thinks for a moment.*) This may sound weird, but maybe part of it has to do with the approval stuff. I would really worry about what my parents and friends would think. Like we can't manage our money or we're not successful.

T: Okay, good. You're really getting out what it would mean to you if your husband should spend money unwisely. It sounds like two important aspects are the effect on your kids and the disapproval of your parents and friends. Let's see if we can take it farther. What would it mean to you if your parents or certain friends did disapprove and think you weren't successful?

C: Well, I'd feel like I was a failure.

At this point, it appears that one important source of Donna's worry involves her connecting her self-worth to approval of significant others. This, of course, is consistent with her worry about being late for fear of the doctor's disapproval. It therefore appears useful to keep this in mind as a possible aspect of her other worries. In addition, Donna's fear of a move to a smaller house contains other fears about her children's welfare that don't appear related to the approval theme.

As a homework assignment, Donna was given a copy of Ellis' (1987) *How to Stop Worrying and Start Living* tape and asked to listen to it and to try to apply the concepts presented to her worry about her husband losing his job. In addition, Donna was instructed to continue using the relaxation tape once a day.

Session 5

C: That Ellis is quite a character! What a voice!

T: Right. He is a unique character! What did you think about the ideas on the tape?

C: Well, it made sense. I did try to apply it to the worry about my husband losing his job.

T: Can you tell me how it seemed to apply?

C: Well, I guess I really do think Bill must not lose his job and that it would be too awful to stand if he did.

T: Okay, I see it that way, too, that those do appear to be two major ways of thinking that fuel your worry. What about the self-worth connection?

C: Oh yeah, I do also tell myself I would be a failure if we had to sell our home.

T: So there you have it in a nutshell. You have a negative event that anybody would strongly prefer not to happen, and then shift to the belief that it must not happen, it would be terrible and intolerable if it did, and that you would be less of a person.

C: I never heard it spelled out so concretely in those words, but I think I really do feel that way.

T: Can you see how the same three beliefs get applied to your fear of disapproval related to what people might think of you if you had to sell your house?

C: I guess it's the same. I must not be disapproved of. I couldn't stand it. It would be terrible and I would be terrible.

T: Exactly! And according to REBT theory, it's because you hold these beliefs that you probably overestimate how likely it would be that you would be rejected by your friends and family.

C: I'm not sure what you mean.

T: Well, it appears that when we define an event as terrible and impossible to bear or deal with, we are definitely viewing it as dangerous, as we discussed a few sessions ago. Then we become hypervigilant, constantly preoccupied with any sign of the danger, and in effect, that's what worry is all about.

C: So are you saying that to control my worry, I have to change these ways of thinking?

T: That's right. But the relaxation can help facilitate a mental state less vulnerable to worrisome thoughts, and there are several other techniques that are also very important in changing both your basic beliefs, and the worry process itself. We'll talk more about those soon.

The remainder of this session was spent discussing an event that happened during the week and applying a similar REBT analysis as with the issue discussed above. For homework, Donna agreed to continue practicing the relaxation tape and to examine another major worry.

Session 6

Donna reported that her relaxation practice was going well, and that she was attempting to use it in stressful situations. Donna also reported that she had listened to Ellis' worry tape again and did, indeed, apply the concepts to her worry about failing at developing her medical transcription business.

We discussed this in detail, and then made a "letting go" relaxation tape, eliminating the tension component and combining some of the muscles while focusing on feelings of tension release. Donna agreed to practice this tape once a day. In addition, I gave her a copy of Ellis' (1993) *How to Be a Perfect Nonperfectionist* tape.

Session 7

My agenda for this session was to review Donna's homework and experiences applying REBT to her worries during the week, and then to spend the majority of the session doing imaginal exposure to Donna's worry about her husband losing his job. The imagery that we used is a combination of rational-emotive imagery and prolonged exposure as described by Barlow and his colleagues (e.g., Craske et al., 1992). Prolonged exposure consists of the client imagining the relevant scene long enough to facilitate habituation and/or cognitive restructuring. With GAD clients, the current recommended time for exposure is approximately 30 minutes.

> **T:** Okay, Donna, you're really doing well with the relaxation and rational thinking. Now I'd like to introduce a technique to help you desensitize yourself to some of the catastrophic images that you've described as frequently popping into your mind when you worry. What seems to happen when we worry is that we try to avoid really thinking about our worst fears, though mental pictures of these worst fears may pop up for a brief instant and then we shut it off by trying to distract ourselves in some way. So it's just long enough to get you anxious, but not long enough to get desensitized to it.

> **C:** What do you mean by desensitize?

> **T:** Good question. It's kind of like watching a horror movie and getting really scared. What would happen if you watched it ten more times all the way through?

> **C:** I guess it wouldn't be so scary after a while.

> **T:** That's usually what happens. Also, in the imagery we'll do, we'll work on applying your relaxation and rational thinking skills so that the final outcome of the scene will involve you imagining yourself coping with your worst fear without being devastated.

> **C:** I think I understand, but it doesn't seem like much fun!

We talked some more about the rationale for the imagery, and Donna agreed to give it a try. We agreed on which image in her chain of worry images she would use for practice in this session.

> **T:** Okay, Donna, I'd like you to imagine that your worst fear came true. Bill lost his job, couldn't find another one that paid enough to make house payments, and you had to sell the house. Now, let's zero in on the image of your parents disap-

proving of you and Bill for mismanaging your finances. They're at your house, sitting at the kitchen table with you.

C: I can see them all right. They look so disappointed in me!

T: What are they saying? Can you hear their words?

C: It's the old "we told you so" routine. My mother's voice sounds so sad. It's like she's failed or something.

T: What thoughts are going through your mind right now?

C: I'm thinking, "I can't stand their disapproval, this really is awful. I'm such a disappointment to them. I feel like a real failure." I'm getting very anxious and depressed.

T: Okay, what's going on in your body?

C: My neck and shoulder muscles are really tight. My stomach has a knot in it. My mouth is dry.

T: What about your heart? Is it beating faster?

C: It's starting to speed up.

T: Okay, just hold that image. Focus on your parents' facial expression, their voices; all the thoughts that you mentioned. What's going on in your body?

Donna was able to continue focusing on this image for about 25 minutes. At that point she reported a slight decrease in her discomfort level.

T: Okay, Donna, now go ahead and apply your coping skills. Challenge the thoughts, see if you can relax some of the tension from your shoulders and neck. (*Pause*) Now try to capture the feeling of being very disappointed that your parents are disapproving. Try to actually change the anxiety and depression to disappointment. Disappointment that your parents are disapproving. Disappointed, and perhaps sad, that you have to sell your home and move to another location.

C: This is really hard to do!

T: I know. Just keep working on it. You're doing fine. (*Several minutes pass*)

c: Okay, I'm not feeling quite as bad now.

t: Okay now, how about also seeing yourself being verbal with your parents, taking control and ending their visit.

c: Okay, they're gone now. That feels better.

t: Good job! Let's go a little further before we stop. Think of some alternatives to the outcome of having to sell your house. Can you think of other, more likely outcomes? Also, is it possible that your parents would be more supportive than you predicted?

I am trying to accomplish a lot with Donna in this session. We are working on habituation to an aversive image, trying to promote integration of cognitive, physical, and emotional reactions. We're also trying to revise unrealistic probability estimates and catastrophic views of feared negative outcomes. Finally, we're attempting to enhance Donna's sense of self-efficacy so she can cope with her worst fears. It is important to note that my assumption is that Donna felt better at the end of this imaginal exposure, not because the A (activating event) changed (i.e., Donna's parents leaving), but rather because Donna changed her thinking about her parents' disapproval and her thinking about herself (i.e., "I can be assertive and have some control over the situation.")

For homework, Donna agreed to listen to the tape of the imagery at least three times before the next session, and to rate her peak and end-of-tape emotional discomfort levels on a scale from 0 to 10. In addition, we also discussed how to continue applying relaxation techniques in more stressful situations and to intervene in the worry process.

Session 8

We began by reviewing Donna's experience of the imagery practice. I was pleased that in the third practice, Donna's end-of-tape discomfort rating had come down significantly, from a 6 to a 3. The remainder of the session involved applying imaginal exposure to Donna's worry about not succeeding at developing her medical transcription business.

As in the previous session, the homework assignment was to listen to the tape of the imaginal exposure conducted in this session, and to continue applying relaxation skills.

Session 9

Donna reported difficulty getting her discomfort level to decrease very much to the second worry scene. Possible reasons for this were discussed, and she agreed to keep practicing the following week. It appeared that difficulties with keeping the image from shifting to other related images and distractions from family members were likely contributors to Donna's imagery practice being less effective than her practice the week before.

The remainder of the session was spent developing a list of avoidance behavior related to Donna's worry about Bill losing his job. Donna agreed to add to her list if she discovered other avoidance maneuvers during the following week.

Session 10

The focus of this session was on reviewing Donna's homework, particularly the list of worry-related avoidance behavior. Donna presented the following list of avoided activities:

1. Discussing finances with her husband, Bill;
2. Paying bills;
3. Balancing the checkbook;
4. Spending money on personal items (e.g., clothes); and
5. Reading newspaper articles about companies laying-off employees.

These activities were rated from 0–10 as to how anxious she predicted she would become by doing each activity. We then ordered the activities into a short hierarchy from least to most anxiety-provoking, as follows: (a) balancing checkbook; (b) discussing finances with Bill; (c) reading newspaper articles about companies laying-off people; (d) paying bills; and (e) spending money for personal items.

For homework, Donna agreed to do the first two hierarchy items, preceding each activity by writing out the ABC's and doing rational-emotive imagery on them.

Session 11

Donna reported that her letting-go relaxation practice continued to go well, and that she was noticing less overall muscle tension. We then discussed Donna's experience with behaviorally confronting her worry.

   T: Well, how did you do with paying the bills and discussing finances with Bill?

   C: I payed the bills, but it really got me worried. I did use the relaxation and it seemed to help. When the worries about moving out came up, I tried to tell myself we would survive, and that I could stand my parent's disapproval. I think it helped.

   T: That sounds really good. You're really starting to use your skills to deal with your worry differently.

   C: Yeah, but I totally blew it with the financial discussion with Bill. I had plenty of opportunities, but I just avoided it.

   T: Did you down yourself? Are you downing yourself for not doing that?

   C: Not really, amazingly enough. I just feel frustrated that I didn't bring up the discussion. I know it's something I need to do.

   T: Well, how about if we look at how you might have talked yourself out of doing it.

   C: I don't know . . . I just thought, "This will really be uncomfortable, we're not good at handling these kinds of financial discussions." Bill doesn't like it either, because I get so freaked out.

   T: I think you have it right there. Sounds like you're saying it's too uncomfortable, I'd better put it off.

   C: I guess. That's the way it felt. When I'm already worried about things and feeling anxious, I don't want to be more uncomfortable.

   T: Naturally, but what happens if you let yourself avoid it?

   C: It hangs over my head . . . I know it's part of working on the worrying. If I avoid dealing with it, I reinforce my belief that the situation is too awful to handle.

   T: Right. So, in a sense, you perpetuate your worry problem, and in the long run probably have to deal with more discomfort.

C: I can see what you're saying, but it's so hard to face this financial issue.

T: Right. But as you can see, it will be harder to face the more you put it off. So we need to help you tolerate the short-term pain for long-term gain.

C: I'll have to keep reminding myself of that.

The remainder of this session was spent using rational-emotive imagery in preparation for the next two hierarchy activities assigned for the following week.

Session 12

This session focused on reviewing Donna's homework. She was particularly pleased, and somewhat surprised, at how reading the relevant newspaper articles and paying bills was not as difficult as she imagined. The remainder of the session was spent trying to address a philosophical issue with which Donna had apparently been struggling.

C: I'm really pleased with my improvement so far. Bill agrees that I'm not worrying as much. I'm definitely sleeping better.

T: That's great! Your weekly records certainly suggest that you are doing better.

C: But, you know, I was watching TV this week. There was a news program on AIDS, and I got to thinking I should be worried and depressed about this and for other really bad things in the world, like the Bosnian situation.

T: So, it seems almost like the ethically correct thing to do to be worried and depressed about tragic events in the world?

C: Yes, it does, sort of. I mean, I can't just say these things are no big deal, that it doesn't matter.

T: Of course not. You wouldn't expect to feel positive or neutral emotions about clearly bad things in the world. But let's suppose you get really depressed and worried about the AIDS epidemic. How would that help you?

C: Well, of course, it wouldn't help, but it just seems like morally I should, we all should, be upset.

T: It sounds like you have the belief, "If I really care about people and events in the world, in order to be a responsible, ethical person, I should be really worried and depressed when really bad things happen."

C: Well, I think I do believe that. Doesn't a really caring person get emotional about tragic events?

T: It depends on what you mean by "get emotional." This gets back to the difference between facilitative and debilitative emotions. Remember when we first started working together, and you were worrying and depressed most of the time?

C: I do remember, of course, but isn't it different with really tragic events?

T: Well, let's play it out. Let's suppose you get really worried, anxious, depressed, maybe even guilty for being spared tragedy in your own life. How would this emotional state lead to ethically good results?

C: I don't know! I guess it wouldn't help my family. I'd just be a wreck around my husband and kids.

T: So in a sense, rather than it being an ethically appropriate response, your being dysfunctional would really be adding another unit of misery to the world.

C: Wow, I never thought of it like that! I see what you mean.

T: I can identify with your question, though. During the Vietnam War, I used to be depressed about babies being killed over there. I thought, "What right do I have to be happy when babies are dying and families are suffering in Vietnam?" After struggling with this and doing a lot of reading, I finally came to the conclusion that my feeling depressed wasn't helping the babies in Vietnam or anybody else. In a true sense, by being depressed, I was adding another unit of misery to the world, and not making it a better place.

C: Well, shouldn't we do something to change bad conditions?

T: That would be ethically responsible. In my situation, I got out of the Air Force as a conscientious objector, and became a VISTA volunteer. This, of course, is ancient history, back in the early seventies.

C: Very interesting. I know what you're going to say next. Couldn't I work better at changing the world if I'm not depressed and worried all the time.

T: Right. If you maintain the facilitative emotions of concern, sadness, and regret, you can determinedly channel your sensitivity and compassion into constructive action.

C: Like volunteering for the Portland Cascade AIDS Project?

T: Right.

This session had a very different flavor to it than the other sessions. It seemed to be the case that as Donna became less preoccupied with her daily worries, she was able to think more about philosophical issues related to dealing with truly bad and tragic events in the world. I also took the risk of some personal self-disclosure. In this case, it seemed to show Donna that I understood her concerns. I had struggled with similar issues myself, and presented one possible solution to dealing with the issue of how to respond to tragic events in life.

For homework, I suggested that Donna listen to Ellis' (1990) tape, *Rational Living in an Irrational World,* and read portions of Ellis' (1988) *How to Stubbornly Refuse to Make Yourself Miserable About Anything, Yes Anything!*

Session 13

During this session, we discussed Donna's reaction to Ellis' tape and book, furthering her view of ways to deal with particular tragic events in the world. We also discussed termination, and decided to make the next two sessions on an every other week basis. Now that Donna appeared to be coping much better emotionally, we discussed practical skills, including problem-solving and assertiveness. Donna was actually a pretty good problem solver when she wasn't so anxious and depressed. This observation was consistent with Davey's (1994) finding that there was no relationship between worrying and social problem-solving skills.

In addition, as over the course of therapy, Donna's belief that she must always perform well and have approval to be worthwhile appeared to have been significantly altered. She was better able to implement the assertive skills that she had previously learned in an assertiveness class.

Sessions 14–16

These sessions were spent reviewing the techniques learned in therapy, and continuing to apply them to everyday problems and concerns. During Session 15, Donna was given the same set of self-report inventories that she had completed at the beginning of therapy. Her PSWQ score had gone from 65 to 47, supporting her apparent decrease in frequency of worry and her increased self-efficacy in controlling the worry process. Similarly, her STAI score had dropped from 58 to 43, suggesting less generalized anxiety. Her BDI score for depression was 8, within the normal range.

In the final termination session, I asked Donna to try to put in her own words the most helpful things she had learned in therapy. Donna's response was as follows:

C: Well, the specific techniques, writing out the ABC's, doing the imagery, . . . doing the things I was avoiding. All of these, I think, gave me tools so I felt more in control and not so helpless. Overall, I think I'm not as hard on myself, not so worried about what other people think of me. It was also really helpful to see that I don't have to be depressed to prove that I'm a sensitive person. As I talk about this, I think I've come a long way—not perfect, though!

T: I'm glad to hear you put all these things into words. You've really worked hard in therapy.

We then discussed Donna's concerns about possible relapse, and ways to cope with setbacks, such as coming back for booster sessions in the future.

CASE DISCUSSION

Unique Aspects of the Case

Donna's case nicely illustrates many of the phenomena or characteristics described by recent conceptualizations of GAD. For example, the use of inference chaining illustrated the potential usefulness of getting at the themes that may underlie a variety of specific worries (Shadick et al., 1991). In Donna's case, this was the approval theme, translated into the irrational belief that one must have the approval they desire in order to be worthwhile and happy. Further, that approval was the central theme for Donna is certainly consistent with Borkovec et al.'s (1991) hypothesis that social-evaluative and self-worth issues may be an important aspect of GAD.

Another salient aspect of Donna's treatment was her profitable use of audiotapes. Ellis' tapes on worry, perfectionism, and living rationally in an irrational world appeared to be important contributions to our in-session work.

Critical Incidents and Therapist's Response to Client

If one event in the therapy with Donna was to stand out as particularly significant, I think it would be our discussion about whether one should be worried and depressed in response to tragic life events. It is my impression that Donna had been doing a lot of critical thinking, partly stimulated by the therapy, but also as an outgrowth of her own previous readings and religious/philosophical questioning. It seems that our discussion in Session 12 facilitated Donna's deeper understanding that it was ethically acceptable not to be emotionally debilitated and still be a caring, responsible person. It appeared to me that this insight further strengthened her resolve to really practice applying her REBT worry-control skills to everyday life problems.

I had a variety of responses to Donna over the course of therapy. Mainly, I liked her. Donna was sincere in her desire to make changes, and she complied delightfully well with homework assignments. All in all, she had many traits that would be attractive to most therapists.

There were times, however, that I became irritated with Donna, when she seemed to perseverate on particular worries. What helped me most at these times was just to work on accepting myself with these reactions, and then reminding myself of how I also have difficulties with some of my own worries, in spite of being well armed with REBT skills!

Complexities and Subtleties of REBT

Several aspects of Donna's therapy illustrate therapeutic issues that can, at times, be complex and/or subtle. One example is Donna's shame and self-downing about her problem with worry and anxiety. This problem about a problem is, of course, familiar to REBT therapists, and the practical benefits of delineating this and working on it early in therapy were notable with Donna. In a sense, addressing it seemed to quickly facilitate our therapeutic relationship, as it helped Donna to see that I was on her side. She could thus more readily disclose her problems and insecurities as she began to work at self-acceptance. In addition, this increased self-acceptance appeared to greatly facilitate Donna's ability to work on tolerating the disapproval of significant others.

Another typical REBT discrimination, that is, the difference between facilitative and debilitative emotions, seemed quite helpful when Donna and I discussed her sense of responsibility about being disturbed when confronted with news of tragic events in the world. Without this distinction between facilitative and debilitative emotions, Donna may have been resistant to giving up feeling worried and depressed about certain events if she thought the alternative was to feel emotionally indifferent.

Finally, REBT's unique delineation of discomfort anxiety as a central emotional problem provided a therapeutic avenue for helping Donna understand why she avoided carrying out certain homework assignments and why she avoided worry-related activities, for example, discussing finances with her husband.

REFERENCES

American Psychiatric Association. (1980). *Diagnostic and statistical manual of mental disorders* (3rd ed.). Washington, DC: Author.
American Psychiatric Association. (1987). *Diagnostic and statistical manual of mental disorders* (3rd ed., rev.). Washington, DC: Author.

American Psychiatric Association. (1994). *Diagnostic and statistical manual of mental disorders* (4th ed.). Washington, DC: Author.

Barlow, D. H. (1988). *Anxiety and its disorders*. New York: Guilford.

Barlow, D. H., Rapee, R. M., & Brown, T. A. (1992). Behavioral treatment of generalized anxiety disorder. *Behavior Therapy, 23*, 551–570.

Beck, A. T., Epstein, N., Brown, G., & Steer, R. A. (1988). An inventory for measuring clinical anxiety: Psychometric properties. *Journal of Consulting and Clinical Psychology, 56*, 893–897.

Beck, A. T., Ward, C. H., Mendelsohn, M., Mock, J., & Erbaugh, J. (1961). An inventory for measuring depression. *Archives of General Psychiatry, 4*, 561–571.

Bernard, M. E. (1990, June). *Validation of General Attitude and Belief Scale.* Paper presented at the World Congress on Mental Health Counseling, Keystone, CO.

Borkovec, T. D. (1985). The role of cognitive and somatic cues in anxiety and anxiety disorders: Worry and relaxation-induced anxiety. In A. H. Tuma & J. D. Maser (Eds.), *Anxiety and the anxiety disorders* (pp. 463–478). Hillsdale, NJ: Lawrence Erlbaum.

Borkovec, T. D., & Costello, E. (1993). Efficacy of applied relaxation and cognitive-behavior therapy in the treatment of generalized anxiety disorder. *Journal of Consulting and Clinical Psychology, 61*, 611–619.

Borkovec, T. D., Shadick, R. N., & Hopkins, M. (1991). The nature of normal and pathological worry. In R. M. Rapee & D. H. Barlow (Eds.), *Chronic anxiety: Generalized anxiety disorder and mixed anxiety-depression* (pp. 29–51). New York: Guilford.

Brown, T. A., & Barlow, D. H. (1992). Comorbidity among anxiety disorders: Implications for treatment and DSM-IV. *Journal of Consulting and Clinical Psychology, 60*, 835–844.

Brown, T. A., O'Leary, T. A., & Barlow, D. G. (1993). Generalized anxiety disorder. In D. H. Barlow (Ed.), *Clinical handbook of psychological disorders* (2nd ed., pp. 137–188). New York: Guilford.

Burns, D. D. (1980). *Feeling good: The new mood therapy.* New York: Morrow.

Butler, G., & Booth, R. G. (1991). Developing psychological treatments for generalized anxiety disorder. In R. M. Rapee & D. H. Barlow (Eds.), *Chronic anxiety: Generalized anxiety disorder and mixed anxiety-depression* (pp. 187–209). New York: Guilford.

Butler, G., Cullington, A., Hibbert, G., Klimes, I., & Gelder, M. (1987). Anxiety management for persistent generalized anxiety. *British Journal of Psychiatry, 151*, 535–542.

Butler, G., Fennell, M., Robson, P., & Gelder, M. (1991). Comparison of behavior therapy and cognitive-behavior therapy in the treatment of generalized anxiety disorder. *Journal of Consulting and Clinical Psychology, 59*, 167–175.

Butler, G., & Mathews, A. (1983). Cognitive processes in anxiety. *Advances in Behaviour Research and Therapy, 5,* 51–62.

Craske, M. G., Barlow, D. H., & O'Leary, T. A. (1992). *Mastery of your anxiety and worry.* Albany, NY: Graywind.

Davey, G. C. L. (1994). Worrying, social problem-solving abilities, and social problem-solving confidence. *Behaviour Research and Therapy, 32,* 327–330.

DiNardo, P. A., & Barlow, D. H. (1988). *Anxiety Disorders Interview Schedule—Revised (ADIS-R).* Albany, NY: Graywind.

Dryden, W., & Yankura, J. (1993). *Counselling individuals: A rational-emotive handbook* (2nd ed.). London: Whurr.

Ellis, A. (1980). Rational-emotive therapy and cognitive behavior therapy: Similarities and differences. *Cognitive Therapy and Research, 4,* 325–340.

Ellis, A. (1987). (Speaker). *How to stop worrying and start living.* [cassette recording]. Washington, DC: Psychology Today Tapes.

Ellis, A. (1988). *How to stubbornly refuse to make yourself miserable about anything—yes, anything!* Secaucus, NJ: Lyle Stuart.

Ellis, A. (1990). (Speaker). *Rational living in an irrational world.* [cassette recording]. New York: Institutue For Rational Emotive Therapy.

Ellis, A. (1993). (Speaker). *How to be a perfect nonperfectionist.* [cassette recording]. New York: Institute For Rational Emotive Therapy.

Eysenck, H. J. (Ed.). (1967). *The biological bases of personality.* Springfield, IL: Charles C Thomas.

Eysenck, H., & Eysenck, S. (1975). *Eysenck Personality Questionnaire.* San Diego, CA: Educational and Industrial Testing Service.

Heide, F. J., & Borkovec, T. D. (1983). Relaxation-induced anxiety: Paradoxical anxiety enhancement due to relaxation training. *Journal of Consulting and Clinical Psychology, 51,* 171–182.

Kranzler, G. (1975). *You can change how you feel.* Eugene, OR: RETC Press.

Lipsky, M., Kassinove, H., & Miller, N. (1980). Effects of rational-emotive therapy, rational-role reversal, and rational-emotive imagery on the emotional adjustment of community mental health center patients. *Journal of Consulting and Clinical Psychology, 48,* 366–374.

Lovibond, S. H., & Lovibond, P. F. (1992). *Self-report scales (DASS) for the differentiation and measurement of depression and stress.* Unpublished manuscript.

Malouff, J. M., & Schutte, N. S. (1986). Development and validation of a measure of irrational belief. *Journal of Consulting and Clinical Psychology, 54,* 860–862.

Meyer, T. J., Miller, M. L., Metzger, R. L., & Borkovec, T. D. (1990). Development and validation of the Penn State Worry Questionnaire. *Behaviour Research and Therapy, 28,* 487–495.

Rapee, R. M. (1991a). Generalized anxiety disorder: A review of clinical features and theoretical concepts. *Clinical Psychology Review, 11,* 419–440.

Rapee, R. M. (1991b). Psychological factors involved in generalized anxiety. In R. M. Rapee & D. H. Barlow (Eds.), *Chronic anxiety: Generalized anxiety disorder and mixed anxiety-depression.* New York: Guilford.

Robinson, E. L. (1989). The relative effectiveness of cognitive restructuring and coping desensitization in the treatment of self-reported worry. *Journal of Anxiety Disorders, 4,* 197–207.

Roemer, L., Borkovec, M., Posa, S., & Lyonfields, J. (1991). *Generalized anxiety disorder in an analogue population: The role of past trauma.* Poster presented at the annual meeting of the Association for Advancement of Behavior Therapy, New York.

Sanderson, W. C., & Barlow, D. H. (1990). A description of patients diagnosed with DSM-III-R generalized anxiety disorder. *Journal of Nervous and Mental Disease, 178,* 588–591.

Sanderson, W. C., Beck, A. T., & McGinn, L. K. (1994). Cognitive therapy for generalized anxiety disorder: Significance of comorbid personality disorders. *Journal of Cognitive Psychotherapy, 8,* 13–18.

Sanderson, W. C., & Wetzler, S. (1991). Chronic anxiety and generalized anxiety disorder: Issues in comorbidity. In R. M. Rapee & D. H. Barlow (Eds.), *Chronic anxiety: Generalized anxiety disorder and mixed anxiety-depression.* New York: Guilford.

Sanderson, W. C., Wetzler, S., Beck, A. T., & Betz, F. (1994). Prevalence of personality disorders in patients with anxiety disorders. *Psychiatric Research, 51,* 167–174.

Shadick, R. N., & Borkovec, T. D. (1991). *Generalized anxiety disorder and comorbid personality disorders: Prevalence and treatment.* Poster presented at the annual meeting of the Association for Advancement of Behavior Therapy, New York.

Shadick, R. N., Roemer, L., Hopkins, M. B., & Borkovec, T. D. (1991). *The nature of worrisome thoughts.* Poster presented at the annual meeting of the Association for Advancement of Behavior Therapy, New York.

Spielberger, C. D., Gorsuch, R. E., & Lushene, R. E. (1970). *Manual for the State-Trait Anxiety Inventory. (Self-evaluation questionnaire.)* Palo Alto, CA: Consulting Psychologists Press.

Warren, R., & Zgourides, G. D. (1991). *Anxiety disorders: A rational-emotive perspective.* West Nyack, NY: Allyn & Bacon.

Yankura, J., & Dryden, W. (1990). *Doing RET: Albert Ellis in action.* New York: Springer Publishing Co.

Zinbarg, R. E., Craske, M. G., & Barlow, D. H. (1993). *Therapist's guide for the mastery of your anxiety and worry.* Albany, NY: Graywind.

CHAPTER 3

Using REBT to Overcome Depression

Paul A. Hauck and Patricia McKeegan

> I want to register a complaint about the word depression. . . . Melancholia, as opposed to depression, would appear to be a far more apt and evocative word for the blacker forms of the disorder, but it was usurped by a term with such a bland tonality that it lacks any magisterial presence, used indifferently to describe an economic decline or a rut in the ground, a true wimp of a word for such a major illness.
>
> —*William Styron*

STYRON'S WORDS, reported as a prelude to Walen and Rader's (1991) personal accounts of their battles with depression, appear to reflect the thoughts of many clients struggling with depression: "Nothing is right with me—or the world! The situation is hopeless and will never change." Indeed "depression" does seem an inadequate word to capture the all-encompassing feelings of emptiness and blackness these clients experience.

The National Comorbidity Survey (Kessler et al., 1994) reports a lifetime prevalence of major depressive episode of 17.1%; a lifetime prevalence of 14.9% for major depression; and, a 6.4% prevalence rate for dysthymia. Annual incidence rates reported by the Epidemiologic Catchment Area Study (Regier & Robins, 1991) found approximately 1 case of major depression per 100 men and

2 cases per 100 women. The higher prevalence of depression in females has been a consistent epidemiological finding across numerous national and international studies (see, e.g., Kessler, McGonagle, Swartz, Blazer, & Nelson, 1993; Kessler et al., 1994; Paykel, 1991). Rates in men and women are highest in 25- to 44-year-olds; for both men and women rates decrease over age 65 (*Diagnostic and Statistical Manual of Mental Disorders* [DSM-IV], American Psychiatric Association, 1994). Prevalence rates for major depression in the United States appear unrelated to ethnicity, education, income, or marital status (APA, 1994). In recent years, international studies of depression and dysthymia have yielded lifetime prevalence rates ranging from 3.3% in Seoul to 17.1% in the United States (Kaelber, Moul, & Farmer, 1995); rates for both major depression and dysthmyia were generally higher for women than for men (Weissman et al., 1993).

Although depression may begin at any age, the average age for a first episode is in the mid-20s (Kaelber et al., 1995). Of note, the appearance of the first depressive episode predicts the likelihood of developing a subsequent depressive episode. About 50%–60% of individuals who experience one depressive episode will have a second; individuals who have experienced two episodes have a 70% chance of having a third; those who have experienced three episodes have a 90% chance of a fourth (APA, 1994).

According to the DSM-IV, depressive episodes are marked by depressed mood, markedly diminished ability to experience pleasure, feelings of worthlessness and/or guilt, fatigue, and inability to think or concentrate. In addition, clients may report insomnia (or hypersomnia), weight loss (or gain), and recurrent suicidal ideation. Walen's (Walen & Rader, 1991) account of her own depression includes the following journal entries: "I have a sense of being a speck in the void. . . . There is a huge gulf between me and all others. . . . My reality is that I live alone—and I always will . . . I can't feel connected" (p. 223) and, "I want to die and today I got to the point of laying out plans. . . . Lots of thoughts about death today. Pictures of myself hanging in the basement" (p. 222).

Given the pain and devastation inherent in depression, it is critically important for the practitioner to be alert to its signs and symptoms. Diagnosis, however, is only the first step. It is also highly important that the practitioner be conversant with effective models and techniques for treating depression.

BRIEF REVIEW OF MODELS FOR
CONCEPTUALIZING DEPRESSION

In the following sections, we offer capsule reviews of several models of depression that have influenced the work of mental health practitioners. Specifically, we discuss contributions made by Freud, Beck, and Ellis.

Freud's View

Freud (1950) offered a theory for conceptualizing depression that retained considerable prominence in the mental health field, until it began to receive critical scrutiny by a number of researchers and theoreticians in the 1950s and 1960s. According to Freud's view, depression was the result of retroflected hostility. It went something like this: A daughter is angry with her mother. She feels guilt and wickedness because of this totally unacceptable emotion and therefore turns that anger toward herself, which serves as a punishment for her rejection of her mother.

From this model stems the view that depressed individuals have a "need to suffer." For years, this "need to suffer" was viewed as an explanatory construct that was able to effectively account for depressive symptomatology such as severe self-criticism, interpreting positive events in a negative way, and suicidal ideation.

Beck's Model

Beck (Beck, Rush, Shaw, & Emery, 1979) has described his early attempts to scientifically validate the psychoanalytic conceptualization of depression. Although his initial findings appeared to support the retroflected hostility and "need to suffer" hypotheses, later studies yielded results that could not easily be reconciled with these concepts. He found, for instance, that "the depressed patient was more likely than the nondepressed to avoid behaviors evoking rejection or disapproval in favor of responses eliciting acceptance and approval by others" (Beck et al., 1979, p. ii). Beck ultimately concluded that depressed patients do not have a "need to suffer," and began to search for alternative explanations for the symptoms that they typically present. Beck's work led to the formulation of a cognitive theory and therapy of depression (Beck et al., 1979; Young,

Beck, & Weinberger, 1993). According to this system, depressive symptomatology stems from a psychological substrate which includes (a) the cognitive triad, (b) schemas, and, (c) cognitive errors (faulty information processing).

The day-to-day experience of the depressed client is colored by negatively biased cognitions in three spheres. The "cognitive triad of depression" (Young et al., 1993) induces the client to regard himself, the world, and the future in negative terms. Thus, he sees himself as worthless, unlovable, incompetent, and the like, views the environment negatively, and sees the future as hopeless.

Beck's model asserts that an important predisposing factor in the development of depression is the presence of early schemas. Beck (1967) defined a schema as follows:

> A schema is a (cognitive) stucture for screening, coding, and evaluating the stimuli that impinge on the organism. . . . On the basis of this matrix of schemas, the individual is able to orient himself in relation to time and space and to categorize and interpret experiences in a meaningful way. (p. 283)

Particular dysfunctional schemas may lie dormant for long periods, but can be activated by specific environmental stressors. In depression, for example, the client's conceptualization of a specific situation is distorted to "match" the prepotent dysfunctional schemas. Young (1990) has emphasized the importance of identifying these early maladaptive schemas in the treatment process.

The cognitive errors (faulty information processing) in the Beck model of depression refer to the depressed client's tendency to maintain his belief in the validity of his inferences, despite evidence to the contrary. Thus, his conceptualization of life events is structured in a "primitive" manner, where broad global judgments, absolutistic thinking, and negative inferences prevail.

Young and colleagues (1993) view effective cognitive therapy as proceeding in two phases. The first phase, which emphasizes symptom reduction, begins by focusing on eliciting automatic thoughts (cognitive errors), testing automatic thoughts, and identifying maladaptive schemas that structure the client's reality. Behavioral techniques are viewed as especially useful in the early stages of treatment. Frequently used techniques include activity scheduling, mastery and pleasure exercises, diversion methods, and role-playing. The second phase of treatment is aimed at relapse prevention. This is referred to as the schema-focused phase of treatment and its focus is on modifying the client's early maladaptive schemas. The emphasis here is on early developmental patterns, long-term interpersonal difficulties, the client–therapist relationship, and emotive exercises. It is assumed that such an emphasis will make the client less vulnerable to another depressive episode.

Ellis' Approach

Ellis (1962) was a pioneer in recognizing the ideological underpinnings of emotional and behavioral disorders. Originally trained as a psychoanalyst, Ellis became dissatisfied with the results he was obtaining with patients in his psychoanalytic practice and subsequently formulated the therapeutic approach now known as rational emotive behavior therapy (REBT) (Yankura & Dryden, 1994). With respect to the genesis of psychological disturbance, REBT accords a central role to the irrational beliefs to which an individual adheres. Within the REBT literature, such beliefs are often described as being composed of an absolutistic demand (expressed verbally as a should, must, or have to) and an absolutistic evaluative conclusion (e.g., negative person-rating, awfulizing, and I-can't-stand-it-itis) (Dryden & DiGiuseppe, 1990; Dryden & Yankura, 1993). Irrational beliefs can be characterized as (a) dogmatic in nature, (b) illogical, (c) inconsistent with reality, and, (d) impediments to the attainment of personally meaningful goals. When the irrational beliefs that an individual holds are triggered by negative circumstances of personal significance, that individual will be likely to experience one or more inappropriate (or unhealthy) negative emotions, such as anger, anxiety, depression, guilt, or shame.

REBT seeks to help individuals replace their irrational beliefs with more rational ones. Rational beliefs tend to reflect a person's wants and preferences, and can be contrasted with irrational beliefs insofar as they are (a) flexible and relativistic, (b) logical, (c) consistent with reality, and, (d) more often facilitative of goal attainment. When an individual subscribes to rational beliefs and encounters negative circumstances, he or she will be less likely to experience significant emotional and behavioral disturbance. Instead, the individual will likely experience one or more *appropriate* (or healthy) negative emotions, such as annoyance, concern, sadness, remorse, or regret (Dryden & Yankura, 1993). These feelings are still negatively toned, but they typically do not cause significant disruptions in a person's functioning and may serve as an impetus to change negative conditions that are open to modification.

Two aspects of Ellis' theoretical system have special relevance to the conceptualization and treatment of depression. First, Ellis (1977, 1987) has maintained that negatively distorted inferences tend to be by-products of the irrational beliefs to which an individual subscribes. He therefore asserts that these inferences usually cannot be accorded primacy in the etiology of depression. Second, Ellis (1987) has made the case that REBT—by virtue of the fact that it quickly and specifically focuses on addressing clients' irrational beliefs—may be more efficient and result in more pervasive and longer-lasting changes for depressed individuals than therapeutic approaches which tend to initially place a heavy emphasis upon correcting distorted negative inferences.

We turn now to discussion of a specific rational-emotive model for understanding and treating depression.

A CLINICAL REBT MODEL FOR ASSESSING AND TREATING DEPRESSION

Based on my own clinical experience and influenced by the theoretical systems developed by Ellis (1962, 1977) and Beck (1963; Beck et al., 1979), I (P.H.) have formulated my own three-factor model of depression (Hauck, 1971, 1973). According to this model, depression can be caused by (a) self-blame (the "bad me" approach), (b) self-pity ("poor me"), and (c) other-pity ("poor you").

Each of these three factors can be viewed as a cognitive/emotional process, underpinned by particular irrational beliefs to which the depressed individual subscribes. Self-blame (which is practically synonymous with feelings of guilt), for instance, typically arises from the following sort of thinking pattern (Hauck, 1971, 1973; Walen, DiGiuseppe, & Dryden, 1992):

1. I have failed, sinned, or accidentally hurt someone.
2. I *should* be perfect and not do bad things.
3. I am, therefore, a *bad person* and deserve punishment.

In considering how this sequence of thoughts and beliefs leads an individual into depression, it is important to first note that the initial thought ("I have failed, sinned, or accidentally hurt someone") appears descriptive in nature and essentially represents a person's interpretation of events in which he or she may have been personally involved. In and of itself, it is usually not sufficient to cause depression. The second and third steps, however, encompass an absolutistic self-directed demand ("I *should* be perfect...") and an absolutistic evaluative conclusion ("I am, therefore, a *bad person*..."). These steps represent the components of an irrational belief (Dryden, 1990), which (according to the REBT view) will lead to self-blame and concomitant depression when it is brought to bear upon the individual's interpretation of events.

Similarly, self-pity is activated by a sequence of thoughts and beliefs that takes this general form (Hauck, 1971, 1973; Walen, DiGiuseppe, & Dryden, 1992):

1. I have been thwarted in getting my way.
2. I *must* have what I want.
3. It's awful if I don't get it. Poor me!

Again, the reader will note that steps two and three of this sequence include an absolutistic demand (in this case directed at the world and the person's life conditions) and an absolutistic evaluative conclusion (which takes the form of awfulizing in this illustration).

Finally, other-pity comes into play when an individual engages in the following sort of thinking pattern (Hauck, 1971, 1973; Walen, DiGiuseppe, & Dryden, 1992):

1. Someone has experienced a serious misfortune.
2. Bad things *must not* happen to other people when they don't deserve it.
3. The world is an *awful* place for allowing such things to happen.

The three-factor model I have presented here offers a number of notable advantages with respect to the treatment of depression. First and foremost, it is fairly non-complex and thus readily comprehended by many clients. Once they are taught the model, they are better able to be active collaborators in their own therapy. Second, it enables the clinician to quickly "diagnose" the type of depression an individual suffers, by identifying the particular factors that are operative for that person. This, in turn, facilitates decision-making about the types of rational-emotive interventions most likely to be of help to the client.

My years as a practicing psychotherapist have demonstrated to my satisfaction that most cases of depression can be subsumed under this three-factor scheme. I would, however, note that I am referring mainly to cases of depression preceded by readily identifiable negative life events, and not to depressions that are essentially organic in nature. Although cognitive-behavioral interventions may have utility in treating depressions appearing to be largely biological in origin, it is important to recognize that such cases may often call for pharmacotherapy. Frequently, individuals suffering from biologically based depressions reap the most benefit from a combination of effective psychotherapy and antidepressant medication.

General Assessment and Treatment Strategies

The assessment procedure that I (P.H.) generally employ when working with depressed individuals is fairly simple and straightforward. First, of course, I glean basic background information. Then, after ascertaining that a given client is indeed experiencing depression and obtaining agreement from the client to target this for change, I proceed to teach the client the three-factor model. Following this, I generally prompt the client to engage in "self-diagnosis," meaning that I ask him or her to try and identify the main method(s) by which he or she is bringing on depression. Thus, quite early on in therapy, I begin the process of psychoeducation that is central to REBT and engage the client in the treatment process.

As noted above, most clients have no difficulty in understanding the three causes of depression and can easily identify which one, two, or three methods they themselves are employing. After obtaining this information, I then typically determine which condition the person mainly suffers from and would like to address first. Generally, I follow this lead and work with the client on the condition so identified. This involves showing the client the irrational beliefs underpinning the particular condition, and then presenting arguments to counter these beliefs. When progress is made in this area, we move on to address the other sources of depression of relevance to the client.

Intervention

REBT places an emphasis on helping clients overcome their emotional and behavioral problems (including depression) by showing them how to identify, dispute, and replace their operative irrational beliefs. REBT theory holds that when clients surrender their irrational beliefs in favor of more rational ones, they are able to minimize their present-day disturbances and make themselves less vulnerable to future ones.

Specific procedures for helping clients to surrender and replace their irrational beliefs have been described in great detail in other sources (see, e.g., Dryden & DiGiuseppe, 1990; Walen, DiGiuseppe, & Dryden, 1992). This being the case, the following sections shall be devoted to explicating the rational arguments used with clients to counter the irrational ideas behind their self-blame, self-pity, and other-pity.

Self-blame. Of the three conditions leading to depression, self-blame appears to be the most frequent cause of depression. Self-blame (and its consequent feelings of intense guilt) represents one of the most uncomfortable psychological experiences that people can endure (Hauck, 1973, 1979a, 1984; London, 1993). Once we hate ourselves for our actions or thoughts, we immediately reduce our capacity to function effectively in many areas.

In helping clients suffering from self-blaming depression, it is important to show them that they create their guilt feelings through two steps: (a) they note that they have acted badly, and (b) they *decide* that they are a *bad person* for having acted in this way. Once they can see this, they are taught the following arguments against their negative self-rating:

1. Separate the rating of your behavior from your self. The "self" is the sum of all the judgments that can be made of an individual. They run into the millions and therefore cannot be tallied accurately. We can condemn greed, for instance, and not condemn the person who acts greedily, since that is only one of his or her many traits.

2. Self-blame and guilt do not help you alter your behavior for the better. In fact, the more one blames oneself for misdeeds, the more one's misconduct is likely to increase. This is because negative self-rating will cause you to see yourself in an increasingly poor light, such that you lose faith in your ability to improve and do better. Also, the worse you think of yourself, the less you will allow success and accomplishment to enter your life. After all, these are the fruits saved for deserving human beings, not "bad" ones.

3. Refraining from engaging in self-blame is not equivalent to refusing to take responsibility for acting bad. You can eschew negative self-rating while still accepting responsibility for your actions—then, you can choose to work on changing any traits you may have that contributed to your acting badly in the first place.

4. Rather than attributing any personal wrongdoing to your being a bad or evil person, you can choose to recognize that poor conduct is almost always due to one of three variables: (a) stupidity (not having the intelligence to know better); (b) ignorance (having the intelligence to know better but lacking opportunities that would have allowed one to learn certain facts or master particular skills); or (c) emotional disturbance (having both the intelligence and skill to do right, but being disturbed to the extent that right and wrong cease to be relevant issues).

5. Self-blamers can be viewed as actually being quite conceited. While they often readily extend forgiveness to others for misdeeds or errors, they vigorously condemn themselves when they commit the very same sorts of acts. This is because they apply one set of (superhuman) standards to themselves, and another set of (plebeian) standards to other people. Others are expected and allowed to be fallible and error-prone; they, however, *must never* make mistakes. By inference, they are placing themselves in a special, superior position relative to the rest of humankind.

When clients gain some skill in countering their guilt and self-blame, they open the way for themselves to become more self-accepting. This, in turn, will likely make them less vulnerable to future depressive episodes.

Self-pity. This is another extremely common cause of depression. In essence, self-pity results when a person awfulizes about frustrations and other negative life conditions that they encounter. The following arguments have been useful for helping clients to surrender their awfulizing and eradicate their self-pity:

1. When you awfulize, it is akin to rating negative circumstances as being 101% bad—in other words, you are saying that the negative circumstances you are facing are completely off the scale of badness. Obviously, nothing can be more than 100% bad.

2.   In fact, it is highly unlikely that any set of circumstances that you face are 100% bad, as things could almost always be worse than they are.

3.   When you awfulize, you are typically applying several implicit *meanings* to your negative conditions: (a) they completely shut the door on the possibility of ever again attaining any happiness or satisfaction in life, (b) they absolutely cannot be coped with, and (c) they are "badder" than they *should* be. From a rational perspective, none of these meanings has any validity. First, even under very bad conditions, it is still probable that you can creatively find ways to attain some degree of happiness and satisfaction. Second, even highly negative circumstances can be coped with—all the more so if you refrain from compromising your coping capacity by awfulizing. Finally, there is no sense in saying that what is *should not* exist. If things are bad right now, that is exactly the way they should indubitably be.

4.   Awfulizing only makes a bad situation worse. By awfulizing, you create unnecessary misery for yourself and thus compound the emotional discomfort prompted by your negative conditions.

Other-pity.   Although other-pity may be the least common means by which people depress themselves, it still occurs with enough frequency to warrant the clinician's attention. Like self-pity, other-pity also involves awfulizing—although this time, the awfulizing is applied to the negative conditions inflicted on people other than oneself. There are a number of cogent arguments that can be used with clients who are depressing themselves through other-pity:

1.   Awfulizing about the negative conditions faced by another person causes *you* to become depressed and thereby brings additional, needless emotional misery into the world. In fact, if the other individual becomes aware that you are depressed, you may become yet another cross that they have to bear.

2.   When you depress yourself through awfulizing and other-pity, you compromise your own ability to be an effective problem-solver. Thus, even if it is your desire to be of aid to some person who is facing dire straits, you will be less well able to carry this off.

3.   When you awfulize about the negative conditions faced by another, you turn yourself into a poor role model. Your own awfulizing may serve to reinforce the awfulizing and self-pitying that the other person may be inclined to engage in. This only serves to make their circumstances worse.

The section that follows presents the case of a depressed client whom I (P.H.) saw in therapy. As will be seen, a number of the rational arguments outlined above were employed during the course of treatment with this individual.

CASE ILLUSTRATION: DEPRESSION FROM SELF-BLAME AND SELF-PITY

Clara was a middle-aged female on her third marriage, and it too was floundering. She was a 52-year-old white female, gentle by disposition, civil, courteous, and fair. Her previous marriages ended when she could no longer endure the dominating ways of her husbands and decided to divorce them. Throughout her marriages she apparently adopted a passive strategy, which, she believed, would get her husbands to be more gentle with her. Little did she realize that it contributed to their having more control over her.

In time she suffered from episodes of guilt and self-pity. No matter how hard she tried, the more unhappy her marriages became. On the one hand she blamed herself for failing to make a success of her best efforts. On the other hand, she felt depressed from self-pity for all the heartbreak life dealt her.

In my work with Clara, I placed a strong emphasis on helping her to overcome her self-blaming tendencies. However, given the nonassertive stance she had developed in her relationships, it also proved important to provide her with guidelines for assertive behavior.

Her complaints during an early session were of her third (and current) husband:

CLARA: He seemed like such a nice man while we courted, but then, after about 6 months he began complaining about the money I was spending for household needs and clothes for myself. When I explained I wasn't being unreasonable he became loud and repeated his accusations that I was selfish, didn't care for him, and had no business spending any money without his approval.

DR. H: How did things go after that?

CLARA: Worse. I felt I must have done something to bring this on, that I was making the same errors I made in my first two marriages and I didn't know how to proceed.

DR. H: You felt guilty and depressed?

CLARA: Oh yes, I often do.

DR. H: If I tell you how people become psychologically depressed, would you try to diagnose your own problem?

I then explained the three causes of depression and Clara readily identified self-blame as one cause and suggested she might also pity herself. We agreed to work together on these things.

CLARA: I know I feel guilty a lot, because why else would I be treated so unkindly by everyone I live with? In three marriages I've always been told I was the selfish one.

DR. H: That fits. If you hear something negative about yourself often enough, you may come to believe it.

CLARA: I sure did; and I still do. I don't know why, though. I think I'm a good and decent woman who cares for others, but if that's true, why am I always so unhappy in my relationships?

DR. H: I think I know. But first, let me tell you the three principles of human interaction. One, you get the behavior you tolerate. Two, others will not change until you change first. And three, change your excessive tolerance of others' inconsiderate behavior toward you.

CLARA: But Dr. Hauck, I just can't do what you ask, because I would feel terribly guilty if I stood up for myself as you suggest.

DR. H: Then let me tell you how people create their feelings of guilt.

CLARA: Yes, do. I need to know how I do that.

Here, I have started the process of teaching Clara some guidelines for assertive behavior. As might be expected, given her tendency to feel guilty, she has difficulty with the notion of standing up for herself. I proceed to show her where her guilt feelings come from.

DR. H: Guilt is created in two steps, not one. First, you must believe you have done something bad.

CLARA: That's easy to do. I'm always doing stupid or self-centered things.

DR. H: I seriously doubt that. If I understand you correctly, I think your problem is that you are nice to a fault. But, even if I agreed with you, I'd still have to disagree that behaving badly makes you a bad person.

To feel guilty, therefore, you must do something you believe is wrong, evil or sinful *and* you must also think that you, as a person, are totally bad too. That's how you create the feeling of guilt.

If you never hate yourself again for any negative behavior you have done or might commit, you will never feel guilty again. Mind you, however, you'll still *be* guilty of negative behaviors because you are human. But if you never rate yourself by your actions again you will never feel guilty, inferior, or depressed from that source again.

For homework I want you to practice talking yourself out of feeling guilty by not condemning yourself. Ask yourself if you behaved badly because you were deficient, ignorant, or disturbed, and then accept yourself as a fallible human being who occasionally has to behave poorly, not because you're evil but because you're imperfect and can never avoid all mistakes.

In addition to the above homework, I also suggested to Clara that she obtain and read my book, *The Three Faces of Love* (Hauck, 1984). This book focuses on showing people how to encourage cooperation, respect, and love from their partners. At her next session, 2 weeks later, Clara came in with a smile and I sensed she had done her homework and had made progress.

CLARA: I've been thinking a lot about what you've been saying, especially about how I might not have been a loving person after all, even though I was doing everything I could to please Ralph.

DR. H: Did you read *The Three Faces of Love?*

CLARA: I did. And it opened my eyes to what you were saying, that we should be tolerant of mean behavior no more than twice, because that's how we teach our partners to take advantage of us.

DR. H: And not feel guilty when we refuse to tolerate such behavior.

CLARA: Right. That's the hardest part of it.

DR. H: How so? Didn't you remember my advice about not blaming yourself for upsetting him? You can't disturb others you know, only frustrate them. Never forget the difference between the two.

CLARA: That's what I tried to remember, but it was so hard. When I refused to give him my whole paycheck he got furious and told me how unfair I was.

DR. H: And then you felt it was your fault that he was upset?

CLARA: Yes. I know what you said, but I automatically felt that he wouldn't be so upset if I hadn't refused him this favor. Am I wrong?

DR. H: No, you're not wrong. Of course he would not have gotten angry if you had given him your paycheck. However, that doesn't excuse him from his responsibility to control his anger. That's his problem, and that's his decision, not yours. He could have talked himself into feeling sorry for himself, or proud of you for being assertive, or simply accepted the fact that the world is unfair and no one gets everything they want and that mature people accept disappointment gracefully. He didn't do any of those. He chose to get mad, just like he chose to drink coffee this morning, or to add sugar, or to have a cigarette and to watch the news.

Neurotics always want people to change their behaviors in certain ways so that they, the neurotics, won't have to put up with frustrations. They love it when they can convince us that we are at fault for their upsets and therefore it's we who have to behave differently so they will feel better. Until we refuse to go along with that nonsense they will never appreciate how they make themselves upset and that they had better talk themselves out of whatever discomfort they talked themselves into.

CLARA: You don't mean to tell me that people never become upset simply because people treat them badly and say things that are very unkind, do you?

DR. H: Are you asking me if there are any exceptions to my point that people never disturb us emotionally, only we do that?

CLARA: Yes.

DR. H: No, there are no exceptions. But just a second, if you want to include infants and young children who simply don't have the experience or intelligence or the ability to think clearly for themselves, I think we could make a case for them being unable to protect themselves from upsets about their frustrations. But, when we're talking about older adolescents and grown-ups, I maintain that all the people in that group are certainly responsible for choosing to upset themselves over what happens to them.

CLARA: And you're saying that it doesn't much matter whether somebody's threatening me such as my husband did, or cursing me and yelling at me? You mean I'm not supposed to get upset by any of that stuff?

DR. H: You can get upset about anything as much as you like. But you can't rationally claim that the thing that's happening to you is the reason why you are upset. It is simply easier to talk yourself into disturbances when the frustrations are very severe and your life is in danger or somebody is saying really nasty and ugly things about you. Under those circumstances it's enormously easy to get upset, because the frustrations are so much more forceful. But the point still remains true that we are talking ourselves into disturbances. They don't happen to us unless we make mountains out of molehills over them.

CLARA: And the same goes for depression and feeling guilty?

DR. H: Absolutely. As I mentioned in one of our previous sessions, we make ourselves psychologically depressed by saying three different kinds of things to ourselves. The first is that we hate ourselves and blame ourselves because we have done something we are ashamed of or strongly disapprove of. The second is that we pity ourselves over what the world is handing us, and the third is heartbreak for other people and the suffering they are going through. In other words, we get psychologically depressed because we blame ourselves, pity ourselves, or pity others. If we never did any of those we'd never be severely psychologically depressed.

CLARA: That doesn't sound right. People aren't able to avoid all disturbances, are they? Isn't it natural for people to get upset?

DR. H: It's perfectly natural for them to get upset and one would expect them to. I am not saying that people should not become sad or quiet or seek some privacy while they nurse their wounds when something very bad happens to them. If we don't have any feelings we would be acting as though we were made out of iron and stone. We are not. We are humans and we have feelings and we are going to react with sadness, irritation, and annoyance to the negative things that happen to us.

CLARA: But you have just been telling me that we should not upset ourselves over anything and that when we are upset we're always the one who are doing it. Now you say it's all right to get upset.

Here, Clara is struggling to understand the REBT principle of self-responsibility for one's own emotional disturbance (Dryden & Yankura, 1993), as well as when it's "all right" versus "not all right" to be upset about negative life events. At this juncture, I decide to highlight the distinction between inappropriate (or unhealthy) and appropriate (or healthy) negative emotions.

DR. H: Let me explain an important distinction to you. I think that your question is an excellent one. There are reasonable emotional responses to frustrations and then there are unreasonable ones. If somebody bangs into your new car and you're annoyed, irritated or saddened by that event I would find nothing wrong with that. Why shouldn't you be upset to that degree? You'll have to have it fixed, rent another car in the meantime and so forth. With these additional frustrations, why should you jump for joy?

CLARA: But now you are saying it's okay to be upset?

DR. H: If you are appropriately emotionally upset that's one thing. We as psychotherapists and counselors don't make an issue out of that. Being sad and irritated or annoyed or disappointed are perfectly sensible reactions for people who have feelings. Life is filled with frustrations of that magnitude, which bring on reactions you have on and off all the days that you live. What we as mental health providers are trying to teach people not to do is to make their frustrations more serious than that. We don't want to talk ourselves into thinking things are tragic when, in fact, they are only sad. Or that they are unbearable and catastrophic when they are only annoying or irritating. When you talk to yourself in extreme terms you are going to get mightily upset. When you talk to yourself in more realistic ways by referring to things as being only sad, irritating, or annoying you don't become mightily disturbed, you simply become appropriately disturbed and unhappy. We could live with appropriate emotional reactions for a lifetime without ever creating more problems for ourselves or without suffering greatly. It is the extreme reactions, those which come from defining every frustration as unbearable, catastrophic, terrible, and horrible that we want to avoid. And, by refraining from such definitions you tend not to blame yourself, to pity yourself, or pity others.

CLARA: Well, just how would that apply in my case?

DR. H: Take the case of your feelings of guilt, for example. In the past you have tended to give in to everyone else's wishes because otherwise you would have felt that, because you were doing yourself a good turn, that would be a selfish act and that would make you a bad person.

CLARA: That's right, that's often what I did. I think I was too kind.

DR. H: Precisely. Now my point is that had you not made a mountain out of a molehill and put yourself down because you were being somewhat self-centered, you wouldn't have gotten depressed, you wouldn't have given in to others, and you would have made yourself more contented and enjoyed life more.

CLARA: You mean even if I honestly believed I was selfish?

DR. H: Sure. I don't think you would have been selfish, actually, but let's assume that you were. In your case, when you believe that you have been selfish or immoral or whatever, you think that's unbearable and then you get mighty upset over it.

CLARA: Well, what should I have done?

DR. H: Calm down, first of all, and realize that no matter what you did it can't upset you unless you let it. And second, talk yourself out of believing that acting selfishly or immorally is the end of the world and makes you a bad person. If you think you have behaved badly then ask yourself why you did it and what you might do in the future to avoid such bad behavior. Whipping yourself over your immoral or selfish behavior doesn't do a lot about changing it. To change your behavior you have to think about what you're doing and what you might be able to do instead. People who blame themselves all the time are simply smearing themselves with verbal filth and not thinking constructively at all. Remember, nothing you can do can make you a bad person. It only makes you human. We always have a right to be wrong and when we commit a sin or perform an unethical act we are doing what fallible human beings do.

CLARA: And what am I supposed to do then, just simply say it doesn't matter?

DR. H: Nonsense. It does matter. Immoral and unethical behavior are not to be condoned. We have to accept the fact that sinning, crime and violence, and all kinds of other assorted deeds are totally undesirable and we don't want to put up with them. But, until we change them, let's not hate ourselves and make everything worse. Let's accept ourselves as mistake-making human beings who can think clearly enough and have energy enough to do something about our mistakes.

CLARA: Do you suppose this is probably why I have always felt so inferior?

DR. H: It certainly is part of the picture, but not all of it. You just suggested that you struggle with feelings of inferiority. Actually, in many ways your problems have not been only feelings of inferiority but also feelings of conceit. You have actually felt that you are better than others.

CLARA: But that's ridiculous. I continually feel I am less capable and less deserving than other people. How can you say that I'm conceited?

DR. H: Because you're judging yourself more harshly than you would other people who committed the same mistakes.

CLARA: What do you mean by that? Are you saying that I'm harsher with myself than with others?

DR. H: Very often, yes. For example, suppose your best friend came to you and said that she had feelings of disgust with her husband, she was ready to leave him, and was going back on her marriage vows. How would you talk to her?

CLARA: Well, I would tell her that her feelings are understandable and that she's a good person and had been putting up with him for a long time and she shouldn't hate herself and so forth.

DR. H: Isn't that interesting? You would be very understanding of your friend, you would be forgiving, you would still think of her as an acceptable person and you wouldn't think she's bad, would you?

CLARA: Oh no, of course not.

DR. H: Yeah, but look what you've been saying to yourself. Those things that we just described your girlfriend doing are, in fact, what you have been doing. Yet you're able to forgive her and tell her not to hate herself, but you can't do that for yourself. Can you now figure out why I'd describe you as conceited?

CLARA: No, I can't. It's the last thing in the world I would describe myself as.

DR. H: Then why do you judge your friend by such kind and reasonable standards but refrain from doing that for yourself? You don't think she's bad because that's all we can expect from a peasant like her. She's just a normal mortal human being. But you, you're apparently not supposed to behave like most normal human beings do. We have to judge you by godlike, angelic, and superhuman standards. Who said you were such a high and mighty person that we had to judge you by standards of perfection?

CLARA: Oh my, I just never thought of this thing in that light. I hear what you're saying, but it just doesn't make any sense.

DR. H: It's a new idea to you, that's all. Think about it very carefully and see whether or not what I'm saying doesn't make sense.

The reader should be aware of the constant need to press the client on every issue that appears to be irrational. Obviously, this doesn't have to be done all at once, but it needs to be done quite directly, in respectful language, with as much brevity and clarity as possible. The therapist's debate should be clear and to the point. This is what Clara was finally benefiting from. But, as any experienced counselor knows, what appears to be understanding during the therapy session itself, turns into lukewarm conviction after the session is over. By the time the next appointment roles around, in a week or 2, sometimes a great deal of what was said previously has been forgotten. This happened in Clara's case, and she continued to experience difficulties with guilt feelings. The disputation of her guilt-producing notions was attempted in the next two sessions, but this time not about how she could keep herself from getting depressed as much as how she could keep herself from being used unfairly by her husband. A prior analysis of her previous marriages indicated that she had a habit of being a very tolerant person who did not protest unfairness until it got to the point where she found it unbearable. At that juncture it was simply too late for her to change the behavior of the men she had spoiled. They would fight back vigorously against what they thought were unfair restrictions. Things went from bad to worse until two divorces took place. Therefore it was not only time to teach her how not to be depressed, but also how not to be so passive and indulgent of her partners.

The following is a partial transcript from a later session, which deals with the matter of assertion and its relationship to depression.

DR. H: Well, how have you been since I saw you last time, Clara?

CLARA: I'm trying to apply what you tell me, but I must say it's a lot harder than it sounds.

DR. H: I understand that. In our business we say that to explain what to do is easy but to change is not.

CLARA: I couldn't agree more. The way you've been explaining my situation to me sounds as though you've been living next door and you see the situation exactly as it is.

DR. H: And now it's advisable for you to learn to change the kind of person you are.

CLARA: What are you talking about?

DR. H: It would be to your benefit to learn how to be more assertive and less passive. In other words, learn how to get tough and not let people push you around. Your major problem has always been that you're nice to a fault.

CLARA: But I always wanted to show my husbands that I loved them and I showed that love by being very nice and helpful, as much as I possibly could be.

DR. H: There's nothing wrong with that Clara, as long as you don't overdo it. What you fail to understand, and millions of people don't seem to understand, is that love can be expressed in three ways, not one. First, we can show our love by being nice to people when they are nice to us and in this way we show them gratitude. That's one of the more commonly accepted ways of showing that we love somebody. We do nice things in return.

CLARA: I try to do that all the time.

DR. H: Yes, I know you have and that's the problem. You didn't know when to stop.

CLARA: Well, when do you stop?

DR. H: When you begin to spoil the other person. That's the same as rewarding them for being unkind to you.

CLARA: You mean if I'm always nice I am teaching my husbands that they can get away with something?

DR. H: Of course. If you reward bad behavior you encourage more of it. Self-pity and other-pity are other conditions which lead to your depression. It's important for you to stop being so tolerant of negative behavior.

CLARA: I don't follow you. How does that lead to depression?

DR. H: When you pity others you aren't about to stand up to them, that's why. And if you pity yourself for the negative outcomes you then receive, you end up depressed, not intolerant.

CLARA: So what do I have to do?

DR. H: Change two irrational ideas into rational ones. To talk yourself out of pitying yourself, stop believing that not getting your way is absolutely unbearable. No doubt, when your husbands disappointed you, your thoughts went something like this, "Poor me. What did I do to deserve this? Everything I try turns out badly. Why do I have such bad luck?," and so on.

Then you did a similar thing when you attempted to deny your men their wishes. They would doubtlessly feel self-pity, look gloomy, depressed, hurt, unhappy, and then your heart would go out to them and, lo and behold, you probably thought you had to be upset and disturbed over their sorrows. That would lead to other-pity. Both types of pity—self and other—cause depression.

What I recommend instead is that the next time people do something bad to you and you believe that they don't know that it's wrong, talk to them once and, perhaps on another and separate occasion, discuss it with them a second time. Reason with them, go the extra mile, forgive seventy-times-seven as it says in the Bible, and then see if they don't change when you're patient and understanding. That is the second way in which we can show love, patience, and understanding. But it's generally not advisable to talk to others about the frustrations they are giving you more than twice.

CLARA: You mean I'm supposed to talk to them about a problem only two times?

DR. H: Right. No more than twice. If you continue to talk about a problem and never do anything else about it they then learn from you that you're only going to complain. That's easy enough for them to put up with. Why should they change and go through the effort and discomfort of changing for you if all they have to do is listen to your complaints and then go on and act the way they always have?

CLARA: But why wouldn't someone change after you have talked to them?

DR. H: Because they are either immature or emotionally disturbed. When you talk to people and they don't change, it is usually for one or both of these reasons. Mature people or undisturbed people can listen, can admit they are wrong, and are much more willing to go along with you when they understand that they have been behaving badly.

CLARA: But suppose talking to them one or two times doesn't help. Then what should I do?

DR. H: Then you use the third form of love, which is firmness or toughness. It goes like this. If someone does something bad to you and talking to them twice doesn't help, do something equally annoying to them. But, it must be done without anger, guilt, other-pity, fear of rejection, fear of physical harm, or fear of financial harm.

CLARA: My goodness—that's a tall order, isn't it?

DR. H: Indeed it is, but you are never going to be an assertive individual unless you control those six conditions which will defeat you every time.

CLARA: How's that?

DR. H: Well, look at it this way. If you try to stand up for your rights with anger you're going to be aggressive. If the person you are dealing with has any tendency to get angry he or she will certainly act against you just as vigorously as you have acted against them. That's no way to get cooperation. That's a good way to start a war.

The second condition, guilt, will surely stop you dead in your tracks if you want to get tough with someone because you're going to feel like a heel for what you're doing.

The third condition, other-pity, will also cause you to back away from being tough, because your heart is going to break for the inconvenience you're putting another person through. Just imagine how a mother might feel if she tells her daughter she can't go to a dance because she was disobedient. Then, as the girl leaves to go to her room, weeping and with her shoulders slumped, the mother gives in because she feels so badly for the girl.

The fourth condition is fear of rejection. If you're going to be afraid that someone is going to reject you, and that rejection hurts, you're certainly not going to get very tough with them.

Fears of physical and financial harm are in a different category. They are realistically painful consequences. The other four are not. Being yelled at, feeling guilty, pitying others, or being rejected, for example, are basically all harmless. But you can truly get hurt by negative physical or financial consequences when another person can wield those against you. I strongly recommend that you back down and give in until circumstances change for the better. But I don't think you should if you are dealing with feelings of anger, guilt, other-pity, or rejection.

CLARA: You're telling me that if I had stood up to my husbands in the past I could have saved my marriages?

DR. H: Quite possibly. They may well have respected you more, and from respect can come love. When they discovered that they could manipulate you they lost respect for you and therefore they lost their love.

CLARA: I don't understand that.

DR. H: I have found that most adults do not love people they can push around. Instead, they look down on them because they are weak. This creates feelings of disgust or dislike, rather than love. Therefore, if you want to be loved, first get the other person to respect you—and that means to make them mildly afraid of you.

CLARA: Mildly afraid? You mean I'm going to get somebody to love me if I make them afraid of me?

DR. H: That's exactly what I'm saying. But it can't be great fear, it must be mild fear, the kind of fear they experience when they know you are not going to put up with their unfairness and that you are going to respond by making them as uncomfortable as they made you. That's the third way to show love—with firmness that brings on respect. And the way you achieve that is to meet two conditions: one, you've got to have the power to make somebody uncomfortable, and two, you have to have the courage to use that power.

CLARA: And that's how I make people love me?

DR. H: I can practically guarantee you that you would have done better with your marriages had you tried loving your past partners by being tough from time to time rather than always being agreeable and believing that the more you do for somebody the more they are going to love you. As I said before, you neglected yourself in your marriages and you spoiled the fellows you lived with. That's happening again in this marriage.

Clara has now been introduced to several bodies of knowledge about her psychological dynamics, which can help her considerably toward having more success in all relationships, and which will serve to relieve her depression.

I have continued to see Clara, but now at a frequency of once a month. She knew what she had to do and I wanted to give her the time she needed to apply what she had learned during our weekly or semi-monthly sessions. At this writing a half year has passed and definite changes have occurred.

Protesting her displeasure has increased. No longer does she suffer frustrations silently. Now she debates, complains, and disagrees. When once she would have felt very guilty for daring to express her views, now she does it easily and with confidence. It was generally her attitude that her husband was immature, self-centered, and very impractical, but she hardly dared to admit those feelings, even to herself.

As that process continued, her husband hardened in his resistance in yielding to her. Rather than acquiesce as she habitually was prone to do, she met him head-on and stood her ground as I had trained her to do. Her "just reasonable" contentment level was her guide as to whether she was ethical in her pursuit. That cured her of the guilt which had played so central a role in her depression.

It was obvious after my last three sessions with her that she was heading for a divorce. She gave all she could without reaching the point of resentment and she would give no more. If her husband does not yield his desires and try to satisfy her to a reasonable degree, she will surely leave him. She knows this is a likely eventuality and it does not trouble her greatly. In my view this therapy was highly successful.

CONCLUSION

The case of Clara is very typical of a whole group of people we therapists see who are basically decent, hard-working, and responsible, but who turn out to be miserable and disturbed because they engage in excessive self-blame and feed into neurotic and inconsiderate behavior from others. To be of assistance to such individuals, the therapist must first focus on the dynamics of depression as presented in the three-factor model outlined above. It is also highly important to teach these clients how to stand up for themselves, and how to combat and confront the people who have always treated them so poorly (Hauck, 1979b; Madsen & Madsen, 1980). To do that they need to learn the following three rules of assertion:

1. If others do a good thing to you do something equally good to them. $(+ = +)$
2. If others do something bad to you and don't realize they are behaving badly, reason with them, but only on two separate occasions. $(- = + \times 2)$

3. If others do something bad to you a third time and talking to them twice did not help, do something equally annoying to them, but it must be without anger, guilt, other-pity, fear of rejection, fear of physical harm, or fear of financial harm. $(- = -)$

These guidelines for assertion focus on the behavioral aspect of the curative process. It is simply not enough for our clients to talk themselves out of being depressed. They also ideally need to talk themselves out of being passive and continually rewarding with kindness, understanding, and endless patience the people who are mistreating them. A two-pronged cognitive *and* behavioral attack usually has to take place in order to get the results we are looking for. This idea was recently underscored by Ellis (1995), when he announced that he was changing the initials of his system from RET to REBT (the B standing for Behavior).

Although REBT has been criticized at times for placing too much emphasis on cognitive disputing of irrational beliefs (Lazarus, 1989), the reality is that it has almost always accorded behavioral methods an important place within treatment. Quite often, behavioral exercises are suggested to clients as a particularly powerful vehicle for countering irrational philosophies. In addition, these exercises frequently have the potential to help clients develop valuable skills (such as those related to assertiveness) and attain desired outcomes within their interpersonal environments.

With its emphasis on the sorts of cognitive and behavioral interventions described in this chapter, REBT is able to help a great many depressed individuals to overcome their present-day depressive episodes. Importantly, however, it is able to go even further than this by encouraging clients to accomplish a deep-seated, pervasive, and enduring change in their basic personal philosophies. When clients commit themselves to attaining such change, they will be able to greatly reduce their vulnerability to future depressive episodes—as well as to the host of other emotional and behavioral disturbances that afflict so much of humankind.

REFERENCES

American Psychiatric Association. (1994). *Diagnostic and statistical manual of mental disorders* (4th ed.). Washington, DC: Author.

Beck, A. T. (1963). Thinking and depression. *Archives of General Psychiatry, 9*, 324–333.

Beck, A. T. (1967). *Depression: Causes and treatment.* Philadelphia: University of Pennsylvania Press.

Beck, A. T., Rush, A. J., Shaw, B. F., & Emery, G. (1979). *Cognitive therapy of depression.* New York: Guilford.

Dryden, W. (1990). *Rational-emotive counselling in action.* London: Sage.

Dryden, W., & DiGiuseppe, R. (1990). *A primer on rational-emotive therapy.* Champaign, IL: Research Press.

Dryden, W., & Yankura, J. (1993). *Counselling individuals: A rational-emotive handbook.* London: Whurr.

Ellis, A. (1962). *Reason and emotion in psychotherapy.* Secaucus, NJ: Lyle Stuart.

Ellis, A. (1977). The basic clinical theory of rational-emotive therapy. In A. Ellis & R. Grieger (Eds.), *Handbook of rational-emotive therapy* (pp. 3–34). New York: Springer Publishing Co.

Ellis, A. (1987). A sadly neglected cognitive element in depression. *Cognitive Therapy and Research, 11*, 121–146.

Ellis, A. (1995). Changing rational-emotive therapy (RET) to rational emotive behavior therapy (REBT). *Journal of Rational-Emotive and Cognitive-Behavior Therapy, 13*(2), 85–89.

Freud, S. (1950). Mourning and melancholia. In *Collected papers (vol. 4).* London: Hogarth Press and the Institute of Psychoanalysis.

Hauck, P. A. (1971). An RET theory of depression. *Rational Living, 6*(2), 32–35.

Hauck, P. A. (1973). *Overcoming depression.* Philadelphia: Westminster.

Hauck, P. A. (1979a). *Brief counseling with RET.* Philadelphia: Westminster.

Hauck, P. A. (1979b). *How to stand up for yourself.* Philadelphia: Westminster.

Hauck, P. A. (1984). *The three faces of love.* Philadelphia: Westminster.

Hauck, P. A. (1991). *Overcoming the rating game.* Philadelphia: Westminster.

Kaelber, C. T., Moul, D. E., & Farmer, M. E. (1995). Epidemiology of depression. In E. E. Beckham & W. R. Leber (Eds.), *Handbook of depression* (2nd ed.) (pp. 3–35). New York: Guilford.

Kessler, R. C., McGonagle, K. A., Swartz, M., Blazer, D. G., & Nelson, C. B. (1993). Sex and depression in the National Comorbidity Survey: I. Lifetime prevalence, chronicity and recurrence. *Journal of Affective Disorders, 29*, 85–96.

Kessler, R. C., McGonagle, K. A., Zhao, S., Nelson, C. B., Hughes, M., Eshleman, S., Wittchen, H.-U., & Kendler, K. S. (1994). Lifetime and 12-month prevalence of DSM-III-R psychiatric disorders in the United States: Results from the National Comorbidity Survey. *Archives of General Psychiatry, 51*, 8–19.

Lazarus, A. A. (1989). The practice of rational-emotive therapy. In M. E. Bernard & R. DiGiuseppe (Eds.), *Inside rational-emotive therapy: A critical appraisal of the theory and therapy of Albert Ellis* (pp. 95–112). San Diego, CA: Academic.

London, T. (1993). The case against self-esteem. Evanston, IL: Garfield.

Madsen, C., Jr., & Madsen, K. C. (1980). *Teaching/discipline.* Boston: Allyn & Bacon.

Paykel, E. S. (1991). Depression in women. *British Journal of Psychiatry, 158*(Suppl. 10), 22–29.

Regier, D. A., & Robins, L. (1991). Introduction. In L. Robins & E. Regier (Eds.), *Psychiatric disorders in America* (pp. 1–10). New York: Free Press.

Walen, S. R., DiGiuseppe, R., & Dryden, W. (1992). *A practitioner's guide to rational-emotive therapy.* New York: Oxford University Press.

Walen, S. R., & Rader, M. W. (1991). Depression and RET: Perspectives from wounded healers. In M. Bernard (Ed.), *Using rational-emotive therapy effectively* (pp. 219–264). New York: Plenum.

Weissman, M. M., Bland, R., Joyce, P. R., Newman, S., Wells, J. E., & Wittchen, H. (1993). Sex differences in rates of depression: Cross-national perspectives. *Journal of Affective Disorders, 29,* 77–84.

Yankura, J., & Dryden, W. (1994). *Albert Ellis.* London: Sage.

Young, J. E. (1990). *Cognitive therapy for personality disorders: A schema-focused approach.* Sarasota, FL: Professional Resource Exchange.

Young, J. E., Beck, A. T., & Weinberger, A. (1993). Depression. In D. H. Barlow (Ed.), *Clinical handbook of psychological disorders: A step-by-step treatment manual* (pp. 240–277). New York: Guilford.

CHAPTER 4

Michael: A Developmental REBT Approach in the Treatment of ADHD

Patricia McKeegan

F IFTEEN-YEAR-OLD Michael strode into the office smiling like a California-surfer version of the Cheshire cat. His sun-streaked hair fell over his eyes, and his lanky frame was bronzed from weeks of summer sun and "hanging out" at the beach near his home. As he angled himself onto the couch, his smile broadened into a wide grin. At this point he could no longer keep his secret.

"Hey, I didn't know you had seen Darren (referring to an adolescent from his school). He told me this afternoon that he had come to see you a couple of times."

"Well, Michael, remember when you and I talked about confidentiality? How what gets talked about here stays here?"

"Oh yeah, sure. I know you can't tell me that Darren was here, but that's okay—I know he was here 'cause he told me! And that's not really what I'm excited about anyway."

"Oh?"

"Well, Darren told me he only came a couple of times and then he quit, and I've figured out what that's all about."

"You've got it figured out?"

"Sure! In therapy you have to look at yourself. I don't think Darren was ready to look at himself."

In this brief exchange Michael demonstrated that he had internalized a primary insight germane to rational emotive behavior therapy (REBT): We need to look at ourselves to find the source of emotional disturbance.

Adolescents in general, and adolescents with attention-deficit hyperactivity disorder (ADHD) in particular, tend to be woefully lacking in insight about their own contributions to their emotional upsets. And yet, Michael articulated this understanding in a quite matter-of-fact manner.

Michael and I have had a long-term therapeutic relationship that began when he was 8 years old. From the developmental perspective, the therapeutic endeavor has spanned a good portion of Michael's middle childhood, his early adolescence, and now, his mid-adolescence. REBT theory, in concert with a developmental focus, has guided the implementation of therapeutic strategies. During this 8-year period, Michael and I have met for as many as 35 consecutive sessions (in the very beginning of therapy) to as few as one or two sessions to tackle a new problem. Although most of the meetings were individual therapy sessions, Michael also participated in a 10-session structured social skills training group with three other boys diagnosed as ADHD when he was 9 years old. Intervention strategies included preplanned re-entry into therapy at key developmental points (for example, his move to the middle school at age 11, and his move to the high school at age 14). Although the focus of this chapter will be on Michael and the benefits he derived from REBT, the reader should know that his mother was also seen intermittently throughout the same period with two primary foci: How to manage Michael's often difficult behavior, and how to deal with her own upsets relative to Michael's behavior. In addition, contacts with school personnel were undertaken when appropriate.

Michael is not presented here as *the* typical child with ADHD—there is no typical child or adolescent with ADHD. Many children diagnosed with ADHD manifest all three of the primary symptoms of this disorder—inattention, hyperactivity, and impulsivity—but they do so to varying degrees; others warrant the diagnosis by virtue of the inattention component alone. Usually, by the time a child with ADHD is seen for psychotherapy, a variety of interpersonal and academic problems have emerged. Before introducing Michael and his particular presenting problems, an overview of ADHD, emphasizing a historical review of the diagnostic criteria and a brief examination of pertinent research, is presented.

OVERVIEW OF ATTENTION-DEFICIT HYPERACTIVITY DISORDER

The 1990s has witnessed a surge of interest in ADHD. Both the professional literature and the lay press reflect the growing consensus that ADHD is not simply a disorder of childhood (as was previously thought), but also a syndrome that often continues into adulthood. This finding brings yet another perspective to a disorder that has been through several reconceptualizations since its first mention in 1902, when it was referred to as defective moral control (Barkley, 1990). This brief review begins with the most current conceptualization of ADHD, and ends with a perusal of current treatment issues.

Diagnostic Criteria

The *Diagnostic and Statistical Manual of Mental Disorders*, fourth edition (DSM-IV; American Psychiatric Association, 1994) requires the presence of inattention and/or hyperactivity-impulsivity in its current conceptualization of attention-deficit/hyperactivity disorder. In a minor departure from DSM-III-R (1987), the DSM-IV delineates criteria that allow for coding of the disorder as "Predominantly Inattentive Type," "Predominately Hyperactive-Impulsive Type," or "Combined Type."

From a historical standpoint several terms have been used to describe children whose primary difficulties are restlessness, impulsivity, and poor concentration. Minimal brain damage, hyperactivity, hyperkinetic reaction of childhood, and minimal cerebral dysfunction have been the classifications most commonly employed (Henker & Whalen, 1989). Early conceptualizations of ADHD emphasized the overactivity or restlessness of these children (Barkley, 1989). With the publication of the 1980 edition of the *Diagnostic and*

Statistical Manual, third edition (DSM-III; American Psychiatric Association, 1980), the psychiatric community recognized the centrality of attentional difficulties to the disorder and changed DSM-II's hyperkinetic reaction of childhood to attention deficit disorder. The defining symptomatology remains intact to the present: developmentally inappropriate inattentiveness, impulsivity and overactivity, and onset before the age of 7. In DSM-IV, as in previous editions, Attention-Deficit/Hyperactivity Disorder is listed in the section on "Disorders Usually First Evident in Infancy, Childhood or Adolescence," although current criteria include terminology such as "fails to finish duties in the workplace," which permit coding of the adult-status syndrome.

It should be noted that it is typically the secondary problems of ADHD (poor peer relationships, academic underachievement, low frustration tolerance, poor self-concept and/or aggression or conduct problems) that bring the ADHD youngster to the attention of the clinician.

Prevalence

Prevalence estimates for ADHD have ranged from 3 to 5% of the school-age population (DSM-IV, 1994) to as high as 20% (e.g., August & Garfinkel, 1989). Such variable findings result from differences in criteria, raters, measuring instruments, and cutoff points on assessment instruments (Wicks-Nelson & Israel, 1991). A consistent finding is that males are more frequently diagnosed than females. Ratios range from 4:1 to 9:1, depending on the population sample (i.e., general population or clinic samples (DSM-IV, 1994)).

Research on Attention-Deficit Hyperactivity Disorder

An exhaustive review of the research on ADHD is beyond the scope of this chapter. The reader interested in a general review of the research findings is referred to Henker and Whalen (1989). Causal hypotheses range from prenatal trauma to sugar consumption to parenting style (Kendall & Braswell, 1993), and have been reviewed by Barkley (1990) and Braswell and Bloomquist (1991). Douglas and her colleagues (Douglas, 1980, 1983; Douglas & Peters, 1979) posit cognitive processing deficits as central to the difficulties experienced by the ADHD child. Barkley (1990) agrees and conceptualizes

ADHD as a disorder of response inhibition and related executive functions resulting in deficient self-regulation, impaired cross-temporal organization of behavior, and diminished social effectiveness and adaptation. Research germane to hypothesized biological factors may be found in Anastopoulos and Barkley (1988), and Zametkin and Rapoport (1987). Kendall and Braswell (1993) report that current evidence appears to favor a biological factor in the etiology of ADHD, especially with respect to certain neurochemical transmitters, which appear to effect specific brain regions differentially. This results in underactivity in those regions associated with the regulation and planning of behavior, and overactivity in regions involving the perception of sensorimotor stimulation. Caution is warranted, however, in accepting a "one disorder, one cause" model for ADHD. A multicausal perspective is espoused by Hartsough and Lambert (1982), who argue that "both individual differences in the organic and psychological make-up of the child and individual differences in the family and social environment contribute to whether or not a child is identified as hyperactive" (p. 273).

Developmental Perspective

Although research and clinical findings appear to support the primary symptomatology of restlessness and overactivity, attentional difficulties and impulsivity in ADHD, several authors (e.g., Barkley, 1990; Ross & Ross, 1976) have noted the importance of developmental shifts in symptomatology. As infants, children with ADHD have been described as particularly demanding and irritable and as having difficulties in establishing regular sleep-eat-elimination patterns (Ross & Ross, 1976). The preschool years may be marked by emotional lability and continued irregularity of physiological functioning. Parents frequently report that disciplinary measures that worked with their other children do not seem to work with their ADHD preschooler. Should the child be enrolled in a day-care or preschool program, reports may begin to reach home concerning the child's inattentiveness and/or inappropriate behavior toward peers. Such behaviors tend to become more noticeable as the child enters elementary school. The demands of the classroom environment highlight the child's distractibility, poor social skills, and failure to attend to the tasks at hand. The relationship between ADHD and academic failure is well established, but research has yet to demonstrate the causal links (McGee & Share, 1988). The developmental task of middle childhood—gaining a sense of mastery in an enlarging social world—is thwarted by skills deficits and the development of a poor self-concept. As Ross and Ross (1976) suggest, the cumulative effects of such deficits may become particularly difficult during adolescence. Lambert, Hartsough, Sassone, and Sandoval (1987) found that 80% of adolescents diagnosed as ADHD during the primary school years continued to experience behavioral and/or cognitive-developmental abnormality. Forty-three percent continued to require active treatment. Henker and Whalen (1989) reported that adulthood is often marked by above-average rates of job changes, traffic accidents, marital difficulties, and legal infractions.

Treatment of ADHD

To date, the most carefully researched and efficacious treatment for the primary symtomatology of ADHD is stimulant medication. The most frequently prescribed medication is methylphenidate (Ritalin). Alternative stimulants such as dextroamphetamine (Dexedrine) or pemoline (Cylert) are sometimes used, as is the antidepressant imipramine (Tofranil) (Henker & Whalen, 1989). Tannock, Schachar, Carr, Chajczyk, and Logan (1989) report that approximately 75% of medicated ADHD children show increased attention and reduced impulsivity and activity level. However, the effects of medication alone on the secondary symptoms of ADHD are less encouraging. Although studies indicate some enhancement of adult–child social interactions when medication is used, the effect on peer relationships is less encouraging (Henker & Whalen, 1989). Research on the effects of medication on academic achievement presents a confusing array of findings. Although some early data suggested improvement in the quantity and quality of work completed by children receiving medication, Barkley (1989) and Gadow (1985) suggest that the weight of the evidence does not provide support for significant academic improvement.

Nonpharmacologic interventions of note have included both behavioral and cognitive-behavioral strategies. Behavior modification programs have aimed for improvements in rule adherence, academic effort, and social interaction. Modest efficacy in both home and school settings has been found with behavioral strategies, although generalization of effects remains problematic. Research has not as yet validated positive long-term outcomes for behavioral interventions (Henker & Whalen, 1989; Wicks-Nelson & Israel, 1991).

In a comprehensive review of cognitive-behavioral treatment outcome results, Kendall and Braswell (1993) examined the effect of both subject variables and treatment factors in an attempt to reconcile conflictng findings emerging from the research. Of interest for the purposes of this chapter are the findings that interventions need to take into account both the age and the cognitive development of the child. For example, self-instructional methods are generally not appropriate until the child has established functional covert self-talk (at approximately 5 or 6 years of age in the normally developing child). Children at lower levels of cognitive development (as measured by Piagetian tasks) require more task-specific, concrete interventions, whereas more cognitively advanced youngsters respond best to more abstract interventions. Treatment factors that appear to contribute more favorable outcomes are the inclusion of parents and other family members in treatment, and the coordination of home–school use of problem-solving methods. Use of external behavioral contingencies, as well as the addition of a self-reinforcement component (as per Nelson & Birkimer, 1978), are also viewed as important in treatment outcome. Kendall and Braswell's review ends with a more optimistic conclusion than previous reviews. The authors assert that more information is now available to guide both clinicians and researchers.

Prognosis

The prognosis for children identified with ADHD varies considerably. Weiss and Hechtman (1986) report that, as adults, one-third to one-half apparently do not experience difficulties attributable to their ADHD status as children. The remainder variously demonstrate continuing difficulties with the primary deficits and/or impaired social relationships, depression, antisocial behavior, and drug use. Lambert's (1988) prospective study of ADHD adolescents found significantly poorer educational outcomes and a greater extent of conduct disorders when compared with age-peer controls. Mannuzza, Klein, Bessler, Malloy, and LaPadula (1993) examined adult outcomes of boys diagnosed with hyperactivity as children. Approximately 25% of ADHD subjects never completed high school (versus 2% of controls), and ADHD subjects manifested a significantly higher rate of substance abuse and were 10 times more likely to have an antisocial personality disorder in adulthood.

Using REBT with ADHD

As was previously noted, current research is strongly suggestive of a biological basis for the triad of symptoms (attentional difficulties, impulsivity, and hyperactivity) considered to be the primary problems of ADHD. In addition to these core symptoms, children and adults with ADHD typically experience difficulties in the following areas: generating and following rules, interpreting and responding to social cues, and initiating goal-directed behavior. The core symptoms and their resulting difficulties form the building blocks on which the secondary problems of ADHD are constructed. These include low frustration tolerance (a frequent correlate of anger problems and poor academic achievement), low self-esteem, social and evaluative anxiety, and depression.

Although research points to the efficacy of stimulant medication for the treatment of the primary problems of ADHD, psychopharmacologic treatment has little or no effect on the secondary problems associated with ADHD. REBT, with its emphasis on reducing demandingness on self and others (the "musts" of emotional disturbance), provides the clinician with an array of techniques and strategies for helping the client deal with the secondary problems of ADHD. More specifically, REBT is able to help the client identify, challenge, and replace the beliefs underpinning negative self-rating, low frustration tolerance, and evaluative anxiety. In addition, REBT offers the clinician the flexibility and creative license needed for working with ADHD child clients, who may be particularly difficult to engage in the therapeutic process.

REBT aims for deep philosophically based solutions to clients' emotional and behavioral problems. Such a view calls for the use of "elegant" or "specific" disputation strategies, wherein the client's irrational *evaluative* cognitions of a specific antecedent event are challenged (DiGiuseppe, 1991). The persistent therapeutic challenges to the client's deeply held convictions (his "musts") about the self, others, or the world pave the way for the client to construct a more rational philosophical orientation to the world. However, REBT also acknowledges that certain clients may benefit with more general or empirical disputation strategies (i.e., disputation of the distorted *descriptive* cognition connected with specific antecedent events). In particular, child clients, depending on their level of cognitive sophistication, may more easily grasp disputing that is targeted at negatively distorted inferences. For example, a child's belief that it is terrible to have no friends may be more successfully disputed with the query, "Is it really true that *nobody* likes you?" rather than the more philosophically based query, "What would it mean about you if nobody liked you?" (Linscott & DiGiuseppe, 1994).

The case illustration presented here included several REBT strategies. The reader will note both the use of general disputation strategies (especially during Michael's childhood) and the gradual shift to more specific disputation strategies as Michael matured.

SUMMARY

Kendall and Braswell's (1993) summative statement bears note:

> There is an urgent need to better understand the cognitive/biological under-pinnings of the targeted difficulties, so that intervention efforts can be increasingly refined and the field can become more realistic about the types of issues that are responsive to and appropriate for psychotherapeutic intervention. (p. 51)

ADHD presents as a complex disorder, frequently overlapping with conduct disorder, sometimes presenting clinically with a symtomatology in at least partial accord with pervasive developmental disorder. We are still far from postulating definitive etiological factors. Outcome studies suggest that children with ADHD are, indeed, at risk for adult psychopathology. My own clinical observations suggest that some of these children develop a certain rigidity of thinking as they become adolescents. This inflexible, often perseverative cognitive style may have developed during middle childhood, either as a direct correlate of cognitive processing deficits, or as a maladaptive strategy to cope with a persistent array of overwhelming external stimuli. These observations have led me to entertain working hypotheses regarding the relationship between ADHD and the possible development of various personality disorders for these children.

As has been noted in this brief review, the research has not as yet delineated an ideal treatment for ADHD. However, the available research does provide a reasonable rationale for psychotherapeutic intervention and does propose particular intervention strategies. Rational emotive behavior theory, in conjunction with affective and cognitive theories of development, offers the clinician a unique conceptualization and treatment plan to pursue with children and adults diagnosed with ADHD.

CASE ILLUSTRATION

About Michael

Michael is the older son of college-educated parents. His brother, Mark, is 2 years younger. His parents were divorced when he was 6 years old. Parental concern about specific aspects of development, in particular, delayed speech, oppositional behavior, excessive tantrum behavior, and poor fine-motor coordination, prompted a psychological evaluation when he was 4 years old.

At the time of the evaluation, the Stanford-Binet Intelligence Scale revealed overall intellectual functioning in the high average range (full-scale IQ score of 117). Despite adequate intellectual functioning, the Vineland Social Maturity Scale indicated a 10-month lag in social skills. Although age-appropriate skills were generally evinced in feeding, dressing, and toileting (although Michael was still enuretic), social and communication skills were below expectancy. The examiner noted Michael's "overattention to the obscure details of objects and situations in his immediate environment." She further noted that "something that would not distract other children appears to draw and hold his attention" and that his communicative patterns were sometimes tangential and perseverative. The examiner reported that the evaluation process required much limit-setting and frequent refocusing to the task at hand.

This early work-up is notable in that was to foreshadow the findings of additional psychological and neurological evaluations completed by other examiners. The Wechsler Intelligence Scale for Children-Revised (WISC-R) administered by the school psychologist in Michael's public school when he was seven years old, again resulted in a full-scale intelligence quotient of 117. The examiner wrote that Michael "was frequently distracted by irrelevant features of the testing materials and by his own verbal associations. In addition, . . . he was in almost constant motion while in his seat." A pediatric neurological examination, completed in 1988 when Michael was 9 years old, revealed the presence of some scattered soft neurologic signs.

Michael was first seen in my office in March 1987. At that time he was 8 years old, and was completing the second grade in a suburban public school. Prior to his mother's seeking to engage Michael in psychotherapy, the school had completed a special education evaluation and had determined that Michael was "learning disabled." Because of this classification, Michael was receiving small-group remedial instruction for 40 minutes a day, while remaining in the regular classroom for the remainder of the school day. Michael's presenting problems, as cited by his mother, included poor academic achievement, lack of friends, tantrum behavior, and difficulty initiating and remaining on-task when completing both simple household chores and homework. The overall clinical impression at this first meeting was of a conspicuous immaturity. An articulate and handsome child, tall for his age, Michael appeared poorly coordinated and inadequately focused. Attentional difficulties were easily observed as Michael overattended to office minutia and had considerable difficulty following a conversation geared toward his age level. He had great difficulty remaining seated, for even the briefest amount of time, and would rock to and fro when he did manage to remain seated. Despite his restless behavior, he was able to state a particular problem that was bothering him. Jessica, a classmate, was "always" teasing him in the schoolyard and this upset him. It appeared that Jessica was engaging in fairly typical second-grade behavior, but Michael clearly did not know how to begin to handle the situation. Although Michael was able to state that he felt "mad" at Jessica, it was clear that he also felt incompetent and frustrated by his lack of skill in managing this social dilemma. In this initial session with Michael the following discourse took place:

DR. P: Michael, how do you feel when Jessica calls you a butthead?

MICHAEL: I get really mad!

DR. P: And then what happens?

MICHAEL: I hit her and then she tells the (schoolyard) aide, and then I have to go inside and sit on the dumb bench by the principal's office and then I'm *really* mad.
(Michael recites this litany in a song-song fashion, giving the impression that this chain of events is routine.)

DR. P: That sounds like "two mads" to me.

MICHAEL: Yeah *(sighs)*.

DR. P: It doesn't sound like you have much fun at recess if you're feeling mad.

MICHAEL: No . . . and it's all because of that dumb Jessica!

DR. P: *And,* when you get mad at Jessica, you hit her and that gets *you* in trouble.

MICHAEL: Yep.

DR. P: Michael, suppose if you and I could figure out a way to help you feel "not mad" at Jessica. Would that be a good idea?

MICHAEL: Maybe . . .

In this first session with Michael I wished to convey to him that a psychologist was a special kind of helper, one who could help him figure out ways to handle problems and help him learn ways to "feel good." In addition, in this first brief exchange, a connection was made between feelings and resultant actions, and some foundation was laid for the connection between thoughts and feelings.

As a follow-up to this initial session, Michael's mother was asked to complete a Conners Parent Rating Scale (Conners, 1970) and the Personality Inventory for Children (Wirt, Lachar, Klinedinst, & Seat, 1984). The Conners Teacher Rating Scale (Conners, 1969) was completed by Michael's classroom teacher, as well as his special-education resource room teacher. These inventories, my clinical observations during Michael's initial sessions, and the previous psychological evaluations all pointed to a child manifesting the symptoms of attention-deficit hyperactivity disorder. During the third grade Michael was placed on Ritalin, and he continued this medication until the end of fourth grade. At that point his mother stopped the medication, because she felt uncomfortable with drug therapy.

Michael has not received Ritalin nor any other psychotropic medication since that time.

Implementation of REBT with Michael

At the time I began treatment with Michael in 1987, cognitive-behavioral psychotherapy in general was being viewed as a panacea for the failures of both psychopharmacology and behavioral interventions in the treatment of ADHD. By 1990, however, research findings suggested a more cautious optimism regarding the use of cognitive-behavioral strategies for children diagnosed with ADHD. In particular, the research suggested that ADHD children were demonstrating a pattern of being "consistently inconsistent" in terms of therapeutic outcome. Most clinicians working with these children would consistently agree! From the clinical perspective, these children display inconsistencies across cognitive, emotional, and behavioral domains throughout the developmental period. In addition, they have greater-than-average difficulties implementing emotional and behavioral control across settings and across time. Fortunately, the clinician, unlike the researcher, is free to continually assess the process of change, and has latitude with respect to changing strategies over time.

Rational emotive behavior therapy, with its multifaceted and flexible focus on cognitive, emotional, and behavioral change (Ellis, 1991), offers distinct possibilities for teaching the ADHD child a different way of thinking about the world, and a way to evaluate his own emotional and behavioral response to that world. The fundamental imperative in treating any child is to safeguard the potential for continued optimal development. Therefore, for the REBT therapist engaged in therapeutic work with children, a key question is, "Can REBT therapy during the developmental period minimize the *development* of an absolutistic and imperative personal philosophy, which, according to REBT theory, leads to emotional disturbance?"

The following account of the use of REBT with Michael illustrates the changing goals and therapeutic strategies employed for each of three developmental periods. A few general principles guided the use of REBT throughout the therapeutic endeavor:

1. Maintain a developmental focus in creating a treatment plan.
2. Develop a working alliance with Michael and his mother, which emphasized collaboration.

3. Assess Michael's assets, as well as his liabilities, on a continual basis and implement treatment strategies accordingly.

Middle childhood—Michael (Age 8–11).   Middle childhood is marked by entry into formal schooling and an emphasis on academic and social skills. The child's enlarging social world demands a set of increasingly skillful social behaviors, which, if below expected levels, tend to be quickly noted by adults and peers alike. Michael, at age 8, was not only falling behind academically, but also evinced several behavioral excesses and deficits which made him stand apart from his peers. As noted previously, attentional difficulties included both inability to focus on relevant tasks, as well as perseverative tendencies. He frequently evinced tantrum behavior. Michael's restlessness was noted in squirmy, frequently-off-the-chair motor responses and frequently-off-the-topic verbal responses. Perhaps most significant was his mother's report that he had never had a friend.

The particular goals of treatment for Michael during this period were:

1. Decrease age-inappropriate motoric excesses (e.g., rocking), which set him apart from his peers.
2. Reduce tantrum behavior.
3. Begin a rational-emotive educational experience, wherein Michael could learn through repeated experiences that thoughts, feelings, and behaviors are interrelated (Ellis, 1991).
4. Combine rational-emotive education with a formalized social skills training program to enable Michael to approximate more closely age-appropriate interactions with peers.
5. Teach Michael to monitor self-talk as a means to help himself with academic tasks and social situations.

Getting started. Michael's limited attention span and restlessness were to make therapy challenging. It was clear that limit-setting and a definitive structure to the therapy hour would be required to accomplish our goals. Almost immediately I began to implement strategies for keeping him focused during our sessions, as illustrated by the following exchange:

DR. P: Michael, it's good to see you again. I was wondering, did you think about which name you would like to call me, Dr. McKeegan, or Dr. Pat?

MICHAEL: Dr. Pat.

DR. P: Fine. I like that. And you said last week that you would
            like to be called Michael. Is that right?

MICHAEL: Yeah. Some people call me Mike, but everybody in my
            family calls me Michael. I like Michael.
            *(Because of Michael's extreme restlessness, it was decided
            beforehand to give him something to "fiddle" with, which
            would help him remain seated, at least for brief periods.)*

DR. P: Michael, I've got some clay here. Would you like to
            play with some while we're talking?
            *(Michael accepted the clay and began to roll out "snakes"
            while seated on the floor at a low table. It became apparent
            that this was an effective strategy. His ability to remain
            seated for longer periods [5–10 minutes] was noted.)*

DR. P: Michael, do you remember what kind of doctor I am?

MICHAEL: Yeah. A psychologist.

DR. P: Good remembering. Michael! Now, here comes a re-
            ally hard question. Do you remember what a psy-
            chologist does?

MICHAEL: Helps people . . . Do you know that they are putting in
            new sewer pipes by my house? All the streets are dug
            up. Big sand piles all over the place. Here, give me a
            pencil. I can draw a map.
            *(Michael takes the pencil and begins to draw streets, intersec-
            tions, and piles of sand, all the while describing in detail the
            work of excavation and pipe-laying.)*

This type of divergent conversation was frequent in our early
sessions. During this phase of treatment, Michael would often go
"off topic" and would get "stuck" on lengthy discussions about
unrelated ideas. With care, I reoriented Michael to the topic at
hand.

DR. P: Michael. *{I say his name while touching his hand. I wait
            for eye contact.}* Michael, you said that a psychologist
            helps people. Do you remember what kind of help?

MICHAEL: Helps them be good listeners.

DR. P: Yes, a psychologist can help people be good listeners. Do you remember something else a psychologist does?

MICHAEL: Helps people feel good.

DR. P: Good remembering, Michael. Yes, a psychologist can teach people ways to be good listeners and can teach people ways to feel good about themselves. Let's start right now and see if we can think of some good listening ideas. Let's make a list. What do you think a person has to do to be a good listener?

MICHAEL: Pay attention. Sometimes my teacher yells at the kids to pay attention. There's this kid in my class, Billy. He never pays attention. He's always in trouble. Then he has to go to the principal's office. One day Billy was at the principal's office for the whole day. The principal's office has a bench outside. The bench is made of wood with six legs on it. It's kinda' old. It's got . . .
(Michael again goes off the topic and begins to describe the bench in detail. This time I interrupt and bring him back to the "good listening" discussion.)

DR. P: Michael, let's write down our good listening ideas. Okay? Here's a pencil and here's an index card. Now, let's see, you said, "Pay attention." Is that right?

MICHAEL: Yes.

DR. P: Okay. Write that good listening idea down. *(Michael asks for some help spelling "attention" and writes the phrase down.)* I have a good listening idea. Look at the person who's talking. How should we write that?

MICHAEL: Look at the person.

DR. P: Okay. What else can we put on the list?

MICHAEL: Think about what the person is saying.

DR. P: That's a really good one! Write that one down. I've got another idea. Don't talk about something else. That means like if a person is talking about ice cream, don't start talking about baseball!

MICHAEL: Okay. Don't . . . *(Michael begins to add this item to the list)* . . . talk . . . about . . . something . . . else.

The "good listening" list was left at these four items and Michael was told that he could take the "good listening" card home to remind him how to be a good listener. I then proposed to Michael that we would practice "good listening" when we had our meetings, and that he could earn points (and prizes) for engaging in this behavior. Michael subsequently began each session with 20 points in his "bank." He could earn extra points for "special assignments" (e.g., recalling the good listening list). He would lose points in session by breaking one or more of the "good listening rules." Of note, prizes were kept out of view during sessions in order to minimize a potential distraction. All points could be spent at the end of the session or some could be left in the bank, adding to the purchasing power of the next session.

This contingency management program remained in place throughout these early sessions with Michael, and was modified over time to include other targeted behaviors. Of particular note was Michael's rocking behavior, which he was aware of and which he labeled one of his "weird weird" behaviors that he wanted to work on.

Sessions with Michael's mother focused on setting up a contingency program at home to help reduce the frequency of tantrum behaviors. Over time, the in-session contingency management, in collaboration with the home contingency management program, resulted in less frequent inappropriate behaviors. Nonetheless, both in session and at home, Michael was "consistently inconsistent" and when I would be ready to congratulate myself at the fine progress we were making, Michael would come to a session very unfocused and inattentive.

Current research suggests that contingency management be incorporated into cognitive interventions when working with children diagnosed with attention-deficit hyperactivity disorder. REBT theory acknowledges the complex interplay between cognitions, emotions, and behavior (Ellis, 1991), and asserts that the goal of internalizing a more rational philosophy of life can be achieved by paying attention to thinking *and* emotions *and* behaviors.

Providing an emotional education. As was previously noted, although Michael's intellectual development was above-average, his emotional/social development lagged considerably. Providing a foundation for teaching him the connections among thoughts, feelings, and behaviors was to proceed slowly. A starting point for intervention was the development of a "feelings" vocabulary. Although Michael's knowledge of basic "feelings words" was about on par with that of his peers, he appeared to have great difficulty labeling his own emotions and "reading" the emotions of others. Anecdotal information from Michael and his mother, as well as my own observations, indicated that he did not focus on facial expressions or body language. This often led to inappropriate social overtures on Michael's part. He would, for example, approach another child when that child was clearly absorbed in an activity and was not amenable to conversation. It was clear from Michael's history that there had been a great number of these "misreads" accompanied by negative consequences; the cumulative effect of these episodes left him quite daunted, in even the simplest of social encounters. Michael was 8 years old, and, as previously noted, was friendless.

Barkley (1990) has asserted that ADHD children may fail to integrate their experiences into developmentally appropriate schemata or cognitive templates, which then guide future behavior. I would further argue that failure to develop such cognitive structures has a spiraling effect throughout the developmental period, leaving the child with ADHD to suffer the continual vicissitudes of a developmental clock which is "out-of-step" with peers. For any aspect of therapy with these children, proceeding slowly and reinforcing new concepts under several sets of circumstances may aid in the development of the necessary schemata and enhance the possibilities for generalization.

As early as the mid-1950s Ellis recognized the efficacy of REBT methods with children (Ellis & Bernard, 1983) and, by the late 1960s, several practitioners demonstrated its effectiveness with school-age children (e.g., Glicken, 1968; Hauck, 1967; Wagner, 1965). Knaus systematized an emotional education approach in his 1974 publication entitled *Rational-Emotive Education: A Manual for Elementary School Teachers.*

Michael and I began his emotional education by drawing happy faces and sad faces and embarrassed faces and labeling them. Part of Michael's REBT homework was to collect photographs of people from magazines. He could earn bonus points equal to the number of photographs he would bring to a session. Each session we would spend some time labeling the photographs with the appropriate emotions and gluing the photographs into a "Feelings Book." While we engaged in this activity (which, like the use of clay in previous sessions, had the secondary benefit of enabling him to remain seated for longer periods) we talked about feelings. Do you remember feeling happy this week? Let's write that down in the happy part of the book. Do you remember feeling excited this week? Let's write that down in the excited part of the book. Did you feel angry this week? Do you remember what you were thinking about when you felt angry?

In addition to the Feelings Book, it was necessary to role-play feeling states over and over. Repetition appeared a necessary ingredient to engender some attention on Michael's part to his own and other people's emotions. I might also add that high tolerance for reiteration and lack of inhibition on the therapist's part were also necessary ingredients! "Feelings Detective" was a game we played during several of these early sessions. Michael would enter the office, and without saying a word, I would act out a feeling. Michael would guess the feeling and cite the evidence for choosing that feeling. Then it would be my turn. Michael would act out a feeling. I would guess the feeling and cite the evidence. Such exercises allowed Michael to focus on his own feeling states and concomitant body language, as well as the feeling states of others.

Only when Michael had mastered a basic understanding of his own feeling states and the feeling states of others, could we begin a more thorough analysis of the connections between happenings-thoughts-feelings-behavior (HTFB). This opportunity presented itself quite naturally when during our fifteenth session the following dialogue took place:

MICHAEL: I just hate doing my homework. It's really dumb. I have to do all that work in school and then I have to come home and do more work. I get really mad. The stuff is hard . . . I just *can't* do it!

DR. P: Is that really true—that you *can't* do it?

MICHAEL: Yeah, that's true all right. Like I start doing my math ditto and then I get all mixed up. I can't remember how to do the problems.

DR. P: Michael, it sounds like what you're saying is that you start out doing some of the problems—and you can do *some* of them. Is that right?

MICHAEL: Yeah, but then some of them I can't.

DR. P: Well, then, would it be right to say that some of the problems are easy for you to do and some of the problems are hard for you to do?

MICHAEL: Yeah . . .

DR. P: Well, is it really true, then, that you *can't do your math homework,* or is it really true that *some* problems are hard for you to do?

MICHAEL: Well, it's really true that *some* problems are hard for me to do.

DR. P: But I bet when you were doing that math ditto last night you were telling yourself, "*I can't do this!*"

MICHAEL: Yeah . . .

DR. P: And how did you feel when you told yourself, "I can't do this!"

MICHAEL: I got really mad . . . I ripped the ditto up. Then my mother yelled at me.

DR. P: Seems like things just got worse and worse . . .

MICHAEL: Yeah.

DR. P: So I guess it wasn't so helpful telling yourself, "I can't do this!"

MICHAEL: Nope.

DR. P: Let's try something, Michael. Here, you sit at the desk. Let's pretend you're doing a math ditto. . . . Now, remember what you figured out before—that *some* of the math problems were hard to do, but not all of them.

MICHAEL: Uh huh . . .

DR. P: Well, can you think of something helpful you could tell yourself about the math problems that would not make you mad?

MICHAEL: I don't know what you mean . . .

DR. P:	Well, "I can't do this!" made you feel mad. And it wasn't really true. Can you think of something that was true?
MICHAEL:	Well, *some* of the problems were hard for me . . .
DR. P:	How do you think you might feel if you said, "*Some* of the problems are hard for me."
MICHAEL:	I'm not sure . . .
DR. P:	How do you think you might feel if you said, "*Some* of the problems are hard, and *some* of them are pretty easy."?
MICHAEL:	Maybe I wouldn't feel so mad?
DR. P:	And, if you didn't feel so mad, would that be a good thing?
MICHAEL:	Well, my mom wouldn't yell at me. And then I wouldn't get punished.
DR. P:	And maybe if you were not *feeling so mad* you could get the easy problems done, and then maybe mom could help with the hard ones . . .
MICHAEL:	Hmm . . . mm
DR. P:	You see, when we think about a problem in a *helpful* way, we don't get so upset . . . I think we should do a thinking experiment. What do you think about that?
MICHAEL:	A thinking experiment?
DR. P:	Yes. Suppose you tried thinking about the math homework in a more helpful way for a *whole week.* Then next week we could see if the helpful thinking *really* helped you not to get so mad about the math homework. That would be our thinking experiment.
MICHAEL:	Okay.
DR. P:	Let's do this. Let's write down a helpful way of thinking on this index card . . . *(With some help Michael writes "Some of the math problems are hard for me to do, but some of them are easy.")*

DR. P: Okay, Michael. Let's try this. Take the Helpful Thinking card home and tape it to the desk where you do your homework. It will remind you to think about the math homework in a helpful way. And you can tell yourself again and again, "*Some* of the math problems are hard, but *some* of them are easy." And you can tell yourself, "I'll do all the easy ones first, and then I can get some help with the hard ones."

In this excerpt, I attempted to help Michael deal more effectively with some of the frustration he encountered in relation to his school work. I provided him with an elementary introduction to the concept of "self-talk" (which would be reinforced and further developed in our subsequent work), and showed him how some types of self-talk would be more helpful to him than others. Here, the reader will note that Michael was helped to correct his distorted *descriptive* cognition ("I can't do this!") rather than the presumed-present irrational *evaluative* cognition (". . . and that's awful!"). Rather than engage an 8-year-old in discourse about the "unawfulness" of incompleted homework, I opted to gently introduce the idea that changing the way you think about a problem can be beneficial. Teaching the client to use rational self-statements is an intervention frequently used with REBT clients who lack the cognitive sophistication to engage in actual disputing of irrational beliefs (Ellis, 1979; Yankura & Dryden, 1990). The concept that happenings-thoughts-feelings-behavior are connected was repeated frequently with Michael, in an attempt to "stamp in" an appropriate schema which would help him deal more effectively with future problems.

The idea of an "experiment" appealed to Michael and the process of designing thinking experiments was to be repeated many times throughout therapy. Homework assignments represent a very important component of REBT, both with children and adults (DiGiuseppe & Bernard, 1983; Walen, DiGiuseppe, & Dryden, 1992). I did not, however, use the phrase "homework assignment" with Michael, choosing instead to ask him to run an "experiment." Dryden and Yankura (1995) suggest that when working with clients who have negative associations to the phrase "homework assignments," it is desirable to employ a term for such assignments that is neutral or has positive connotations.

Concluding the initial phase of treatment. Weekly individual therapy sessions with Michael continued for approximately 1 year during this initial phase of treatment. Near the end of this 1-year period I approached a colleague with the idea of running a structured 10-week social skills training program for Michael and other children in our joint practice who were diagnosed with ADHD. Between the two of us we had four boys (ages 9 through 11) diagnosed with attention-deficit hyperactivity disorder. Each of these children had received several months of REBT-based individual psychotherapy. I reasoned that the group approach would offer Michael and these other youngsters a chance to reinforce what they had already learned during individual sessions, and would offer valuable practice in what still was the most difficult challenge for each of them—negotiating interpersonal relationships. The 10-week program focused on the happenings-thoughts-feelings-behavior paradigm (Knaus, 1974) with a particular emphasis on the interpersonal skills that the boys or their parents had cited as problematic. These included initiating and maintaining conversations with peers, approaching and joining into already-formed peer groups, and handling the inappropriate behaviors of peers (e.g., teasing). At the end of this 10-week intervention, Michael and I had several individual sessions, during which we discussed and elaborated on what had occurred during the skills workshop. Michael, now nine-and-a-half years old, had made good progress in therapy. Motoric excesses and tantrum behavior had all but disappeared. Michael had taught himself to monitor frustrating situations (a frequent antecedent to his tantrum behavior) and was able to use self-talk to produce a more rational response to such situations. He was still somewhat awkward in social situations with peers, but appeared to be less apprehensive about such encounters. The good rapport that had developed between us enabled Michael to experiment with joke-telling and some rather sophisticated verbal repartee. Therapy sessions were reduced to once every two weeks and then once a month. Summer was approaching and Michael and his family were set for a camping trip to the Grand Canyon. Michael and his mother and I decided that a "therapy vacation" was in order. We agreed that we would meet for future "check-ups" as needed. There were a few scattered sessions over the next 2 years, but we did not meet on any consistent basis until Michael was ready to enter middle school and begin the sixth grade. Michael was now almost 12 years old.

Early adolescence—Michael (Age 12–14).   The foremost developmental task of the adolescent period is identity achievement—the internalization of a unique and relatively stable sense of self (Erikson, 1968). Of note, the process of individuation is predicated on the competencies achieved during earlier developmental periods, and continues into young adulthood. Several major developmental shifts occur during early adolescence which act in concert to bring into focus two key questions for the adolescent: "Who am I?" and "Where is my place in this world?"

The newly emerging ability to "play with ideas" typically leads the adolescent to question parents' values; some adolescents envision far superior systems of government or religion. Piaget refers to the adolescent's insistence that reality submit itself to such idealistic constructions as formal operations egocentrism (Inhelder & Piaget, 1955/1958). Elkind (1981) describes two facets of adolescent egocentrism which have a direct bearing on the social world of the adolescent. The ability to imagine what others may be thinking leads to the belief that others are as concerned and critical of the adolescent's behavior and appearance as adolescents themselves are. Elkind refers to this phenomenon as the *imaginary audience*. A second aspect of adolescent egocentrism is called the *personal fable*. Adolescents often believe that their particular ideas and feelings are so unique that no one else could experience anything like them. The young adolescent's increased self-focus is typically accompanied not only by a preoccupation with the reactions of others (notably peers), but also with an increase in approval neediness and self-rating. As we shall see, Michael was to find the scrutiny of peers quite difficult.

Michael begins middle school. Michael's mother telephoned me just prior to his starting into the sixth grade. She wondered what could be done to make his transition from elementary school to middle school as smooth as possible. She had been in contact with Michael's special education resource room teacher, who had made some suggestions, including setting up a meeting with Michael's guidance counselor at the middle school. She asked me to join this meeting. The middle school was organized to accommodate varying ability levels, and students were assigned to "teacher teams" to help offset the apprehension associated with changing classrooms after each 40-minute period. The "teams" permitted the students to share many of their classes with the same cohort of students. At the middle school meeting we discussed Michael's academic progress, his particular scholastic assets and liabilities, and his still-apparent social awkwardness. He had made considerable academic progress and, although he was still quite disorganized, his skills were at and above grade-level. He was very interested in school, and especially liked math and science. His resource room teacher "pushed" for Michael to be included with the most capable students, and I suggested that he might find greater social acceptance within this group. With some reluctance, the middle school counselor agreed, and Michael began middle school assigned to a "team" composed of the most capable sixth-grade students, while still receiving resource room support. It seemed a worthwhile risk to try presenting Michael to the world of middle school as a bright, socially awkward youngster, rather than as a needy "special-ed" youngster. We hoped it would work.

Treatment goals for early adolescence. During his transition to middle school Michael and I saw each other for a total of 12 sessions, over a span of 4 months. Together we formulated the following treatment goals:

1. Continue Michael's rational-emotive education and reinforce independent use of self-talk and disputation strategies.
2. Increase self-acceptance and decrease negative self-rating.
3. Review and practice basic social skills previously taught (e.g., making a phone call; beginning and ending a conversation).
4. Reinforce appropriate study skills (including time management).

Although it had been more than a year since Michael and I had had a session, he was quite comfortable with his return to treatment and it was clear that he had remembered the "routine" of the therapy hour. Michael hadn't yet started the sixth grade, and he came to this first session with a long list of questions relative to what would await him in middle school. "Is it true that all the kids smoke pot in the bathrooms?" "How can you tell if a girl likes you?" "If you go into the boys' room alone will you get beat up?" Of note, not one of Michael's queries concerned the academic demands that would be placed on him!

It appeared futile to begin the disputation of anxiety-producing "boys' room cognitions" without first consulting an "expert." Fortunately, I knew just such an expert. Another client, whom I shall call Keith, was approximately 18 months older than Michael, and was just completing the seventh grade in the same middle school. After consulting with the parents of both boys, all agreed to a joint session.

Michael eagerly awaited his consultation with Keith, and generated an even longer list of questions for his special consultant. When I joined the boys for the scheduled joint session (although I noted my presence was hardly necessary!), it was evident that Keith benefited from his role as mentor to a younger child, and that Michael took in every bit of sage advice that Keith offered.

Armed with Keith's view of the middle-school scene, Michael began to get a more realistic view of what lay ahead for him in the coming weeks and he appeared less apprehensive about being assaulted or being coerced into unwanted activities. It appeared that Keith's input helped to counter some of the anxiety-provoking awfulizing cognitions to which Michael subscribed. In subsequent sessions he turned his attention toward his subjective distress at not being "cool" and being rejected by his peers. The focus of therapy at this point was not to downplay the importance of peer relationships, nor to deemphasize the very real possibility that Michael would be rejected by at least some of his peers, but to reinforce the following rational ideas: (a) Although not everyone might like him, that would not prove that he was a terrible, unlikeable person; and, (b) that if other kids teased or taunted him, such episodes would only be upsetting if he allowed them to be. In the following dialogue these ideas are reviewed and Michael is encouraged to generate his own self-talk in order to be less upset about such incidents.

DR. P: Michael, remember we said that it is probably true that not every single kid in the middle school is going to like you?

MICHAEL: Yeah . . . .

DR. P: And what does that mean?

MICHAEL: Some of the kids will like me, and some of the kids won't?

DR. P: Okay, good. And what about those kids who won't like you?

MICHAEL: What about them?

DR. P: Yes, what will their not liking you say about *you?*

MICHAEL: Maybe they just don't really know me. Or maybe they just don't like the same things that I like.

DR. P: That's a good way to think about it, Michael. Both of those ideas are helpful ideas. Remember, you and I have choices—we can use helpful thinking or unhelpful thinking when someone doesn't seem to like us. Do you remember what unhelpful thinking is?

MICHAEL: The thinking that makes us feel bad?

DR. P: Exactly! Like, if I was thinking, "Mary doesn't like me. That means I am a no-good person, because otherwise Mary would like me." How might I feel if I did that kind of thinking?

MICHAEL: Sad . . . maybe mad . . .

DR. P: And does it feel good to feel sad or mad?

MICHAEL: Nope . . . you might even have less friends if you're sad or mad all the time.

DR. P: That's a good point! Well, if helpful thinking helps us to fell good, how come we don't choose to think helpful thoughts all the time?

MICHAEL: We forget?

DR. P: Yes, we forget, and sometimes it's really hard to do. Like maybe someone teases us and BOOM! We're feeling mad before we know it!

MICHAEL: Oh yeah! That happens to me!

DR. P: And then what do you do?

MICHAEL: Well, I try to remember some of the helpful thinking to help me calm down.

DR. P: Like . . . ?

MICHAEL: Well, like I tell myself if some kid calls me a jerk, that doesn't make me a jerk. Sometimes I think about that thing you told me when I was a little kid, "Sticks and stones can break my bones . . ."

DR. P: ". . . but names can never harm me."

MICHAEL: (*Laughs*) You use that, too?

DR. P: You bet!

This excerpt illustrates that now, at age 12, Michael is becoming increasingly able to benefit from more philosophically based interventions. This shift in the way Michael was able to think about and evaluate a possible negative event was related to his ongoing cognitive development and increased capacity to engage in abstract thinking. In the present instance, our work together helped to lay the foundation for a philosophy of self-acceptance. Michael was able to see that negative judgements from peers did not have to lead him into negative self-rating.

Michael made a fairly good adjustment to the middle school, and had made progress with respect to the treatment goals we formulated together. In particular, he was usually successful in employing rational self-talk on those occasions when the social environment proved rejecting, and was developing the ability to dispute self-downing cognitions when they crept up on him. Therefore, we agreed to terminate our regularly scheduled appointments. At this point Michael was 3 months into the sixth grade in middle school.

I was, however, to see Michael again before he left middle school. Just as he was completing the eighth grade, I received a phone call from his mother that brought him back to treatment.

Dealing with a setback. Michael's mother called to say that Michael was cutting classes and that the school psychologist indicated he was exhibiting phobic behavior. When I met with Michael he admitted to cutting classes, and then gleefully explained how he had figured out a whole system wherein he was able to cut *most* of his classes while the school was only able to tabulate cuts for *some* of the classes. Because the skillful execution of this masterful plot took on a reinforcing life of its own, it took some probing to find out why it had all begun. Michael indicated that the primary problem was that he had difficulty dealing with negative affect, in particular, anger (which he apparently experienced on a fairly regular basis because of "stupid" teachers), and that sometimes he just needed time out to regain control. In addition, he sought to escape the anxiety he associated with the school cafeteria. Within this relatively unstructured setting, he was particularly fearful of being evaluated negatively by his peers. These aforementioned problems are fairly typical complaints of early adolescents. They *all* seem to have "stupid" teachers and scrutinizing peers. For Michael, however, the frequency, intensity and duration of his angry and anxious feelings were quite disruptive. We discussed the anger in session:

MICHAEL: I was so mad at Mr. (*Name*) (*the computer teacher*) that I took my disk home and put it on the stove and burned it.

DR. P: Well, I guess you were pretty burned up!

MICHAEL: (*Laughs*) Yeah . . . very funny!
            You know, he really is an asshole. I ask him one question about a new program we're using, and he screams at me like I'm an idiot or something.

DR. P: And you felt angry about that?

MICHAEL: You're damn . . . oops!. You're darn right I felt angry. The guy's an idiot!

DR. P: Is Mr. (*Name*) an idiot or is he a-computer-teacher-who-sometimes-yells-at-kids?

MICHAEL: What do you mean?

DR. P: Well, I don't think the behavior you have described is "idiot behavior" but it sure sounds like computer-teacher-who-sometimes-yells-at-kids behavior.

MICHAEL: I don't think I understand . . .

DR. P: Well, does Mr. (*Name*) yell at other kids?

MICHAEL: Oh yeah, he yells at a couple of kids *every* period.

DR. P: So, what do we know about this guy? We know that for some reason he chooses this not-so-great way of teaching about computers. For some reason, he gets himself upset and yells at kids. It would be better, perhaps, if he did *not* do this, but he does.

MICHAEL: So . . .

DR. P: So, unless he can find a way to not get himself upset in the future, he will probably continue to behave like a computer-teacher-who-sometimes-yells-at-kids.

MICHAEL: Oh, great!

DR. P: Well, the situation is not hopeless! Remember, you and I have choices about how to react to someone else's behavior. What would be some helpful thinking about Mr. (*Name's*) behavior?

MICHAEL: "Welcome to Monday. Another week with the idiot!" No . . . just kidding! Maybe something like, "Welcome to Monday. Be prepared. Mr. (*Name*) will launch an attack today. That will be Mr. (*Name*) doing his computer-teacher-who-yells-at-kids thing. It would be nice if he wouldn't do that, but he probably will. And I'll just tell myself to chill."

DR. P: Sounds good to me. And just think—you won't have to burn any more disks or throw away that "A" you're working on.

At a developmental period during which all adult values are suspect, and the inherent unfairness of life presents itself in technicolor, it is a therapeutic challenge not to minimize the adolescent's reactions, but to suggest that such intense negative affect ultimately interferes with the adolescent's goals.

Focusing on fears. Although Michael could appreciate that his intense angry responses were ultimately self-defeating, he was not as willing to give up his by now well-practiced avoidance responses to deal with anxiety-provoking situations. He still had not found a peer group with which to connect, and had, at different times, tried to affiliate with a cabal of "Dungeons and Dragons" aficionados, a street-wise group of rappers, and a bunch of kids "who just drink beer and talk about sex." He was not interested in sports (and, indeed, was somewhat motorically clumsy), so after-school sports activities were not a feasible option for him. He expressed concern about starting high school in the fall, and reported that, on the day of the high school orientation, he felt so nauseous that he did not accompany his class, but stayed behind in the middle school. He also reported difficulty entering a local delicatessen, because other kids might be there. His mother reported his refusal to eat in restaurants. And Michael admitted that he would not eat in front of anyone except his mother and brother.

Several behavioral interventions were deployed concurrent with rational self-statements to help Michael cope with his social/evaluative anxiety. The behavioral interventions took the form of graduated risk-taking exercises. Because cheesecake was one of Michael's favorite foods, he and I made a "cheesecake date" for one therapy session in the office. After reviewing specific cognitions that created and maintained his anxiety about eating in public and practicing replacing them with more rational self-talk, Michael and I moved to a small anteroom with a table and chairs. Here we devoured most of a very delicious cheesecake! Subsequent to this, the following session was conducted in a local fast-food chain, and he "successfully" ate a hamburger. In collaboration with his mother, Michael agreed to a contingency program for joining the family for restaurant meals. Within a few weeks Michael resumed eating lunch in the school cafeteria and, although he was still anxious in this setting, he was more willing to work at confronting this fear head-on.

However, Michael continued to express extreme anxiety about starting high school in the fall, and began to argue for moving out-of-state to live with his father and attending high school there. Part of Michael's evaluative anxiety centered around getting lost in the very large high school building, and being overwhelmed by the numbers of students. It was now summer and Michael agreed to visit the high school with me, walk the halls, and find his assigned class-rooms. We spent about 2 hours in the building exploring every possible area from the art room to the science labs to the pool. One could almost see Michael making a cognitive map of the school, and as our visit continued, he expressed greater comfort with being there. However, as we finished this in vivo session, he declared that he still wanted to go live with his father. He stated matter-of-factly that he had spent all these years with his mother, only seeing his father occasionally, and now it was time to get to know his father better. He presented his argument logically and denied that this was an avoidance strategy.

The therapist's dilemma. My therapeutic instinct was to push onward and continue to work toward modifying Michael's anxiety-producing cognitions through in vivo exposure and rational dia-logue. I suggested to Michael that not confronting the "monster of anxiety" head-on could make matters worse. He only restated his argument, asserting that as a male child he would now be more comfortable living with his male parent.

As anyone who works with adolescents knows, you don't "push" 14-year-olds into much! I argued with myself to come up with some solution to this conundrum. I reminded myself that the goal of any therapeutic endeavor is the long-term well-being of the client. I also reminded myself that if I were to *demand* that Michael solve his anxieties by *my prescriptions only*, then I would be modeling an abso-lutistic approach, which might be ultimately problematic. REBT includes an emphasis on empiricism, and argues for continual reality-testing (DiGiuseppe, 1991). If, in Michael's case, the reality was that you do not solve a problem by running away from it, then perhaps we needed to collect the data! I spoke with Michael's mother and suggested that if she insisted that he remain with her, he would probably blame every problem he ran into in the high school on her. If, however, we let him spend some time with his father, he might discover on his own that escape behavior was not the solution. After all, it was likely that Michael would encounter anxiety-provoking activating events and social difficulties out-of-state as well as in-state! Michael's mother ultimately agreed with me and, with some trepidation, she prepared for his move to his father's home some 300 miles away. We worked out an agreement with Michael that this was an experiment: Should his schoolwork suffer, he would return home at the end of one semester.

Michael thus began the ninth grade in a small-town parochial high school. On his occasional weekends back at his mother's home we would schedule an appointment to see how things were going. As might be expected, there was an initial "honeymoon" period and Michael sang the praises of living in his new community, of his new-found friends, of how well he was doing in his classes, and so on. In early spring, however, he experienced a minor disagreement with a peer and complained that his father was not home enough. He wanted to return home. His mother explained to him that making such a move in the middle of a semester would not be tenable, as the out-of-state curriculum differed significantly from that of his home school. I reminded Michael that he had made an agreement: Barring academic failure, he would complete the year living with his father. When he joined his mother in the waiting room after that evening's session, he just growled, "Bad session."

About 3 weeks later Michael was on spring break and was home with his mother. The following dialogue ensued when we met for one of our "check-up" sessions:

MICHAEL: You know, it was really good that I went back to stay with my father.

DR. P: Is that so . . . ?

MICHAEL: Yes! I was doing a lot of thinking and I figured out that when you're upset about something there are three levels of action possible. You can just live with the upsetment, you can avoid the situation that is upsetting you, or you can deal with it. Dealing with the problem is better. Remember that kid I was telling you about? The guy I had that fight with? Well, I just spoke to him about it—and that was that. It was no big deal. He's like my best friend now. And, you know what else? I pulled a 96 on my last math test.

DR. P: Well, congratulations on that great math grade! And congratulations on doing that heavy-duty thinking about that problem with your classmate. I think you're on to something there!

Michael completed his ninth grade year out-of-state, eager to return home for the summer. He said he was looking forward to going to the local high school for tenth grade. With some help from his mother he had lined up a summer job hauling outboard motors and bait at a local fishermen's dock.

Middle adolescence—Michael (Age 15–16).   Toward the middle of adolescence the teenager enters what Josselson (1980) terms the *rapprochement* phase of the individuation process. Having achieved some separateness from parents, there emerges a partial and conditional acceptance of adult authority. There is no longer a need to "fight the enemy at every turn." Instead, there is a growing awareness that adults may be valuable consultants. This developmental shift was noted in one of the first sessions Michael and I had upon his return home. He explained to me how he had handled one of the frequent angry outbursts of his boss at the dock. "You know," said Michael, "I just tell myself, 'That's Tom being Tom.' Oh, by the way, I have you to thank for that thought." At the end of this particular session, which had remained steadily problem-focused, Michael stood up to leaved, shook my hand, and stated, "Good session tonight. I learned a lot. Thank you."

Treatment goals middle adolescence.   Currently, Michael and I are meeting on an every-other-week basis. His tenth-grade year in his local high school has been quite successful, academically. He achieved "High Honors" for the first marking period. Although still somewhat subjectively uncomfortable in social situations involving groups of people, he is fairly comfortable in one-on-one social encounters. Although an examination of the normative developmental data would point to some social deficits, to the untrained eye he looks and acts like any other high school sophomore. Michael has stated that he needs to work on two problem areas right now and these have become the focus of the current intervention:

1. Work on becoming less shy around girls.
2. Work on becoming more flexible in some of my thinking patterns.

These treatment goals are stated pretty much as Michael articulated them. From the developmental perspective, it is important that Michael take increasing responsibility for the therapeutic endeavor, and this he has been able to do quite comfortably. Since the very beginning of Michael's therapy, at age 8, he has been encouraged to be an active participant in the process. It appears that he has now internalized the idea of therapy as a collaborative venture. Additionally, it is apparent that he has internalized the problem-solving focus of the REBT approach (Dryden, 1990). It is noteworthy that he monitors and assesses his cognitions and is aware that sometimes he comes to hasty, judgmental, overgeneralized conclusions. Even as he states that he wishes to work on "becoming more flexible," he reports that he "catches" himself overgeneralizing, stops and thinks about it, and then adopts a more rational perspective.

Michael liked hearing the idea that everyone struggles against irrational thinking patterns and that such patterns appear to be biologically rooted (Ellis, 1976); this concept seemed to dispel any lingering notions that he was somehow oddly different from his peers. Also, because disputing such irrational thinking was presented as intellectually challenging (and at least as much fun as some of his other intellectual pursuits), Michael eagerly accepted the challenge of modifying his own irrational thinking.

Michael and I are still working on his "shyness around girls" problem. During one session I told Michael a story about "a very famous psychologist" who, as a young man, was very shy around women. To the reader unfamiliar with the often-told tale of the Bronx Botanical Garden and the young Albert Ellis, suffice to say that Dr. Ellis is fond of relating that he would "force" himself to approach a seated female at the Botanical Garden and, after engaging in pleasantries, would invite her to go out with him. He reports that out of 100 women thus approached, only one agreed to go out with him, and then she stood him up. But, as Dr. Ellis reports, all this practice allowed him to eliminate his shyness around women (Yankura & Dryden, 1994).

About 2 weeks after hearing this story Michael reported that he had asked a girl if he could "see" her and she replied that she had a boyfriend. He then added, "I guess that's one down and 99 to go!"

It appears that Michael's shyness around girls is predicated on an irrational belief that goes as follows: I must always say the right thing around girls, because otherwise they will think I'm a jerk—and they'd be right! Disputing this belief both cognitively and behaviorally is the current focus of treatment. As this school year draws to a close, Michael has developed friendships with several girls in his high school. He does not yet have a girlfriend, but reports that he is working on it. If I were to make a prediction for *this* summer . . .

CONCLUSION

It is difficult to correlate the image of the overly active, poorly achieving, friendless 8-year-old boy I first met in 1987 with the articulate, engaging adolescent I know today. Sixteen-year-old Michael appears to be at minimal risk for significant adult psychopathology, thus lessening one of the central concerns of a childhood diagnosis of ADHD. More than that, however, he uses his good intellectual ability to consistently question and challenge what he calls "inflexible thinking." This would appear to bode well for his continued healthy emotional development. His exchanges during the therapy hour (for example, the opening dialogue of this chapter) seem to provide evidence for the existence of cognitive schemata in concert with the philosophical underpinnings of REBT theory.

Human behavior is multidetermined. What role has REBT played in Michael's developmental history? More to the point, what role has REBT played in the seemingly fortuitous outcome thus far? At the present time, Michael's internalization of REBT concepts and use of REBT techniques greatly assist him in better regulating his thoughts, feelings, and behaviors. He has demonstrated that he has been able to generalize cognitive, affective, and behavioral regulation across time and across settings. I would therefore speculate that future developmental tasks will proceed without undue turmoil. I would not have predicted this in March 1987.

REFERENCES

American Psychiatric Association. (1980, 1987). *Diagnostic and statistical manual of mental disorders.* Washington, DC: Author.

American Psychiatric Association. (1994). *Diagnostic and statistical manual of mental disorders* (4th ed.). Washington, DC: Author.

Anastopoulos, A. D., & Barkley, R. A. (1988). Biological factors in attention-deficit hyperactivity disorder. *Behavior Therapist, 11,* 47–53.

August, G. J., & Garfinkel, B. D. (1989). Behavioral and cognitive subtypes of ADHD. *Journal of the American Academy of Child and Adolescent Psychiatry, 28,* 739–748.

Barkley, R. A. (1989). Attention deficit-hyyperactivity disorder. In E. J. Mash & R. A. Barkley (Eds.), *Treatment of chhildhood disorders* (pp. 39–72). New York: Guilford.

Barkley, R. A. (1990). *Attention-deficit hyperactivity disorder: A handbook for diagnosis and treatment.* New York: Guilford.

Braswell, L., & Bloomquist, M. L. (1991). *Cognitive-behavioral therapy with ADHD children: Child, family and school interventions.* New York: Guiford.

Conners, C. K. (1969). A teacher rating scale for use in drug studies with children. *American Journal of Psychiatry, 126,* 884–888.

Conners, C. K. (1970). Symptom patterns in hyperkinetic, neurotic and normal children. *Child Development, 41,* 667–682.

DiGiuseppe, R. (1991). Comprehensive cognitive disputing in RET. In M. E. Bernard (Ed.), *Using rational emotive therapy effectively: A practitioner's guide* (pp. 173–195). New York: Plenum.

DiGiuseppe, R., & Bernard, M. E. (1983). Principles of assessment and methods of treatment with children: Special considerations. In A. Ellis & M. E. Bernard (Eds.), *Rational-emotive approaches to the problems of childhood* (pp. 45–88). New York: Plenum.

Douglas, V. I. (1980). Higher mental processes in hyperactive children: Implications for training. In R. M. Knights & D. J. Bakker (Eds.), *Treatment of hyperactive and learning disordered children* (pp. 65–92). Baltimore: University Park Press.

Douglas, V. I. (1983). Attentional and cognitive problems. In M. Rutter (Ed.), *Developmental neuropsychiatry* (pp. 280–320). New York: Guilford.

Douglas, V. I., & Peters, K. G. (1979). Toward a clearer definition of the attentional deficit of hyperactive children. In G. A. Hale & M. Lewis (Eds.), *Attention and the development of cognitive skills* (pp. 173–248). New York: Plenum.

Dryden, W. (1990). *Rational-emotive counselling in action.* London: Sage.

Dryden, W., & Yankura, J. (1995). *Developing rational emotive behavioural counselling.* London: Sage.

Elkind, D. (1981). *Children and adolescents: Interpretive essays on Jean Piaget* (3rd ed.). New York: Oxford University Press.

Ellis, A. (1976). The biological basis of human irrationality. *Journal of Individual Psychology, 32,* 145–168.

Ellis, A. (1979). The practice of rational-emotive therapy. In A. Ellis & J. M. Whiteley (Eds.), *Theoretical and empirical foundations of rational-emotive therapy* (pp. 61–100). Monterey, CA: Brooks/Cole.

Ellis, A. (1991). The revised ABC's of rational-emotive Therapy (RET). *Journal of Rational-Emotive & Cognitive-Behavior Therapy, 9,* 139–172.

Ellis, A., & Bernard, M. E. (1983). An overview of rational-emotive approaches to the problems of childhood. In A. Ellis & M. E. Bernard (Eds.), *Rational-emotive approaches to the problems of childhood* (pp. 3–43). New York: Plenum.

Erikson, E. H. (1968). *Identity: Youth and crisis.* New York: Norton.

Gadow, K. D. (1985). Relative efficacy of pharmacological, behavioral, and combination treatments for enhancing academic performance. *Clinical Psychology Review, 5,* 513–533.

Glicken, M. D. (1968). Rational counseling: A dynamic approach to children. *Elementary School Guidance and Counseling, 2,* 261–267.

Hartsough, C. S., & Lambert, N. M. (1982). Some environmental and familial correlates and antecedents of hyperactivity. *American Journal of Orthopsychiatry, 52,* 272–287.

Hauck, P. A. (1967). *The rational management of children.* New York: Libra.

Henker, B., & Whalen, C. K. (1989). Hyperactivity and attention deficits. *American Psychologist, 44,* 216–233.

Inhelder, B., & Piaget, J. (1958). *The growth of logical thinking from childhood to adolescence: An essay on the construction of formal operational structures.* New York: Basic Books. (Original work published 1955)

Josselson, R. (1980). Ego development in adolescence. In J. Adelson (Ed.), *Handbook of adolescent psychology* (pp. 188–210). New York: Wiley.

Kendall, P. C., & Braswell, L. (1993). *Cognitive-behavioral therapy for impulsive chidren.* New York: Guilford.

Knaus, W. J. (1974). *Rational emotive education: A manual for elementary school teachers.* New York: Institute for Rational Living.

Lambert, N. M. (1988). Adolescent outcomes for hyperactive children: Perspectives on general and specific patterns of childhood risk for adolescent educational, social, and mental health problems. *American Psychologist, 43,* 786–798.

Lambert, M. M., Hartsough, C. S., Sassone, D. & Sandoval, J. (1987). Persistence of hyperactivity symptoms from childhood to adolescence and associated outcomes. *American Journal of Orthopsychiatry, 57,* 22–32.

Linscott, J., & DiGiuseppe, R. (1994). Rational emotive therapy with children. In C. W. LeCroy (Ed.), *Handbook of child and adolescent treatment manuals* (pp. 5–40). New York: Lexington.

Mannuzza, S., Klein, R. G., Bessler, A., Malloy, P., & LaPadula, M. (1993). Adult outcome of hyperactive boys: Educational achievement, occupational rank, and psychiatric status. *Archives of General Psychiatry, 50,* 565–576.

McGee, R., & Share, D. L. (1988). Attention deficit disorder-hyperactivity and academic failure: Which comes first and what should be treated? *Journal of the American Academy of Child and Adolescent Psychiatry, 27,* 318–325.

Nelson, W., & Birkimer, J. C. (1978). Role of self-instruction and self-reinforcement in the modification of impulsivity. *Journal of Consulting and Clinical Psychology, 40,* 148–154.

Ross, D. M., & Ross, S. A. (1976). *Hyperactivity: Research, theory, and action.* New York: Wiley.

Tannock, R., Schachar, R. J., Carr, R. P., Chajczyk, D., & Logan, G. D. (1989). Effects of methylphenidate on inhibitory control in hyperactive children. *Journal of Abnormal Child Psychology, 17,* 473–491.

Wagner, E. E. (1965). Rational counseling with children. *School Psychologist, 9,* 3–8.

Walen, S. R., DiGiuseppe, R., & Dryden, W. (1992). *A practitioner's guide to rational-emotive therapy.* New York: Oxford University Press.

Weiss, G., & Hechtman, L. T. (1986). *Hyperactive children grown up.* New York: Guilford.

Wicks-Nelson, R., & Israel, A. C. (1991). *Behavior disorders of childhood* (2nd ed.). Englewood Cliffs, NJ: Prentice-Hall.

Wirt, R. D., Lachar, D., Klinedinst, J. K., & Seat, P. D. (1984). *Multidimensional description of child personality: A manual for the Personality Inventory for Children* (rev. by D. Lachar). Los Angeles: Western Psychological Services.

Yankura, J., & Dryden, W. (1990). *Doing RET: Albert Ellis in action.* New York: Springer Publishing Co.

Yankura, J., & Dryden, W. (1994). *Albert Ellis.* London: Sage.

Zametkin, A. J., & Rapoport, J. L. (1987). Neurobiology of attention deficit disorder with hyperactivity: Where have we come in 50 years? *Journal of the American Academy of Child and Adolescent Psychiatry, 26,* 676–686.

CHAPTER 5

REBT and Panic Disorder with Agoraphobia

Joseph Yankura

> I feel as if I cannot breathe—it's as if I'm suffocating. The harder I try to fill my lungs with air, the worse this feeling gets. I feel my heart beating rapidly and I have pains in my chest. I get very dizzy and everything seems unreal—almost like I'm looking at the world through gauze. It feels crazy, and I'm sure that I'm going to go completely over the edge and lose control of myself. I get very scared and I feel like I have to do something to stop these awful feelings, but I don't know what to do. I frantically look around to see if anyone is there who might help me. I want to escape, to just run away from what I'm experiencing—and I feel afraid that this time, something absolutely terrible is going to happen to me!

T HIS DESCRIPTION OF A PANIC ATTACK was provided by a panic disorder sufferer named Angela, whose rational emotive behavior therapy (REBT) treatment is described further on in this chapter. Angela's description is similar in its basic features to those provided by many people with panic disorder (PD). By definition (as per the *Diagnostic and Statistical Manual of Mental Disorders*, fourth ed.

[DSM-IV]; American Psychiatric Association, 1994), individuals with panic disorder live in dread of their next panic attack. This is understandable, given the strange, unexpected physiological symptoms, the discomfort of intense anxiety, and the fears of impending doom that PD sufferers experience during a panic attack. Many individuals with panic disorder engage in avoidance of sensations and experiences they associate with such attacks, or of situations in which escape might be difficult or help unavailable in the event of an attack. Individuals with panic disorder often suffer severe impairments in quality of life (Markowitz, Weissman, Quellette, Lish, & Klerman, 1989) and are the most frequent users of mental health and medical services (Boyd, 1986). It is not uncommon for PD sufferers to have multiple admissions to hospital emergency rooms.

For many years, the nature and etiology of panic attacks, panic disorder, and agoraphobia were poorly understood. As a result, psychotherapeutic treatments often produced rather weak outcomes for clients, and relapse rates tended to be high. Currently, however, highly effective cognitive-behavioral treatments can help individuals with PD to greatly reduce the frequency, intensity, and duration of their panic attacks, as well as overcome the lifestyle restrictions stemming from agoraphobic avoidance.

The present chapter will first review general material pertinent to the diagnosis and treatment of panic disorder with agoraphobia (PD-A). Contemporary treatments for this disorder will then be described. The general cognitive-behavior therapy (CBT) approach to conceptualization and treatment will be presented in some detail, as features of this approach are often incorporated within a rational-emotive treatment package for PD-A. Following this, the REBT approach will be discussed, and an illustrative case presentation provided. This material will illuminate some important differences between the general CBT and REBT approaches.

PANIC DISORDER WITH AGORAPHOBIA: DIAGNOSTIC CRITERIA AND DEMOGRAPHIC INFORMATION

In discussing the diagnosis of panic disorder with agoraphobia, it is first necessary to describe the DSM-IV (American Psychiatric Association, 1994) criteria for panic attacks, as the experience of recurrent attacks is essential to the identification of this disorder. DSM-IV describes a panic attack as

> A discrete period in which there is the sudden onset of intense apprehension, fearfulness, or terror, often associated with feelings of impending doom. During these attacks, symptoms such as shortness of breath, palpitations, chest pain or discomfort, choking or smothering sensations, and fear of "going crazy" or losing control are present. (American Psychiatric Association, 1994, p. 393)

Panic attacks differ from high levels of general anxiety in terms of their sudden and often unexpected onset, and also in terms of their tendency to surge to a peak, usually within 10 minutes or so (Warren & Zgourides, 1991). In addition, general anxiety does not involve the rather dramatic physical changes that accompany panic attacks, and is viewed as being more of a chronic, ongoing condition (Clum, 1990).

As per DSM-IV, in order for an individual to qualify for a diagnosis of panic disorder, panic attacks must be recurrent and must also be followed (for a period of at least 1 month) by one or more of the following features:

1. Persistent concern about having additional attacks.
2. Worry about the implications of the attack or its consequences (e.g., losing control, having a heart attack, "going crazy").
3. A significant change in behavior related to the attacks. (p. 402)

In addition, the panic attacks must not be due to use of a substance (e.g., street drugs or prescription medications) or a general medical condition, and are not better accounted for by the presence of another mental disorder (such as obsessive-compulsive disorder, posttraumatic stress disorder, or a phobia). Here, it is noted that panic attacks often occur within the context of a variety of emotional disorders. It is also noteworthy that the three features described above can be viewed as providing rather clear intervention points for a rational-emotive approach to treatment.

Many individuals with panic disorder experience anxiety or engage in phobic avoidance with respect to situations or places in which escape might be difficult or help unavailable in the event of a panic attack. When such anxiety and avoidance are part of the symptom picture (and are not due to another mental disorder), a diagnosis of panic disorder with agoraphobia (PD-A) is appropriate.

For sufferers of PD-A, typically avoided places and situations can include public transport (e.g., subways, buses, planes), waiting in lines, traveling far from home, restaurants, theaters, and elevators (Barlow & Craske, 1994).

DSM-IV indicates that, while the age for onset of panic disorder can vary considerably, it is usually between late adolescence and the mid-30s. Many experts have noted that the period preceding an initial panic attack may be characterized by stressful life events, and some writers have proposed that chronic stress may predispose certain individuals to panic attacks and the subsequent development of panic disorder (see, e.g., Clum, 1990). The diagnosis of panic disorder (with or without Agoraphobia) is made with females much more frequently than it is with males, perhaps partly because of the fact that males may be less likely to seek treatment for their problems. Thus they go undiagnosed and untabulated.

Research suggests that panic attacks are actually a rather common phenomenon. For example, one study examining the incidence of infrequent panic attacks found that 34.4% of participants had experienced at least one panic attack during the previous year (Norton, Harrison, Hauch, & Rhodes, 1985). Another study, which focused on unexpected panic attacks, revealed that approximately 12% of a large sample of college students reported having experienced one or more panic attacks during their lifetimes (Telch, Lucas, & Nelson, 1989). With respect to the prevalence of panic disorder, DSM-IV reports lifetime prevalence rates between 1.5% and 3.5%. One-year prevalence rates are reported as ranging from 1 to 2%. In community samples one-third to one-half of individuals with panic disorder also have agoraphobia, although a much greater incidence of agoraphobia is found within clinical samples. Given these figures, it is probable that several million individuals have panic disorder (with or without agoraphobia) within the United States alone!

TREATMENTS FOR PANIC DISORDER AND AGORAPHOBIA

Psychopharmacological Treatments

Certain psychotropic medications are commonly prescribed for the treatment of panic disorder with and without agoraphobia. Barlow and Craske (1994), in fact, have noted that almost 75% of patients who seek treatment at the Phobia and Anxiety Disorders Clinic at the State University of New York at Albany are taking some form of medication for their anxiety. The most widely accepted medications for PD sufferers include the monoamine oxidase inhibitor (MAOI) and tricyclic antidepressants, and the high-potency benzodiazepines (Warren & Zgourides, 1991). Also, a relatively new group of antidepressants, the selective serotonin reuptake inhibitors (SSRIs), have received attention in the psychopharmacological treatment of PD.

Although psychotropic medications have demonstrated utility in reducing the symptoms of panic sufferers, there are a number of problems inherent in treating PD solely with medication.

Side effects.   First, some of the drugs used for treating PD have unpleasant side effects. For example, patients beginning a regimen of a tricyclic antidepressant may experience blurred vision, rapid heart rate, and jitteriness. While these side effects generally subside with continued administration, they can be an especially hard pill to swallow for PD patients. This is because PD sufferers tend to be anxiously attuned to any somatic changes that may signal the onset of a panic attack. In fact, up to 25% of PD patients may terminate their tricyclic antidepressant regimen before the point at which they start to benefit from it.

Drug dependency.   The high-potency benzodiazepines (such as Xanax) are fast-acting medications. Patients often experience improvement with respect to their panic symptoms within the first few days of beginning drug administration. Xanax, however, has a short half-life, meaning that its effects wear off relatively quickly. In addition, termination of Xanax can result in a quick recurrence of anxiety symptoms and may also produce withdrawal effects. Because tapering or termination of Xanax can be unpleasant, patients may be at risk for becoming psychologically and physically addicted to the drug.

Relapse.   Rates of relapse tend to be substantial for PD patients who have terminated pharmacotherapy. Clum (1990) has reported a relapse rate of more than 30% for the tricyclic antidepressants, and a 55% rate for the MAOI Nardil. Barlow and Craske (1994) report that approximately one-half of patients using high-potency benzodiazepines will relapse within six months of drug termination. Relapse rates may tend to be higher for pharmacotherapy patients who have not received concurrent psychotherapy.

Lack of coping skills.   Compared with PD patients receiving concurrent, effective psychotherapy, PD patients treated solely with medication are probably far less likely to develop new coping skills for dealing with panic-related problems. Whereas psychotherapeutic approaches (such as REBT) which explicitly teach coping skills may help to boost patients' sense of self-efficacy (i.e., increase their sense that they are able to handle their problems on their own), pharmacotherapy, when it is the sole mode of treatment, may actually teach PD patients that they are helpless to deal with their problems without a vial of pills.

Current cognitive-behavioral treatments (which provide clients with an assortment of coping strategies and techniques) have demonstrated efficacy in relieving the symptoms of panic disorder. These treatments also appear to have lower relapse rates than the current array of pharmacotherapies. Needless to say, treatment that relieves symptoms *and* fosters client independence and self-efficacy is preferable to treatment that often seems to provide only time-limited symptom relief.

General Cognitive-Behavioral Treatment

In this section, the general cognitive-behavioral approach to conceptualizing and treating PD-A will be described. The REBT approach to conceptualization and treatment, which differs in a number of important respects from the general CBT approach, will be presented in a subsequent section.

Cognitive-behavioral approaches that directly target panic symptoms and agoraphobic avoidance have been shown to be highly effective (Clark & Ehlers, 1993; Clark, Salkovskis, Hackmann, Middleton, Anastasiades, & Gelder, 1994; Craske, Meadows, & Barlow, 1994). Before describing these approaches, however, it will first be helpful to describe the cognitive-behavioral conceptualization of panic disorder with agoraphobia. An appreciation of this model will aid the reader in understanding the treatment targets and techniques incorporated within the general CBT approach.

Essentially, the general cognitive-behavioral model takes into account the following elements:

1. Predisposing factors
2. Precipitating factors
3. Disorder-specific factors

These various components of panic disorder with agoraphobia are represented in Figure 5.1.

With respect to predisposing factors, cognitive-behavioral views concerning the etiology of panic attacks and PD acknowledge that some individuals, due to their genetic make-up, may have a *biological predisposition* to experience panic attacks and panic disorder (Clum, 1990; Craske, Meadows, & Barlow, 1994). In addition, an individual's *learning history* may also contribute to a predisposition toward having panic attacks. To cite an example, a person reared in an environment which contributed to the development of chronic health-related worries may be more prone to develop PD than another person reared in an environment in which health issues were kept within a reasonable perspective.

Concerning precipitating factors, the general cognitive-behavioral model recognizes that *stressful life events* (or, more specifically, the individual's views and experience of such events) may often contribute to an initial panic attack. In addition, excessive caffeine consumption and alcohol and drug abuse may lead to physical stress and bodily sensations that may precipitate a panic attack.

Up to this point, we have discussed factors that may be implicated in the onset of an individual's first panic attack. After this initial attack, the development of panic disorder hinges on a number of variables that can be termed to be disorder-specific factors. Individuals who develop PD after an initial attack develop *hypervigilance* for cues that another panic attack is imminent (Barlow & Cerny, 1988; Clum, 1990). In particular, these individuals are hypervigilant for somatic cues that they have learned to associate with panic. Such cues may stem from "normal" activities that lead to certain types of bodily sensations (e.g., shortness of breath or rapid heart beat resulting from physical exertion; sweating and feeling faint from being in a hot, stuffy room). Perceiving particular somatic cues, the individual applies *catastrophic interpretations* to them (e.g., "I'm going to die/go crazy/lose control"). According to the general cognitive-behavioral model, these catastrophic interpretations lead the individual to experience a heightened level of anxiety. This heightened level of anxiety, combined with additional or exacerbated somatic cues, may contribute to the individual experiencing a new panic attack episode.

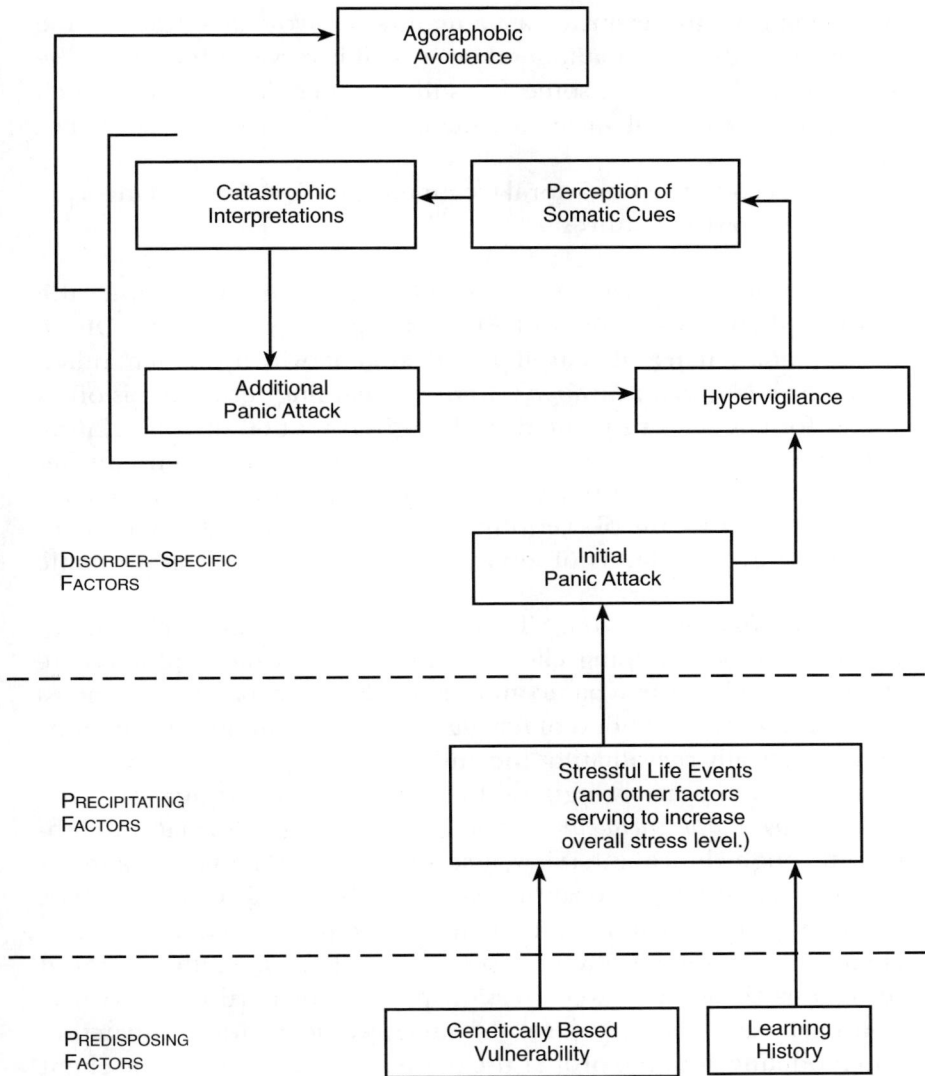

Figure 5.1. General cognitive-behavioral model of panic disorder with agoraphobia.

Panic disorder sufferers may develop agoraphobia if they come to associate particular situations and places with panic attacks, such that they avoid these situations as a means of reducing the likelihood of another attack. Agoraphobic avoidance may also be evidenced with respect to situations in which escape may be difficult or help unavailable in the event of a panic attack. Avoidance and escape behavior tends to be maintained because it is very reinforcing in the short term. In a sense, some PD sufferers may learn to view such behavior as a crucial means of managing the threat of recurrent attacks.

General cognitive-behavioral treatment for PD-A tends to incorporate the following features:

1. *Reeducation about panic attacks.* Early in treatment, the cognitive-behavioral model of PD-A is explained to clients. Often, this explanation in and of itself provides clients with significant relief.

2. *Breathing and relaxation training.* Breathing retraining is often useful for clients with panic disorder, given that 60 to 70% of individuals who panic experience hyperventilation symptoms during attacks. Breathing and relaxation training afford clients the means to develop some control over physical symptoms, and also help them to reduce general levels of anxiety which may contribute to panic attacks.

3. *Cognitive restructuring.* This component of general CBT treatment focuses on helping clients to modify the catastrophic cognitions involved in their panic attacks. Revising probability estimates concerning the likelihood of having panic attacks in given situations and realistically reevaluating the anticipated negative consequences of a panic attack are two goals of cognitive restructuring.

4. *Exposure to interoceptive somatic cues.* Using information gathered through clinical interview, assessment instruments, and a series of body sensation provocation exercises (Barlow & Craske, 1994), the therapist determines the client's feared body sensations. The client then systematically exposes him or herself to these feared sensations through between-session practice of pertinent provocation exercises. The therapist, of course, would provide instruction and modeling as to the proper use of these exercises. After the client has completed a hierarchy of interoceptive exposure exercises, he or she would next be given instruction on confronting avoided activities (such as physical exertion, sex, or drinking coffee) that are associated with feared somatic sensations.

5. *Exposure to avoided situations and places.* For clients who have developed agoraphobic avoidance in connection with their panic disorder, in vivo exposure to avoided situations and places (such as lines at supermarkets, restaurants, movie theaters) is a very important part of treatment. Because clients avoid particular settings be-

cause of anxiety that a panic attack will occur within them, they are instructed to deliberately induce their feared somatic sensations while in these settings, so that they can further desensitize themselves to them. Clients are taught how to use particular techniques (e.g., diaphragmatic breathing) to help themselves deal with any anxiety they experience during in vivo exposure exercises.

Given the treatment strategies and intervention targets outlined above, general cognitive-behavior therapy for PD-A is particularly concerned with assessment of clients' catastrophic cognitions, feared somatic sensations, and avoided activities, situations, and places. In particular, accurate and specific assessment is required in order to construct exposure hierarchies that are personally relevant for clients. For a concise review of assessment procedures for PD-A, the reader is referred to Warren and Zgourides (1991).

In the forthcoming sections, the REBT approach to conceptualization and treatment of PD-A will be reviewed. While the REBT approach overlaps in numerous respects with the general cognitive-behavioral approach, significant differences do exist. These differences, particularly as they relate to treatment issues, will be highlighted for the reader.

REBT AND PANIC DISORDER WITH AGORAPHOBIA

In order to provide the reader with a foundation of important conceptual material, the following discussion begins with consideration of REBT theory as it applies to psychological disorders in general and to anxiety disorders in particular. It then focuses specifically on the application of REBT to PD-A.

The REBT View of Psychological Disorders

REBT theory hypothesizes that all human beings have a biologically based tendency to construct both rational and irrational beliefs about self, others, and the world around them (Ellis, 1976). Rational beliefs are defined within REBT as evaluative cognitions of personal significance which tend to be preferential (as opposed to absolutistic), logical, and consistent with reality. They generally abet the individual's survival and happiness, and tend not to result in significant and enduring emotional distress. Irrational beliefs, on the other hand, are most often absolutistic, illogical, and inconsistent with reality. They usually consist of an irrational premise (frequently expressed in the form of a should, must, or have to), and of one or more irrational evaluative derivatives (e.g., negative person-rating, awfulizing, and I-can't-stand-it-itis). As opposed to rational beliefs, irrational beliefs will frequently result in significant emotional distress and impede an individual's happiness and attainment of personally meaningful goals (Dryden & Yankura, 1993).

Given an innate tendency to construct irrational beliefs, it is likely that all human beings will at least occasionally produce needless emotional upsets for themselves by bringing their irrational beliefs to bear upon negative life circumstances. Such upsets include unhealthy negative emotions such as guilt, depression, shame, anger, hurt, and anxiety. These unhealthy negative emotions can be contrasted with their healthy (but still negatively-toned) counterparts: Remorse, sadness, regret, annoyance, disappointment, and concern (Dryden & Yankura, 1993). Specific sorts of irrational beliefs tend to underpin each of the unhealthy negative emotions; anger, for example, typically involves an other-directed absolutistic premise (e.g., "My husband *should* act more considerately toward me!") and an evaluative derivative that takes the form of negative person-rating (e.g., "He's a *total shithead* for treating me as shabbily as he does!").

For many healthily functioning individuals, significant emotional upsets and behavioral disruptions will be relatively infrequent, mild, and of brief duration. Some individuals, however, experience emotional and behavioral problems on the level of a psychological disorder, where "disorder" is defined as an enduring condition associated with significant levels of distress and functional impairment (see DSM-IV, American Psychiatric Association, 1994). REBT maintains that, compared with more healthily functioning individuals, those with psychological disorders tend to:

1. More readily construct irrational beliefs about negative life circumstances;
2. more often bring these irrational beliefs to bear upon negative life circumstances; and
3. cling to their irrational beliefs with greater tenacity.

In general, REBT tries to help clients to identify, dispute and replace the irrational beliefs which underpin their emotional upsets and behavioral difficulties. The process of disputing irrational beliefs can be implemented through cognitive, emotive, and behavioral channels. Given the characteristics of individuals designated as having significant psychological disorders, REBT recognizes that therapeutic interventions will often have to be particularly vivid, forceful, and energetic in order to be optimally effective (Dryden, 1991; Ellis, 1979a).

The REBT View of Anxiety and Anxiety Disorders

Of the various unhealthy negative emotions listed above, anxiety has the greatest relevance for the present chapter. According to REBT theory, the following cognitive steps are implicated when an individual experiences this emotion (Walen, DiGiuseppe, & Dryden, 1992):

1. Something bad will probably happen. [Negative Inference]
2. It *must* not happen. [Irrational Premise]
3. It would be *awful* if it did. [Irrational Evaluative Derivative]

Note that the first step in this sequence involves a negative inference: "Something bad will probably happen." In the rational-emotive conceptualization of emotional upsets, this inference (which here takes the form of a prediction, or probability estimate) would be viewed as an Activating Event (A) which serves to trigger the individual's irrational belief (B—composed of a premise and derivative) at steps 2 and 3. This then leads the individual to experience the emotional consequence (C) of anxiety. This emotional consequence may then prime the person to have certain action tendencies associated with anxiety, such as avoidance of or escape from the perceived threat at A (Dryden & Yankura, 1993). Figure 5.2 depicts a simple anxiety episode (which can be viewed as social or evaluative anxiety) as per REBT's ABC model.

Ellis (1977, 1980a) has hypothesized that "musturbatory" beliefs lead to negatively distorted inferences. In fact, an interactive relationship exists between the inferences and irrational beliefs implicated in episodes of anxiety. When an individual constructs an irrational belief about a particular negative event (e.g., "I *must* avoid rejection at all costs!"), he or she then becomes hypervigilant for the occurrence of this event. This hypervigilance results in

Activating Event (A)	Beliefs (B)	Consequences (C)
"I will probably experience rejections at the party to which I've been invited."	*Premise:* "I must be approved of and never be rejected by people whom I consider important." *Derivatives:* 1. Negative Self-Rating: "If I experience rejection, it proves I'm no good!" 2. I-Can't-Stand-It-Itis: "I absolutely couldn't tolerate such rejection!"	*Emotional:* Anxiety *Action Tendency:* Avoidance (e.g., make up excuse for not attending party.)

Figure 5.2. A simple anxiety episode as per REBT's ABC model.

misperceptions of events (e.g., if an individual looks hard enough for signs of rejection at a party, he or she will probably perceive some), and increases the frequency with which negative inferences are generated. An increased number of negative inferences then results in more frequent "triggerings" of irrational beliefs. This cyclic relationship between irrational beliefs and inferences is pictured in Figure 5.3.

Compared with individuals who are relatively free of anxiety problems, individuals with anxiety disorders are more prone to construct and then strongly adhere to irrational beliefs about anticipated

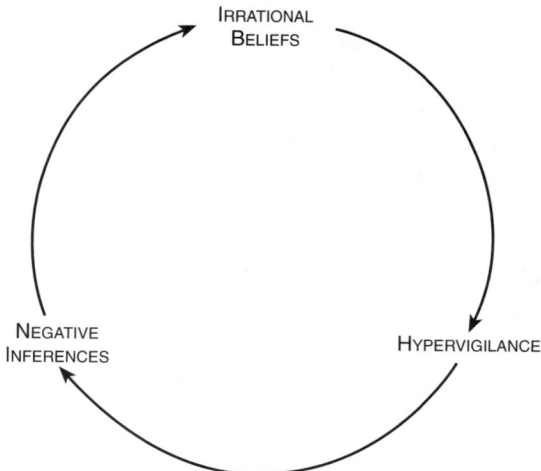

Figure 5.3. Cyclic relationship between irrational beliefs and inferences.

negative future events. Depending on the particular type of anxiety disorder under consideration, these events may include rejection (as in social phobia), contamination (as in obsessive-compulsive disorder), or uncomfortable bodily sensations (as in panic disorder). The mechanisms by which individuals *develop* anxiety disorders can be described as follows:

1.   Through a complex interplay of experiences, familial and cultural norms, and certain hypothesized physiological vulnerabilities (e.g., an overly labile autonomic nervous system), individuals "learn" to rate particular events or circumstances as being "very bad."

2.   Related to their innate tendency to think rationally, they then reasonably and realistically *prefer* that these "very bad" events and circumstances not occur.

3.   Having a comparatively greater innate tendency to think irrationally, however, they easily add absolutistic musts and shoulds (with their associated derivatives of awfulizing, negative self-rating, and I-can't-stand-it-itis) to their reasonable preferences.

4.   Having constructed irrational beliefs about the future occurrence of "very bad" events and circumstances, they are more likely to generate negatively distorted inferences concerning these events. Such inferences include overestimates of the probability that such events will occur, exaggerated views of the "badness" of these events, and underestimates of personal capacity to cope with these events.

5.   Distorted negative inferences trigger irrational beliefs, which then lead the individual to experience anxiety. As noted above, the greater the frequency of negatively distorted inferences, the more often anxiety-provoking irrational beliefs will be triggered. The individual thus suffers frequent anxiety episodes.

6.   Because anxiety episodes are frequent and occur in a variety of contexts, anxiety may come to be associated with a variety of additional circumstances and events, which can then themselves become (sometimes subtle) triggers for anxiety-provoking irrational beliefs.

7.   Given that the experience of anxiety can be very uncomfortable (and may be accompanied by a number of distressing physical symptoms), individuals may engage in a variety of self-defeating strategies to minimize exposure to threatening As. Such strategies can include avoidance, escape, and superstitious behavior. These strategies are self-defeating because they may contribute to a constricted lifestyle and effectively prevent the individual from develop-

ing more rational ways of thinking about "very bad" circumstances and events.

8. The individual may develop a variety of secondary emotional problems in relation to his or her primary problem of anxiety. Such problems may include negative self-ratings (e.g., "I'm a weak, inadequate person for being so anxious and avoidant"), which may make it ever-more difficult for the individual to take steps that would be helpful for combating the primary problem.

The foregoing description must be considered a simplified and abbreviated version of REBT's view of the development of anxiety disorders. Hopefully, however, it has provided the reader with a sense of the complexity of these disorders, and why some individuals develop them while others do not.

Generally, REBT treatment for anxiety disorders involves helping clients to identify, dispute, and replace the irrational beliefs that underpin their anxiety problems. A particularly important component of REBT for anxiety disorders involves accurately identifying the As which clients anxiously avoid, such that meaningful exposure-type homework activities can be designed. REBT favors a flooding approach to exposure exercises, as this is viewed as a means for helping therapy to be briefer and more effective (Ellis, 1991). Clients who take on in vivo flooding exposure exercises provide themselves with the opportunity to challenge their irrational beliefs in the very situations most likely to trigger them.

Having reviewed REBT's approach to the general conceptualization and treatment of anxiety disorders, I will next discuss these issues as they specifically apply to panic disorder with agoraphobia.

REBT Conceptualization and Treatment of Panic Disorder with Agoraphobia

As noted in the previous section, individuals with anxiety disorders tend to construct and then strongly adhere to irrational beliefs about anticipated negative future events. In the case of individuals with PD-A, these irrational beliefs are likely to be centered around the occurrence of future panic attacks. Because certain somatic sensations (e.g., sweating, dizziness, difficulty catching one's breath) come to be viewed as the harbingers of such attacks, irrational beliefs are more specifically focused on the occurrence of these symptoms.

Some typical sorts of irrational beliefs found to be operative with PD-A patients include the following:

- I *must* not experience these uncomfortable physical feelings; it's absolutely awful if I do because they signal the beginning of another panic attack!
- I *must* not experience another panic attack and something absolutely terrible may happen if I do. It would be awful and absolutely intolerable if I were to (faint, go crazy, lose control, be embarrassed, etc.).
- I *must* not have another panic attack, and if I do the feelings I will experience during the attack will be absolutely intolerable!
- Because I may be particularly likely to have another panic attack when in particular situations and places, I *must* avoid being in these situations and places and find it awful and intolerable when I am!
- I absolutely *should* be better able to control my panic symptoms and my avoidance behavior; the fact that I continue to have panic attacks and avoid is proof that I'm a weak, inadequate person!
- I *must* not show others that I am anxious, because if I do they will look down on me and I couldn't bear that!

The reader will note that this list of absolutistic beliefs is focused on (a) the occurrence of certain uncomfortable bodily sensations, (b) the occurrence of actual panic attacks, (c) the anticipated negative consequences of a panic attack, (d) the feelings experienced during an actual panic attack, (e) situations and places in which panic attacks are predicted to be more likely, (f) self-efficacy and self-acceptance issues, and (g) issues concerning disapproval and rejection by other individuals.

How does a person develop PD-A? With reference to the numbered list presented in the section on anxiety disorders, the following steps are probably quite often involved:

1. A complex interplay of experiences, familial and cultural norms, and certain physiological vulnerabilities lead the individual to rate certain physical sensations and conditions as being "very bad." To cite an example, a PD-A client who shall be referred to here as Allison grew up in a family that worried constantly about health issues. Recently, Allison witnessed her father have a heart

attack. He was hospitalized, but died several days later. Allison also had several other relatives who had passed away because of heart problems. At least partly as a result of this background, she "learned" to regard certain sorts of somatic sensations (e.g., tightness in the chest, rapid heart rate, difficulty breathing) as being "very bad."

2.   The individual rationally *prefers* that these "very bad" physical sensations and conditions not occur.

3.   Having a comparatively greater innate tendency toward irrational thinking, the individual adds to his or her preference an absolutistic irrational belief: "I *must* not experience these particular physical sensations and conditions; it's awful and intolerable if I do!"

4.   With this irrational belief in operation, the individual is more likely to be hypervigilant for the physical sensations and conditions rated as "very bad." He or she is also more likely to generate negatively distorted inferences related to these phenomena. In Allison's case, these negatively distorted inferences took the following forms: (a) If I experience chest pains or a racing heart, it's a sure sign that I'm going to have a heart attack; (b) Given my family's history, it's almost certain that I will at some point have a heart attack; (c) I'm helpless to ward off or deal with this eventuality.

5.   Given the individual's hypervigilance for and negative inferences about "very bad" bodily events, his or her irrational beliefs about such events tend to be triggered often with the result that frequent anxiety episodes are experienced. Through chaining of negatively distorted inferences and irrational beliefs (to be discussed in detail below), the individual becomes caught up in a cycle of escalating anxiety and exacerbated physical symptoms. *The result: A full-blown panic attack.* During a very stressful period of Allison's life (the company for which she worked was undergoing structural reorganization and there was a possibility that she would be laid off), Allison began to experience a number of somatic anxiety symptoms. One particular day, she experienced hyperventilation and concluded that she was probably having a heart attack. This negatively distorted inference triggered her irrational beliefs, which led to an exacerbation of anxiety and somatic symptoms. These exacerbated symptoms became a new A, which triggered additional irrational beliefs—the ultimate outcome being a full-blown panic attack.

6.   Having experienced an initial attack, the individual becomes hypervigilant for any cues that may signal the onset of additional attacks. Such cues involve the original somatic experiences rated as "very bad," and may also come to include additional cognitive, somatic, and situational cues. An expanded array of cues leads to an increased likelihood that irrational beliefs and panic attacks will be triggered. Because Allison felt particularly anxious and stressed while at her workplace during its transitional period, she came to regard it as a likely site in which she would experience additional panic attacks. She thus became particularly hypervigilant for signs of panic while at work, and did indeed experience a number of panic attacks there.

7. Having experienced several panic attacks, the individual develops (self-defeating) strategies for minimizing their occurrence. These strategies, which stem from irrational beliefs concerning the "awfulness" of panic attacks, may include avoidance of activities (such as physical exercise) that lead to somatic sensations associated with panic, as well as avoidance of places in which panic attacks may occur. Superstitious behaviors may also develop, as when individuals with PD-A carry "good luck charms" with them (such as Bibles, pills, and personal stereos which act as distractors) to ward off panic attacks. Given the panic attacks she experienced while at work, Allison became avoidant of her workplace. She would call in sick when she awakened in the morning with a "feeling" that a panic attack was going to occur that day, and tried to find excuses for not attending meetings at which her colleagues might witness her having a panic attack.

8. With reference to the PD-A that has now developed, the individual may also develop a number of secondary emotional problems. Allison constructed a number of irrational beliefs related to her panic attacks (and her avoidance), which served to diminish her levels of self-acceptance and self-efficacy:

- I absolutely *should* be able to do something to stop my constant worrying and these attacks I'm having. The fact that I haven't is evidence that I'm a hopeless case and a truly weak person.
- I absolutely *shouldn't* allow these problems to interfere with my work. The fact that I do proves that I'm an incompetent employee.

These beliefs, which eroded Allison's sense of herself as a person with good capabilities, made it more difficult for her to face and take steps to combat her panic-related problems.

As mentioned above in step 5, chaining of inferences and irrational beliefs leads panic attack sufferers into a cycle of increasing anxiety and exacerbated physical symptoms (Dryden, 1991). Actually, the links between negatively distorted inferences (As) and irrational beliefs (Bs) can be depicted as a series of ABC sequences, as in Figure 5.4. This cycle of exacerbation can be viewed as central to an individual's experience of panic attacks, and has important implications for treatment. These implications will receive more detailed consideration in the section below entitled "Focusing on inferences vs. beliefs."

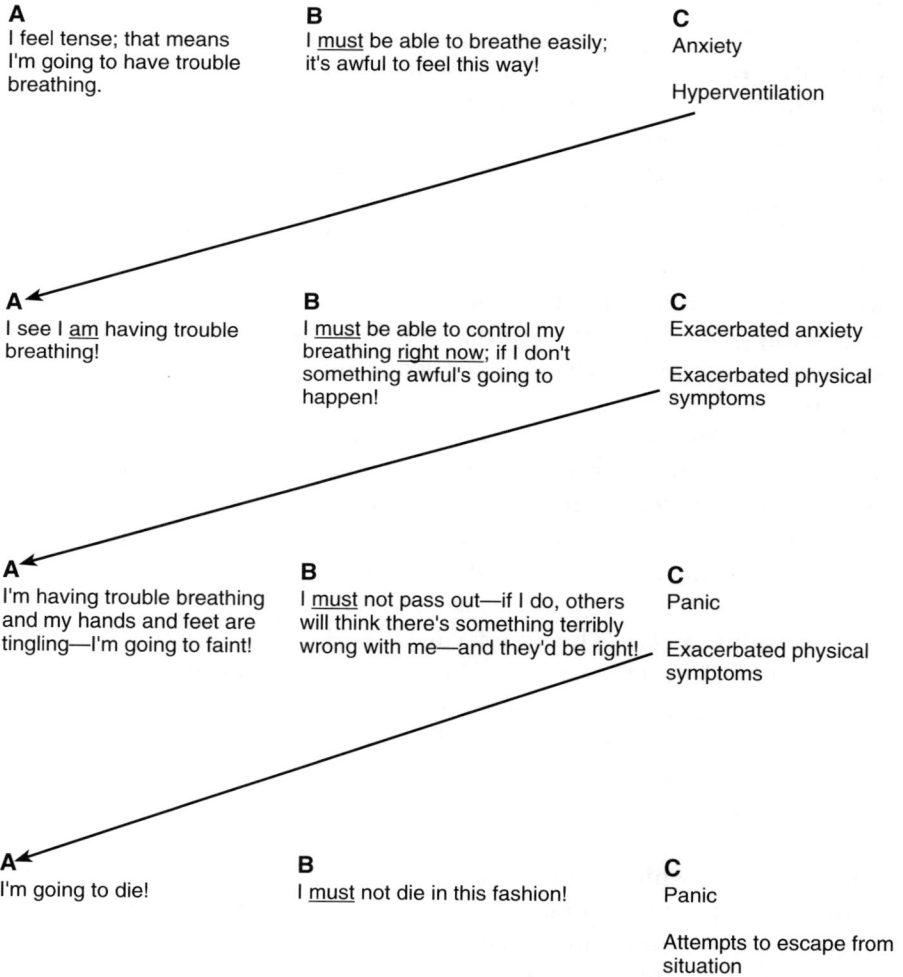

A
I feel tense; that means I'm going to have trouble breathing.

B
I <u>must</u> be able to breathe easily; it's awful to feel this way!

C
Anxiety

Hyperventilation

A
I see I <u>am</u> having trouble breathing!

B
I <u>must</u> be able to control my breathing <u>right now</u>; if I don't something awful's going to happen!

C
Exacerbated anxiety

Exacerbated physical symptoms

A
I'm having trouble breathing and my hands and feet are tingling—I'm going to faint!

B
I <u>must</u> not pass out—if I do, others will think there's something terribly wrong with me—and they'd be right!

C
Panic

Exacerbated physical symptoms

A
I'm going to die!

B
I <u>must</u> not die in this fashion!

C
Panic

Attempts to escape from situation

Figure 5.4. ABC sequences implicated in panic attacks and PD-A.

As indicated in the previous review of current cognitive-behavioral approaches to PD-A, breathing and relaxation training, cognitive restructuring (focused primarily on negatively distorted inferences), and a variety of exposure techniques are important components of treatment. These treatment components can readily be incorporated within what Ellis (1980a) has termed "general REBT." However, "preferential REBT" contains perspectives, emphases, and procedures which rather clearly set it apart from general REBT, or cognitive-behavior therapy. Some of these features, reviewed directly below, can increase the efficacy and efficiency of PD-A treatment.

Focusing on inferences vs. beliefs. Most current cognitive-behavioral treatment packages for PD-A focus on helping clients to challenge and replace the negatively distorted inferences involved in their panic attacks (see, e.g., Barlow & Craske, 1994). Although recognizing that disputing distorted inferences can serve a useful function in the treatment of many emotional disorders, REBT places an emphasis on identifying and disputing clients' irrational beliefs. This is because negatively distorted inferences are viewed as stemming from the irrational beliefs to which an individual subscribes. Thus, it makes clinical sense to focus on eradicating the source of these problematic inferences.

Clients with PD-A can be shown the chain of ABC sequences implicated in their panic attacks, and can be presented with a rationale for focusing on challenging the underlying musts involved in these sequences. Disputing efforts can be particularly focused on irrational beliefs that are operative early on in an ABC chain, such that the chain can be interrupted before it reaches panic proportions (Dryden, 1991).

Clients with PD-A often have musts concerning the intense discomfort of panic attacks which lead them into discomfort disturbance (Ellis, 1979b, 1980b). They also typically harbor irrational demands and evaluations concerning the perceived consequences of having a panic attack. Thus, they believe that they *must* not experience panic attacks because they *must* not lose control, suffer social disapproval, feel helpless, die, and so on. Although many REBT therapists would have little difficulty in mounting rational challenges to most of these musts, it is noted that a significant number would experience difficulty with challenging the belief "I *must* not die." This is frequently because (a) they have personal difficulty with issues pertaining to death and dying and/or (b) they (sometimes accurately) predict that they will encounter client resistance and damage the therapeutic relationship if they attempt to dispute this notion. In the first instance, it would be beneficial for therapists to deal with their own awfulizing about death. With respect to the second instance, it is likely that disputing musts about dying, when implemented in an appropriate manner, can be beneficial for many PD-A sufferers (Warren & Zgourides, 1991). Here, it is noted that rather than charging in and immediately disputing the belief, "I *must* not die," REBT therapists can first explore with the client the "meanings" or consequences he or she associates with dying. In some cases, for instance, an inquiry will reveal a client's fears that if they die, their children will be sad and left without a caretaker. The client's awfulizing about these negative consequences can then be identified as a target for disputation.

Focusing on catastrophizing vs. awfulizing.   In the past, it was not uncommon for the terms "catastrophizing" and "awfulizing" to be used synonymously within the REBT literature. In more recent REBT publications, however, the distinctions between these two cognitive concepts have been clarified (see, e.g., Ellis & Abrams, 1994). *Catastrophizing* refers to appraising a set of circumstances and rating these circumstances as being exceptionally bad. *Awfulizing* refers to the process of perceiving a set of circumstances to be exceptionally bad, and then deciding in one's mind that these circumstances are so awful that:

1. They *must* not exist.
2. They are *more than* 100% bad.
3. They *absolutely cannot* be coped with.
4. They *completely eclipse* any possibility of being happy and/or attaining personally meaningful goals.

A number of contemporary cognitive-behavior therapies for PD-A aim to help clients counter their catastrophizing, meaning that they encourage reappraisals of the "badness" of particular events and circumstances. They attempt, for example, to move clients from rating panic attacks and their consequences as "exceptionally bad" to "not so bad; tolerable." When clients are able to view panic attacks and their consequences as "not so bad" and "tolerable," they may then surrender some of the avoidance behavior they engage in with respect to their panic attacks and view themselves as being better able to cope with them.

There are, however, several potential problems inherent in this approach. For instance, clients exposed to this sort of decatastrophizing may pick up the implicit message that while "not so bad" circumstances and events can be coped with, "exceptionally bad" circumstances and events *are* truly awful and cannot be effectively dealt with. Although REBT therapists may at times work with PD-A clients to help them reassess the "badness" of their panic attacks and anticipated negative consequences, they especially focus on helping them to de-awfulize these things. In particular, they help clients to see that even if particular events or circumstances *can* legitimately be rated as exceptionally bad, it is nevertheless true that:

1. Such circumstances may continue to exist, despite the client's demanding that they disappear.
2. They can never be more than 100% bad, and could almost always be worse than they actually are.
3. They can still be tolerated.
4. They very rarely completely cancel out all opportunities for happiness and satisfaction in life (unless one is referring to death, in which case these issues no longer have relevance).

By directly addressing the awfulizing that PD-A clients may engage in, REBT therapists teach them that they can cope with the problems stemming from their disorder, even if these problems are "very bad." In addition, a focus on de-awfulizing can help clients to deal with "very bad" circumstances that they may have the misfortune to encounter in the future, after therapy has formally ended.

Specific vs. core irrational beliefs. Current cognitive-behavioral treatment packages for PD have demonstrated effectiveness in helping clients to eliminate panic attacks (Rapee & Barlow, 1989). It has been noted, however, that significant general anxiety often remains for PD clients who have completed such treatment (Klosko, Barlow, Tassinari, & Cerny, 1990). This may be, in part, because cognitive-behavior therapies focus largely on modifying the negative inferences implicated in PD, and generally do not deal with the underlying beliefs which comprise an anxiety-producing personal philosophy.

REBT particularly targets the specific irrational beliefs underpinning the negative inferences involved in PD. As noted above, this approach is viewed as eliminating these inferences at their source. However, REBT also emphasizes helping clients to identify and change their *core* irrational beliefs (DiGiuseppe, 1991; Dryden, 1990). Core irrational beliefs can be identified by looking for common themes among the specific irrational beliefs that appear to be implicated in clients' presenting problems. Untreated core beliefs are viewed as having the potential to cause additional and future emotional problems for clients, even if specific irrational beliefs have been dealt with during the course of therapy.

When REBT therapists work with their clients to modify core beliefs, they bring a quality which Ellis (1980c) has termed *pervasiveness* to their therapeutic work. According to Ellis (1980c), pervasiveness means that therapists help clients "to deal with many of their problems, and in a sense their whole lives, rather than with a few presenting symptoms" (p. 415). For clients with PD-A, a dual focus during treatment on both specific and core irrational beliefs may help them to (a) eliminate their panic-related symptoms *and* (b) reduce their vulnerability to general anxiety once therapy has been concluded.

Position on distraction techniques. Cognitive-behavioral treatments for PD-A usually include specific training in diaphragmatic breathing and relaxation techniques. These methods are included to help clients better manage their panic attack symptoms, and may also function to reduce general stress levels.

When clients use these techniques to deal with an actual panic attack or to interrupt their anxious anticipation that a panic attack may occur, they are, in part, engaging in cognitive distraction: By focusing on their breathing or on tensing and relaxing various muscle groups, they turn their minds away from ruminating about the "awfulness" of their panic-related symptoms. Some self-help manuals, in fact, encourage PD sufferers to use other sorts of cognitive distractions (such as counting, thinking of a song, or having sexual fantasies) if breathing and relaxation techniques fail to produce desired effects (see, e.g., Clum, 1990).

There is, however, a fine line between the healthy and unhealthy utilization of distraction strategies. Indeed, they *can* be useful for helping clients to manage physical symptoms and calm themselves to a point where they can effectively deploy cognitive disputing techniques. Unfortunately, some clients overuse distraction strategies, become dependent on them, and develop the belief that they *must* have them in order to cope with panic attacks. When this happens, they may (a) inadvertently reinforce their view that panic attacks are *awful,* (b) prevent themselves from developing a more helpful and rational way of thinking about their attacks, and (c) prevent themselves from seeing that a panic attack *may not* occur, even when they are in a situation where one is expected.

REBT therapists prefer direct cognitive modification strategies over distraction methods, and remain alert to the possibility that their clients are over-relying on distraction methods to cope with uncomfortable experiences and situations. As an example of such overreliance, a given client who is fearful of flying in airplanes may use distraction strategies throughout the entire flight. She is thus actually engaging in a form of avoidance—although her body is on the plane, her mind is someplace else (on a "higher plane," so to speak!).

With respect to incorporating diaphragmatic breathing and relaxation into a treatment package for PD-A, REBT therapists would tend to observe the following guidelines:

1. Teach clients how to use breathing and relaxation techniques partly as a means for showing them that they can exert some degree of control over their anxiety and its concomitant physical symptoms. This will help to foster self-efficacy and counter "helplessness" cognitions.
2. Show clients that they can combine these methods with cognitive disputing techniques. In particular, train them to use these distraction methods to reduce anxiety so that they can more effectively challenge their unhelpful thinking when anticipating or experiencing a panic attack.
3. Help clients to see that it is not an absolute necessity to utilize distraction techniques when a panic attack is experienced. Although an attack can be rated as "very bad," it is not awful and can certainly be survived.
4. Be alert to the possibility that clients may become overly reliant upon distraction methods and take steps to help them develop a more healthy perspective on their use when this is the case.
5. When clients insist that they *need* distraction methods in order to function, attempt to engage them in examining the beliefs that underpin this "need." Show them the self-defeating elements of these beliefs and help them to challenge them.

Graduated vs. flooding approaches. Most cognitive-behavioral treatment approaches for PD-A (e.g., Barlow & Craske, 1994) employ graduated hierarchical exposure to feared somatic sensations and situations. Ellis (1982a, 1983), however, has noted that therapeutic "gradualism" may reinforce in clients' minds the irrational beliefs that (a) it is *awful* to experience emotional discomfort, and (b) therapy absolutely *should* proceed in a relatively easy, painless fashion. REBT therapists generally encourage clients to confront the situations that are most difficult and emotionally uncomfortable for them, as this can facilitate therapeutic efficiency and provide clients with the opportunity to directly challenge and replace their upset-producing beliefs. Therapists can explain these advantages to clients, and also show them that confronting an item at or near the top of their "fear hierarchy" may quickly make it easier to cope with items lower down on the hierarchy.

Despite their preference for a flooding approach to treatment, REBT therapists refrain from dogmatically insisting that clients take on flooding type homework assignments that they may resist completing. Such therapist insistence would be countertherapeutic, as it could damage the therapeutic alliance and serve as a stimulus for clients to engage in negative self-rating (e.g., "I *should* be able to do the flooding exercises my therapist has so strongly recommended to me; the fact that I have not proves that I'm an utter failure!"). Instead, REBT therapists often employ a principle known as "challenging but not overwhelming" when collaboratively designing homework activities with clients who steadfastly refuse to do flooding assignments (Dryden, 1991). This principle represents a form of therapeutic compromise: Clients are invited to choose assignments that are sufficiently challenging to discourage reinforcement of their philosophy of low frustration tolerance, but that they don't experience as being overwhelming. In this way, even in the face of client resistance stemming from discomfort disturbance, therapeutic progress can be facilitated.

Anxiety about therapy. Cognitive-behavioral therapies for PD-A frequently neglect a very important element that can impact on treatment effectiveness: Clients can bring irrational beliefs to their therapy which cause them to experience anxiety (as well as other debilitating emotions) about it (Dryden & Yankura, 1995; Ellis, 1982b). In the case of clients with PD-A, these irrational beliefs may often take the following forms:

1. I absolutely *shouldn't* have to work so hard at therapy; I can't stand the discomfort I have to face in order to get better.

2. I *must* make quick progress in this therapy, since it's supposed to be relatively short term. If I don't, it will prove that I'm a lazy and inadequate person.
3. I *have to* understand the complexities of PD-A the first time my therapist explains them to me; if I don't she'll think I'm a stupid jerk—and she'd be right!
4. I *must* never backslide and experience an exacerbation of my panic symptoms—if I do, it will prove I'm a hopeless case and will never get better.

Readers familiar with REBT's conceptualization of emotional disturbance will see that these various beliefs can contribute to both ego disturbance and discomfort disturbance (Ellis, 1979b, 1980b). If unidentified and untreated, they may create significant obstacles to treatment progress. For instance, clients who see treatment as "too hard" or themselves as "hopeless cases" will probably be prone to prematurely drop out of therapy when the going gets tough. By explicitly recognizing and dealing with clients' irrational beliefs about therapy, REBT therapists are able to prevent negative outcomes such as premature termination and client self-blame and self-downing. They are therefore in an advantageous position relative to cognitive-behavior therapists who neglect to specifically attend to such beliefs.

Dealing with secondary problems.   In addition to dealing with clients' beliefs and upsets about therapy and therapeutic progress, REBT therapists are also attuned to the possibility that PD-A clients may develop secondary problems in relation to their primary problems of anxiety, panic, and avoidance. Secondary problems result when primary problems become a new A in an ABC sequence that leads to an additional layer of emotional disturbance. Thus, clients may make themselves anxious (or depressed, or ashamed) about their panic.

An especially pernicious secondary problem may develop when clients rate themselves negatively for having PD-A. Such negative self-rating can have far-reaching destructive consequences, as it can:

1. Make it more difficult for clients to face and work on the problems that they have.
2. Lead clients to be less than completely self-disclosing about their panic-related problems such that therapists (or other group members, if the client participates in a therapy group) lack information that could be important to treatment.

3. Lead to premature therapy termination, as in the case of clients who regard themselves as too weak or inadequate to ever benefit from any form of treatment.

4. Cause clients to expect that other people will judge them as negatively as they judge themselves, with the result that they restrict social activities and cut themselves off from social supports and pleasures.

When REBT therapists determine that clients are engaging in negative self-rating with respect to their primary PD-A symptoms, they take specific steps to counter this. They show clients their self-downing beliefs, teach them how to challenge these, and encourage them to adopt a philosophy of self-acceptance. A philosophy of self-acceptance will assist clients to derive optimal benefits from therapy while it is in progress, and will also make them less vulnerable to ego disturbance after treatment is ended.

I now will present a case study that illustrates REBT's application to PD-A.

CASE ILLUSTRATION

This case illustration describes my work with Angela, a young woman I saw in therapy at the Institute for Rational-Emotive Therapy (IRET) in New York City. Rather than presenting the case on a session-by-session basis, I describe specific sessions that particularly illustrate REBT's application to PD-A.

Introducing the Client

Angela was a college-educated 28-year-old woman who worked as a supervisor for a telemarketing firm in New York City. She generally liked her job, but often had thoughts about returning to school in order to pursue a graduate degree and enter a profession. Angela was single and had never been married. Although she dated frequently, her relationships with men rarely lasted longer than a few months.

Angela was 20 years old and in college when she had her first panic attack. During this attack (as well as subsequent attacks) she experienced a surge of feelings and sensations that included shortness of breath, pressure in her chest, palpitations, disorientation, and intense anxiety. After several attacks had occurred, she sought help at the college's counseling center. There she received supportive counseling, and a referral to a psychiatrist. She found the counseling to be minimally helpful, and did not follow-up on the psychiatric referral. She believed that her panic attacks meant that she was "losing control" or "going crazy," and was reluctant to squarely face the problems she was experiencing.

Angela essentially "toughed it out" through the remainder of her college career, and developed (on her own) a number of techniques for managing her panic attacks. These techniques mainly consisted of distraction and avoidance strategies. To cite an example, she would carry a tape recorder with her to classes, and would try to seat herself in the rear of the lecture hall, near the exit. Then, if she believed a panic attack was about to begin or if she actually experienced a panic attack, she would leave her tape recorder running (so as not to miss any parts of the instructor's lecture) and quietly leave the lecture hall. She would then wander around the building or the campus while listening to her personal stereo, until the panic attack had subsided or she was convinced that she was not going to have a panic attack. Frequently she returned to the lecture hall only after the class had finished, in order to pick up her tape recorder. Angela also moved from her small off-campus apartment back to an on-campus dormitory, in order to reduce travel distance to classes and the need to take public transportation. With her anxious apprehension about future attacks and an increasing array of avoidance behaviors, Angela qualified for a diagnosis of panic disorder with agoraphobia.

At the time of her first appointment with me, Angela hadn't experienced a panic attack in 2 months. However, she continued to dread the onset of her "next" attack, and persisted in agoraphobic avoidance.

Prior to seeing me, Angela had seen a cognitive-behavioral therapist for treatment. This therapy had continued for approximately 5 months until Angela had terminated it approximately 4 months before her first session at IRET. She had derived a number of benefits from this therapy, insofar as it had provided her with:

1. Accurate information about panic attacks and PD-A.
2. Breathing and relaxation techniques for managing her panic attacks.

3. A more helpful way of thinking about her disorder and her panic symptoms (e.g., she no longer strongly believed that panic attacks meant she was "losing control" or "going crazy").

It appeared, however, that Angela used her breathing and relaxation techniques inconsistently. In fact, their main benefit to her was that they provided her with the knowledge that she *could* exert some degree of control over her panic symptoms if she chose to do so. Also, Angela came to be at odds with her former therapist over particular aspects of her treatment. She felt that her therapist pushed her too hard to engage in certain in vivo exposure activities (such as independently riding the subway through tunnels, which Angela avoided as much as possible), and she resisted becoming engaged in interoceptive exposure exercises. In addition, she claimed that her therapist had become insistent that she go for a psychiatric consultation. With reference to these difficulties, Angela had dropped out of treatment.

Angela had decided to give therapy "one more try" because she was fed up with what she perceived to be an increasingly restricted lifestyle. Specifically, she avoided riding on public transportation and taking trips beyond the borders of New York City out of fear that she might have a panic attack and would not have access to escape or help. A friend of Angela's referred her to IRET. Her treatment at the Institute spanned 5 months, for a total of 16 sessions.

Initial Session

The early part of my first session with Angela was spent in gathering background information and in ascertaining presenting complaints. Angela was encouraged to describe the history of her panic attacks, her current symptoms and problems, and her experience with her prior therapy. In the course of discussing the prior therapy, the following dialogue ensued:

DR. Y: So, it sounds like you and Dr. M. (*the prior therapist*) had some disagreements about how treatment should proceed. Is that why you stopped seeing her?

ANGELA: That's right—she just kept pushing me to ride the subway by myself, and I had a lot of difficulty with that. Finally, Dr. M. started insisting that I go to a psychiatrist for medication—she thought that would help me. But I didn't want to do that—I'm not keen on the idea of using mind-altering drugs.

At this point, I decided not to pursue assessment of Angela's aversion to medication. Instead, I chose to focus on gaining further information about her experience with her previous therapy.

DR. Y:　Did Dr. M. check with you each session to see if you'd done your subway homework?

ANGELA:　Yes, she did. And just about every week, I'd have to tell her that I hadn't done it. I think she actually started to wince each time I told her that. I felt like she was my first-grade teacher, and I was getting an "F" in therapy.

DR. Y:　An "F" in therapy—that's an interesting way to put it! It sounds like your therapy sessions started to become aversive for you. Did you feel like a failure?

ANGELA:　Yup—I felt like a real loser.

DR. Y:　And how do you think and feel about that now? I mean, do you still think you're a loser because you didn't do your homework assignments?

ANGELA:　Yeah, I hate to say it, but I do. I sort of feel like I'm a hopeless case. I mean, I'm able to go to work and everything, but sometimes I really doubt that I'm going to get any better than I am now.

Here, it is apparent that Angela has developed some secondary problems with respect to her prior therapy experience and continuing panic-related difficulties.

DR. Y:　That's understandable—you had some failure experiences in your other therapy, and you started to think of yourself as a failure and a hopeless case. But this is important—if you continue to rate yourself in those terms, how might it impact on your ability to get better?

ANGELA:　What do you mean?

DR. Y:	If you continue to think of yourself as a failure and a hopeless case, is it going to help you or hinder you with respect to getting better?
ANGELA:	Oh—I guess it's going to hinder me.
DR. Y:	In what way do you see that it will hinder you?
ANGELA:	If I really believe I'm hopeless, I won't think that anything—including therapy—will really help me. Then, I'll probably just give up and go bury myself somewhere!
DR. Y:	That's right! You see, you're engaging in negative self-rating. It's like you're saying to yourself, "I *should* have been an A+ client and gotten more out of my therapy—the fact that I fell short and didn't do my homework assignments proves that I'm a real failure and I'll *never* get any better!"
ANGELA:	Mm . . . I guess I am saying that to myself.
DR. Y:	But that statement isn't a fact, it's a belief—in this case, a belief you have about yourself. And we can examine that belief to see if it's helpful and valid. If it isn't valid, and if it blocks you from reaching your goals, you can discard it and find another way of thinking about yourself that will be more helpful and healthy.
ANGELA:	So you're saying I should question my beliefs? I used to work on some of my beliefs with Dr. M.
DR. Y:	Right—there's some overlap between Dr. M.'s approach and REBT. But there's also some important differences—one difference is that we pay special attention to how you think about yourself in relation to your problem and your therapy. Here, I'm saying we should examine your belief that you're a failure, and see if there's a more helpful way for you to think about yourself. By doing so, we can remove one potential obstacle to your improving right at the start.
ANGELA:	That seems to make sense—but where do we begin?
DR. Y:	We begin by examining your assumptions—in this case, your assumption that not doing your therapy

homework makes you a failure and a hopeless case. Is that true?

ANGELA: Well, if you fail at something a number of times, doesn't that make you a failure?

DR. Y: Let's look at this more closely. You were a client in therapy with Dr. M., right?

ANGELA: Right.

DR. Y: And as a client in therapy, you play a certain role in your own treatment. That role involves certain tasks that you undertake. What are some of those various tasks?

ANGELA: Well, with Dr. M., that meant coming to sessions each week on time, doing various readings, practicing relaxation exercises, paying fees, riding the subway, listening to Dr. M. during sessions . . .

DR. Y: Okay, hold it there for a moment. Is it safe to say that given these various tasks, your role as a client was fairly complex?

ANGELA: Hmm . . . I never thought about it like that, but I see that it's true.

DR. Y: And is it also safe to say that you failed at some of these tasks, did quite well with others, and were so-so with still others?

ANGELA: Yes, that's true.

DR. Y: Then how is it legitimate to rate yourself as a total failure and a hopeless case as a therapy client when you really had a mixture of successes and failures?

ANGELA: I think I see what you're getting at . . .

DR. Y: Right—in rating yourself a failure, you're focusing only on the negatives, ignoring the positives, and on that basis giving yourself an overall negative label. Do you see that?

ANGELA: Oh, yes.

DR. Y: Does it make sense to do that?

ANGELA: No, it doesn't when you explain it that way.

DR. Y: So if it doesn't make sense to label yourself a failure
           since you had both failures *and* successes, how could
           you instead more realistically think about yourself?

ANGELA: Someone who sometimes succeeds and sometimes
           fails?

DR. Y: That's right! Do you know what we call someone like
           that?

ANGELA: No . . .

DR. Y: A human being! And as a human being, you can never
           legitimately put a global rating on yourself! The com-
           plexity of all the various roles you play defies such
           ratings!

The session continued with further discussion of self-rating and
self-acceptance issues (Ellis, 1987), and with assignment of relevant
homework. With respect to her negative self-rating, Angela was encouraged to read *Overcoming the Rating Game* (Hauck, 1991). She was
also instructed on how to challenge her negative self-rating when it
occurred. In addition, she was asked to make some notes concerning
the following information related to her PD-A:

1. Typical panic attack symptoms;
2. Typical thoughts about having a panic attack; and
3. Activities, situations, and places avoided with respect to panic
   attacks.

This information was requested in order to tailor treatment to
Angela's particular array of panic-related symptoms and problems. It
assisted in the process of collaboratively identifying treatment goals.

Interim Between Sessions 1 and 5

During the period between the initial session and Session 5 (the
next session to receive detailed description), Angela appeared to
make some progress in overcoming her negative self-rating with
respect to her prior therapy experience. She no longer considered
herself as a therapy failure, but instead more realistically viewed

herself as a person who had simply experienced difficulty with in vivo exposure exercises at a particular point in time. She no longer dwelled on the fact that she hadn't derived greater benefit from her previous therapy.

During her second session, based on interview data and the written information she had provided about her panic-related problems, the following goal list was constructed:

1. Minimize the possibility of experiencing further panic attacks, and be better able to manage them if they do occur.
2. Be concerned but not worried about the possibility of having a panic attack.
3. Be able to more readily counter anxiety and avoidance behavior with respect to riding the subway and bus.
4. Be able to more readily counter anxiety and avoidance about travelling beyond the confines of the city.
5. Be appropriately concerned but not anxious about the possibility of experiencing rejection within a relationship.

With respect to goal 1, Angela's knowledge of breathing and relaxation techniques was assessed and she was given guidelines for their appropriate use. With respect to her second goal, assessment revealed that Angela no longer believed that her panic attacks meant that she was "losing control" or "going crazy." She did, however, continue to worry about future attacks because of (a) the intense discomfort she experienced during them, and (b) the possibility that other people might notice her while having a panic attack and judge her negatively. She worked on her underlying musts concerning discomfort and disapproval, and demonstrated some progress in disputing them during sessions. It was not clear, however, that this progress was contributing to meaningful behavior change. Issues and interventions pertaining to ongoing avoidance and approval anxiety (see goals 3, 4, and 5) are discussed in forthcoming sections.

During Sessions 3 and 4, I discussed with Angela her apparent aversion to psychotropic medication and interoceptive exposure exercises. With respect to the former, she revealed she was afraid that medication-induced physical sensations might trigger a panic attack. Here, it is noted that Angela avoided taking any sort of medication (including aspirin) if it was at all possible to do so. With respect to the second issue, Angela worried that provoking panic symptoms within session would also lead to a full-blown panic attack. Although I suggested that her fears could be dealt with in therapy, she was firm about not trying medication or interoceptive exposure. I decided it was wise not to push on these issues, as Angela's previous therapy experience suggested that this could damage the therapeutic alliance.

Angela and I did, however, reach a compromise of sorts with respect to identifying an activity that would give her exposure to panic-related physical sensations. Understanding the rationale for such exposure and wanting to get into better physical shape, Angela agreed to take up jogging.

Session 5

This session was focused primarily on the role that in vivo exposure exercises would play in treating Angela's PD-A. The cognitive-behavioral rationale for such exercises was reiterated to her, and riding the subway through the underwater tunnel traversing New York City's East River was identified as an exposure activity at the top of Angela's fear hierarchy.

Angela, however, evidenced considerable reluctance to take on this exposure assignment. Again, this reluctance seemed clearly to stem from irrational beliefs contributing to both discomfort and approval anxiety. Angela frankly admitted that, in all probability, she would not do this exercise in the time prior to our next session. She persisted in this position despite review of rational counters to her approval and discomfort-related musts.

At this point I was faced with a choice: Attempt to work with Angela on exposure assignments in a more gradual, hierarchical fashion, or try to find some other means of encouraging her to try the activity at the top of her hierarchy. Here, the "challenging but not overwhelming" principle of homework design proved useful. I decided to offer to accompany Angela on the subway running under the river during our next session, provided that during the subsequent week she would attempt to do so independently. Somewhat surprisingly, Angela agreed to this arrangement. We spent the balance of the session reviewing rational self-statements that Angela could use when anxious on the subway, and we wrote these down on 3×5 index cards that she could carry with her. I wanted her to have these cards ready for handy reference while on the subway, as it was preferable that she not depend on my presence to help her deal with any panic-related symptoms she might experience.

Session 6

As agreed, Angela and I rode the subway under the East River during this session. Not long into the ride, she turned pale and appeared to become very uptight. The following exchange ensued:

ANGELA: Please start a conversation—about anything!

DR. Y: Are you feeling anxious?

ANGELA: Yes, very!

DR. Y: Do you have your 3 × 5 cards with you?

ANGELA: I don't know where they are!

DR. Y: That's okay—you know what to do. What are you telling yourself right now that's serving to raise your anxiety?

ANGELA: That I'm going to have a panic attack!

DR. Y: And if you do have a panic attack? What then?

ANGELA: I'm going to start gasping for air and other people are going to stare at me.

DR. Y: And if they do? What then?

ANGELA: They'll think I'm weird.

DR. Y: And if they think you're weird—what about that?

ANGELA: Then *I'll* think I'm weird.

DR. Y: Let's suppose a few people actually do think you're weird—would that *really* mean you're a weird person?

ANGELA: (*Relaxes a bit*) No . . .

DR. Y: What does it mean?

ANGELA: That they're rating me on the basis of a small bit of my behavior.

DR. Y: That's right. Is that *really* awful?

ANGELA: No—I guess not.

DR. Y: Why not?

ANGELA: (*Appearing less uptight now*) Because they're not the final judges of who's good and who's bad. And besides—I'll probably never see them again once I get off this train—I don't *need* their approval!

DR. Y: Right. Do you think you can review that in your own mind right now? Go over everything that we just talked about.

Angela fell silent as she did this, and later told me that she had concurrently practiced her diaphragmatic breathing. I made a point of commenting favorably on her efforts, and of emphasizing the fact that she had been able to help herself feel less anxious.

Note that when Angela asked me to start a conversation, I responded by asking her a series of questions. This was because (a) I didn't want her to use conversation as a means of simply distracting herself from her anxiety-producing thoughts, and (b) I wanted to prompt her to think her way through to rational self-talk. Although it was impossible to be sure whether Angela was in this instance responding primarily to distraction or to REBT, she did indeed become more relaxed and seemed to have little difficulty with the return trip on the train. The session ended with reiteration of the coming week's homework assignment—going solo on the subway—and brief review of strategies that Angela could use if she started to feel anxious.

Session 7

As she entered the office at the start of this session, Angela looked rather dejected. She slumped into her seat and, fixing her eyes on the floor, reported that she'd failed to do her homework.

Angela had gone to the subway station the previous Wednesday with every intention of riding the subway through the tunnel, but the train was running quite late and she was left waiting on the subway platform for an unexpected extra 7 minutes or so. Her original plan had been to time her arrival on the platform to coincide with the train's arrival at the station, so that she could simply rush through its open doors without any time for anxious rumination. Interestingly, Angela's plan seemed to represent an attempt at *cognitive* avoidance, as its aim was to prevent her from dwelling on her anxiety-producing thoughts. However, the train was late and the plan failed, and Angela did indeed make herself anxious as she waited. Fearing that her anxiety was the prelude to a panic attack, she left the station without completing her assignment.

Noting Angela's dejection about not completing her homework, I engaged her in the following dialogue:

DR. Y: So you weren't able to get yourself on the train—how do you feel about that?

ANGELA: Terrible! Here we went to all this trouble so I could prepare for the train, and I wasn't able to do it! I feel like a real jerk—it reminds me of when I was still with Dr. M. and would return week after week without having done my homework.

DR. Y: So you're downing yourself—you're telling yourself you're a jerk because you didn't do the homework.

ANGELA: (*Sighs*) Yeah—I guess I still haven't gotten over that self-downing business, either. I'm a double-jerk.

DR. Y: I wouldn't agree with you that you're a jerk, but I would say you're giving yourself two problems for the price of one. First, you're downing yourself for not doing the homework, and then you're downing yourself for downing yourself. Look—it's not necessary to be so hard on yourself, and it's certainly not going to be helpful to you. I'd suggest that we review in a step-by-step fashion what you experienced as you tried to do the homework, and focus our efforts on troubleshooting so you'll be better equipped the next time you attempt it. How does that sound to you?

ANGELA: Okay . . . it sounds all right.

Here, I was concerned with the secondary and tertiary problems of self-downing that Angela had constructed for herself, but I believed that troubleshooting her failure to ride the subway in a direct, matter-of-fact way (as opposed to spending time examining and challenging her self-downing beliefs) would represent the most efficient use of session time. I decided, however, that I would be alert to any signs that Angela was distracted from problem-solving by continued self-downing. Had this been the case (and in this instance it wasn't), I would have suggested that we shift our focus to dealing with this issue.

DR. Y: Tell me exactly what you were telling yourself as you became anxious on the platform—let's start with that.

ANGELA: Well, the train was late, and I was thinking that it might be having mechanical problems. Then I started to feel very tense.

DR. Y: Were you feeling anxious at that point as well?

ANGELA: Yes—tense and anxious.

DR. Y: Suppose the train *was* having mechanical problems—what was anxiety-provoking in your mind about that?

ANGELA: Well, if the train wasn't working properly, it might get stuck in the tunnel—and then I'd be trapped!

DR. Y: So you saw yourself being trapped in the tunnel in a disabled train—did you also see yourself having a panic attack?

ANGELA: Yes, that's what I was afraid would happen, especially since I felt myself becoming more and more anxious as I was waiting.

DR. Y: What were you telling yourself about having a panic attack?

ANGELA: Nothing, really. I just imagined myself panicking on the train, curled up in a fetal position, feeling intensely anxious with no place to run.

DR. Y: Well, wait—as you were standing on the platform imagining all of this, there were several things you could have done. What it seems that you *did* do was to imagine the worst—having a panic attack on the train—and then tell yourself that that would be awful and you wouldn't be able to stand it. Suppose instead that you imagined the worst but then really *convinced* yourself that you *would* be able to stand it—would that have helped you to get on the train when it finally pulled into the station?

ANGELA: Yes, I suppose it would have, but I really *don't* believe I can tolerate the feelings I have when I experience a panic attack.

DR. Y: Okay—but let's examine that and see if it's true. Where's the evidence that you wouldn't be able to *tolerate* those feelings?

ANGELA: It's almost excruciating—every time I've ever had a panic attack, I couldn't tolerate it.

DR. Y: But wait a minute—you just made reference to the evidence that you *can* stand the excruciating feelings you experience during a panic attack!

ANGELA: What do you mean?

DR. Y: How many panic attacks would you say you've had in your lifetime? I'm not looking for an exact number, just an estimate.

ANGELA: Oh, I don't know—probably over a hundred.

DR. Y: Okay, you've had over a hundred panic attacks. Are you still alive?

ANGELA: Yes.

DR. Y: Have you experienced any bodily damage as a direct result of those panic attacks?

ANGELA: No . . .

DR. Y: Have they made you psychotic?

ANGELA: No—okay, I see what you're getting at. I *can* tolerate them, because I *have* tolerated them. But they're still excruciating.

DR. Y: I'm not disputing that—no doubt, they are *extremely* uncomfortable. But, it's very important for you to keep distinct in your own mind your actual physical sensations as opposed to your evaluations of those sensations. If you awfulize about your panic attacks and tell yourself that they're absolutely intolerable, are you going to be more or less likely to get yourself on the train?

ANGELA: Much less likely.

DR. Y: Right! That being so, what could you instead tell yourself about your panic attacks that will be more helpful to you?

ANGELA: Umm . . . they're painful, but they're not lethal!

DR. Y: That's right! But think some more—what could you tell yourself about the *pain* of panic that would work more in your favor?

Angela and I continued to work in this fashion to construct a series of rational beliefs that she could use to counter her discomfort anxiety about experiencing new panic attacks. We then used imagery to work through anticipated "rough spots" she might encounter in attempting to ride the train by herself the following week. We next identified a particular time and day for her to execute her assignment, as establishing the specifics of a homework activity can help to increase the likelihood of compliance (Dryden & Yankura, 1995). As the session drew to a close, Angela actually seemed a bit enthusiastic about the prospect of "going solo."

Session 8

It was apparent that Angela was in a positive mood as she walked into the room for this session. Without delay, she happily reported that she had been able to complete her homework assignment of riding the subway through the East River tunnel—and, she hadn't even experienced a panic attack. We reviewed what this experience had been like for her, and how she had dealt with difficult moments she'd experienced. I made certain to recognize her efforts, and we agreed that continued practice of this exposure exercise would constitute appropriate homework.

Session 10

Although Angela reported at Session 9 that she had been taking the train on almost a daily basis, she entered the current session complaining of backsliding—she was again avoiding the train through the tunnel. An inquiry revealed that she had developed the habit of listening to a tape of one of our sessions on her personal stereo when she was on the train, and that she had come to depend on this device to distract her from anxiety-provoking thoughts. Unfortunately, she had misplaced the tape and was unable to find it. We discussed this as both a form of cognitive avoidance and superstitious behavior, and challenged the "need" to distract oneself from anxiety-producing thoughts and avoid all semblance of anxiety. Following this session, Angela was able to resume riding the train with comparatively little difficulty—*sans* stereo.

Session 12

In this session, Angela reported that her current boyfriend had invited her to travel with him for a weekend at his family's ski lodge in upstate New York. Angela had thus far avoided giving him a definite answer, because she found herself in a double-bind situation: On the one hand, she wanted to accept his invitation, but was afraid that she would experience a panic attack during the lengthy car ride and that he would then think she was weird and reject her. On the other hand, she feared that if she declined her boyfriend's invitation, he would believe that she really wasn't interested in him and would then end their relationship. Angela was nearly beside herself with worry about this conundrum, and had no idea as to which way she should turn.

We worked on identifying and challenging the irrational beliefs behind Angela's approval anxiety and fear of rejection, and also examined the probability that her boyfriend would reject her if she did indeed experience a panic attack in his presence. This combination of cognitive interventions proved effective, as Angela was able to conclude that (a) her boyfriend would very likely not reject her, as he was quite compassionate and understanding, and (b) even if he did reject her, it would not be the end of the world nor evidence that she was a worthless human being. We also considered other contexts in which Angela feared rejection, in order to try and reduce her approval-neediness in these other areas as well.

The following two sessions were focused mainly on helping Angela to prepare for the various exigencies that might occur during her weekend away.

Session 15

Angela reported that, despite the fact that she had been anxious at various points during her weekend trip, she was quite happy that she had gone and had had a very good time. She was especially pleased that she had not experienced any panic attacks.

Given that she had only experienced one panic attack in the past 7 months (and no longer dwelled upon the possibility of future attacks), and also given her impression that she had made considerable progress with her agoraphobic avoidance, Angela decided that this was an appropriate point at which to terminate her therapy. Together, we established the following set of goals that she would continue to work toward independently:

1. Maintain progress with using public transportation.
2. Reduce avoidance of travel beyond New York City by planning and going on weekend trips.
3. Continue working on approval anxiety through cognitive disputation and also by engaging in selective self-disclosure about having had panic-related problems.

I believed at this time that Angela would have benefited from additional sessions, particularly given her goals of attacking new aspects of her agoraphobic avoidance and of reducing her approval anxiety within broader contexts. At the same time, however, I recognized that she had developed a good level of knowledge and competence with respect to using rational emotive behavioral methods, and I wanted to encourage her desire to work independently. As such, I did not recommend that we continue treatment, but instead suggested that Angela phone me in three months time to schedule a "check-up" session. She agreed that this seemed a reasonable idea.

Angela did indeed phone me at the end of 3 months, but not to set up an appointment. She wanted to let me know that she had maintained her progress, and had made inroads with respect to the goals set during her last session. She was now traveling out of the city on a fairly regular basis with her boyfriend, and reported that the two of them had grown quite close. In addition, she indicated that she planned to register for some graduate classes (as an initial foray into academic work on this level) during the coming fall. She reported that she was continuing to utilize the cognitive disputation skills she had learned, and that she regularly challenged herself with a variety of exposure-based behavioral assignments.

I let Angela know that I was quite pleased that she had maintained and even expanded upon the progress she had made in therapy, and told her she could telephone me if she ever thought it would be a good idea to have a "booster session."

CONCLUSION

REBT has much to offer in the treatment of panic disorder with agoraphobia. It may be particularly useful with clients who tend to be difficult customers or who have had negative experiences with prior therapy. In addition to helping the client to minimize or eliminate presenting symptoms of PD-A, it can also help to minimize future vulnerability to emotional disturbance.

Despite REBT's apparent effectiveness with PD-A, it must be noted that current cognitive-behavioral approaches incorporate a number of procedures (such as interoceptive exposure) that even some veteran REBT therapists are unfamiliar with. As these procedures appear to be very helpful for many clients, it would be desirable for REBT therapists to add them to their therapeutic armamentarium.

As detailed in this chapter, the REBT approach to treating PD-A differs in a number of important respects from the general cognitive-behavioral approach to treating this disorder. Although the effectiveness of the latter approach has received empirical support (see, e.g., Barlow, Craske, Cerny, & Klosko, 1989; Craske, Brown, & Barlow, 1991), REBT's effectiveness with PD-A has yet to be put to the test with a series of carefully designed, controlled experiments. In particular, it would be useful to know whether REBT's philosophical emphasis truly adds anything substantial to PD-A treatment. For example, does such an emphasis result in more pervasive, longer-lasting changes for PD-A clients?

Research on REBT's effectiveness with PD-A could be facilitated with production of a standard treatment manual for therapists and researchers. Such a manual could be used as a basis for designing treatment-outcome studies which: (a) examine REBT's general effectiveness for clients with PD-A; (b) compare REBT's effectiveness with that of general cognitive-behavioral treatment for PD-A; and (c) compare long-term effects of rational emotive behavioral versus general cognitive-behavioral treatments for PD-A.

REFERENCES

American Psychiatric Association. (1994). *Diagnostic and statistical manual of mental disorders* (4th ed.). Washington, DC: Author.

Barlow, D. H., & Cerny, J. A. (1988). *Psychological treatment of panic.* New York: Guilford.

/>

Barlow, D. H., & Craske, M. G. (1994). *Mastery of your anxiety and panic II* (client manual). Albany, NY: Graywind.

Barlow, D. H., Craske, M. G., Cerny, J. A., & Klosko, J. S. (1989). Behavioral treatment of panic disorder. *Behavior Therapy, 20,* 261–282.

Beck, A. T., & Emery, G. (1985). *Anxiety disorders and phobias: A cognitive perspective.* New York: Basic Books.

Boyd, J. (1986). Use of mental health services for the treatment of panic disorder. *American Journal of Psychiatry, 143,* 1569–1574.

Clark, D. M., & Ehlers, A. (1993). An overview of the cognitive theory and treatment of panic disorder. *Applied and Preventive Psychology, 2,* 131–139.

Clark, D. M., Salkovskis, P. M., Hackmann, A., Middleton, H., Anastasiades, P., & Gelder, M. (1994). A comparison of cognitive therapy, applied relaxation, and Imipramine in the treatment of panic disorder. *British Journal of Psychiatry, 164,* 759–769.

Clum, G. A. (1990). *Coping with panic: A drug-free approach to dealing with anxiety attacks.* Pacific Grove, CA: Brooks/Cole.

Craske, M. G., Brown, T. A., & Barlow, D. H. (1991). Behavioral treatment of panic disorder: A two-year follow-up. *Behavior Therapy, 22,* 289–304.

Craske, M. G., Meadows, E., & Barlow, D. H. (1994). *Therapist's guide for the mastery of your anxiety and panic II and agoraphobia supplement.* Albany, NY: Graywind.

DiGiuseppe, R. (1991). Comprehensive cognitive disputing in rational-emotive therapy. In M. Bernard (Ed.), *Using rational-emotive therapy effectively* (pp. 173–195). New York: Plenum.

Dryden, W. (1990). *Rational-emotive counselling in action.* London: Sage.

Dryden, W. (1991). *Reason and therapeutic change.* London: Whurr.

Dryden, W., & Yankura, J. (1993). *Counselling individuals: A rational-emotive handbook.* London: Whurr.

Dryden, W., & Yankura, J. (1995). *Developing rational emotive behavioral counselling.* London: Sage.

Ellis, A. (1976). The biological basis of human irrationality. *Journal of Individual Psychology, 32,* 145–168.

Ellis, A. (1977). The basic clinical theory of rational-emotive therapy. In A. Ellis & R. Grieger (Eds.), *Handbook of rational-emotive therapy* (pp. 3–34). New York: Springer Publishing Co.

Ellis, A. (1979a). The issue of force and energy in behavior change. *Journal of Contemporary Psychotherapy, 10,* 83–97.

Ellis, A. (1979b). Discomfort anxiety: A new cognitive-behavioral construct, Part 1. *Rational Living, 14,* 3–8.

Ellis, A. (1980a). Rational-emotive therapy and cognitive-behavior therapy: Similarities and differences. *Cognitive Therapy and Research, 4,* 325–340.

Ellis, A. (1980b). Discomfort anxiety: A new cognitive-behavioral construct, Part 2. *Rational Living, 15,* 25–30.

Ellis, A. (1980c). The value of efficiency in psychotherapy. *Psychotherapy: Theory, Research, and Practice, 17*, 414–419.

Ellis, A. (1982a). Must most psychotherapists remain as incompetent as they now are? *Journal of Contemporary Psychotherapy, 13*(1), 17–28.

Ellis, A. (1982b). Psychoneurosis and anxiety problems. In R. Grieger & I. Grieger (Eds.), *Cognition and emotional disturbance* (pp. 17–45). New York: Human Sciences Press.

Ellis, A. (1983). The philosophic implications and dangers of some popular behavior therapy techniques. In M. Rosenbaum, C. M. Franks, & Y. Jaffe (Eds.), *Perspectives on behavior therapy in the eighties* (pp. 138–151). New York: Springer Publishing Co.

Ellis, A. (1987). The evolution of rational-emotive therapy (RET) and cognitive-behavior therapy (CBT). In J. K. Zeig (Ed.), *The evolution of psychotherapy* (pp. 107–133). New York: Brunner/Mazel.

Ellis, A. (1991). Using RET effectively: Reflections and interview. In M. E. Bernard (Ed.), *Using rational-emotive therapy effectively* (pp. 1–33). New York: Plenum.

Ellis, A., & Abrams, M. (1994). *How to cope with a fatal illness.* New York: Barricade.

Hauck, P. A. (1991). *Overcoming the rating game: Beyond self-love—beyond self-esteem.* Louisville, KY: Westminster/John Knox.

Klosko, J. S., Barlow, D. H., Tassinari, R., & Cerny, J. A. (1990). A comparison of alprazolam and behavior therapy in treatment of panic disorder. *Journal of Consulting and Clinical Psychology, 58*, 77–84.

Markowitz, J. S., Weissman, M. M., Quellette, R., Lish, J. D., & Klerman, G. L. (1989). Quality of life in panic disorder. *Archives of General Psychiatry, 46*, 984–992.

Norton, G. R., Harrison, B., Hauch, J., & Rhodes, L. (1985). Characteristics of people with infrequent panic attacks. *Journal of Abnormal Psychology, 94*, 216–221.

Rapee, R. M., & Barlow, D. H. (1989). Psychological treatment of unexpected panic attacks: Cognitive/behavioral components. In R. Baker (Ed.), *Panic disorder: Theory, research, and therapy* (pp. 239–259). West Sussex, England: John Wiley & Sons.

Telch, M. J., Lucas, J. A., & Nelson, P. (1989). Nonclinical panic in college students: An investigation of prevalence and symptomatology. *Journal of Abnormal Psychology, 98*, 300–306.

Walen, S. R., DiGiuseppe, R., & Dryden, W. (1992). *A practitioner's guide to rational-emotive therapy* (2nd ed.). New York: Oxford University Press.

Warren, R., & Zgourides, G. D. (1991). *Anxiety disorders: A rational-emotive perspective.* New York: Pergamon.

CHAPTER 6

REBT for Anger and Hostility

Mark D. Terjesen, Raymond DiGiuseppe, and Jennifer Naidich

LIMITED THEORY and research exists on the topic of anger to guide therapists in the treatment of clients with anger problems. It appears that the mental health community pays little attention to anger as a clinical problem. Professional journals publish about one-tenth the number of articles on anger as they do on depression and anxiety (Kassinove & Sukhodolsky, 1995a). Although there are nine diagnostic categories for depression and anxiety disorders, there are no anger diagnostic categories, and no guidelines to suggest how clients with anger problems should be diagnosed. Only recently have researchers called for separate diagnostic categories for anger disorders. (DiGiuseppe, Tafrate, & Eckhardt, 1994; Eckhardt & Deffenbacher, 1995).

Currently there is a sparse outcome literature to suggest successful interventions for anger problems. Tafrate (1995) reviewed the treatment approaches that have some empirical support in a meta-analytic review of 20 years of published anger research. Specifically, he identified that treatments that target client self-statements, physiological arousal, and behavioral skills all appear to be effective in helping to manage anger. Although studies that combine approaches may be efficacious, the research does not indicate that any combination of treatments is better than any single intervention. Tafrate also reported that no research studies exist to support Ellis' rational emotive behavior therapy (REBT) or Beck's cognitive therapy with anger.

Besides a lack of comprehensive literature, diagnostic categories, and outcome studies to guide interventions, therapists face other problems that make anger difficult to treat. DiGiuseppe, Tafrate, and Eckhardt (1994) suggest that a major obstacle to successful treatment is that angry clients do not arrive at therapy ready to change their anger. They usually want to change the people at whom they are angry. DiGiuseppe and colleagues (1994) maintain that successful anger treatment usually entails exploration of the consequences of the client's emotions, and the generation of new alternative reactions. These maneuvers motivate the client to change. After this phase of therapy is completed, they recommend a combination of REBT focused on the client's demandingness and imaginal, role-play, or in vivo exposure-based interventions. The present case study attempted to test the treatment recommendations made by DiGiuseppe, Tafrate, and Eckhardt (1994).

DiGiuseppe, Tafrate, and Eckhardt (1994) propose that several diagnostic categories be added to the *Diagnostic and Statistical Manual of Mental Disorders—Fourth Edition* (DSM-IV; American Psychiatric Association, 1994) that would identify the scope and duration of dysfunctional anger and the co-occurrence of aggression. They suggest that categories for situational and generalized anger disorder be added and that each of these be further divided into categories for persons who display or fail to display physical aggression. Also, they suggest an additional category of adjustment disorder with angry mood to represent reactive anger problems. An anger disorder would differ from an episode of anger or annoyance, in that someone experiencing an anger disorder gets angry frequently to a degree that results in functional impairment in one or more spheres of activity for a considerable period of time.

REBT VIEW OF ANGER DISORDERS

DiGiuseppe, Tafrate, and Eckhardt (1994) suggest that angry clients often fail to see anger as their problem. In REBT terms, angry clients arrive for treatment seeking consultation to change their negative activating events. This problem exists because anger is an emotion that comes from a self-righteous view of how other people should behave. Because the transgressors have violated the angry person's moral codes, the transgressors are responsible for the outcome, including the client's anger. The problem (anger) would be solved if only the transgressors behaved as they should.

In addition, short-term reinforcement often influences people to believe that anger is a helpful response to difficult social interactions. Anger often motivates people to behave aggressively toward their transgressor. These actions may suppress the transgressor's behaviors temporarily, reinforcing the angry person's emotional reactions and behavioral aggression. The problem, however, is that the anger and aggression have deleterious effects on social relationships in the long run, and the transgressions often reemerge. Kassinove and Sukhodolsky (1995b) reported survey data on American and Russian college students that indicated that 45% of the anger episodes of the respondents ended negatively. The most common negative outcome of anger episodes was that it weakened subjects' relationships with the person who was the target of their anger. Some anger episodes do have positive outcomes. Aristotle said in *The Nicomachean Ethics,* "We praise a man who feels angry on the right grounds and against the right persons and also in the right manner at the right moment and for the right length of time." However, Aristotle advised that few of us can achieve this degree of control over our anger.

Another problem that prevents angry people from seeing anger as a problem is the common acceptance of the value of cathartic anger expression. Most angry clients maintain the false belief that it is desirable to let out their anger and behaviorally express it. Nasty comments or throwing objects are viewed as constructive ways of dealing with anger. Our Western culture and its acceptance of the Freudian hydraulic model of emotional expression (Tavris, 1989; Torrey, 1992), seems to promote the notion that anger must be expressed to dissipate its energy or the energy will build up and explosive behavior will result. Clients believe that holding in their anger will eventually lead to greater anger outbursts. With this idea one can justify one's anger expression and destructive tirades against one's transgressors as necessary for good mental health.

DiGiuseppe, Tafrate, and Eckhardt (1994) believe that a therapist's first agenda is to assess the client's beliefs *about* anger that block the client from taking responsibility for his or her emotional reaction and attending to the disruptive nature of the emotion.

Exploring the consequences of one's anger and deciding if it serves one's needs is the first step of treatment and is consistent with the REBT philosophy of pursuing long-term hedonism. Once a client decides that his or her anger is self-defeating, an alternative emotional response is needed. Many angry clients are perplexed as to how they would feel or act if they surrendered their anger. DiGiuseppe, Tafrate, Eckhardt, and Robin (1995) suggest that therapists help clients develop a new emotional script for the activating events associated with anger. Such a script would include models of how one could feel and act if the activating event recurred. The development of alternative scripts includes the steps of reviewing the behaviors of models, imagining the consequences of the script in the client's life, and imagery to encourage the experience of the script.

Rational emotive behavior therapy distinguishes between the emotional states of anger and annoyance. Anger differs from annoyance on two grounds. First, anger occurs from or with thoughts that are dogmatic absolutistic demands that the world conform to one's desires. Annoyance occurs with cognitions that acknowledge that the world does not comply with one's preferences. Frustrating situations are disappointing and the reality of the frustration is acknowledged. Second, REBT sees anger as a clinically disturbed emotion that is destructive to the individual. Anger leads to intense physiological arousal, distorted judgments, and dysfunctional behavior. Annoyance, on the other hand, leads to moderate levels of physiological arousal, problem solving, and functional behavior to find alternative ways of attaining one's goals or focusing on alternative goals. REBT theory does not see annoyance as a less intense form of anger. Rather, it is a qualitatively different emotional state. Research by Kassinove and Sukhodolsky (1995b) indicates that both Americans and Russians can distinguish between these two emotional states.

Although anger is considered a dysfunctional emotion according to REBT theory, normal persons may experience anger regularly, perhaps once a month. Isolated episodes of anger would not qualify one for the proposed diagnostic category of an anger disorder. In order for a client to be diagnosed as having an anger disorder, the person would have to experience anger more intensely, for longer duration, and more frequently than most people. Presently, there are little data to suggest what the normal parameters are for the experience of anger. What data we do have come from the Kassinove and Sukhodolsky (1995b) studies of American and Russian college students. Using SUDS (Subjective Units of Discomfort Scale) ratings, the mean rating for intensity of anger episodes was around 50, with a standard deviation of 24. Intensity could be inferred from the degree to which a person's angry feelings, thoughts, and images interfere with other routine activities in his/her life. The norming of self-report data that assess this information could tell us more about the normal intensity of people's anger episodes.

Duration of anger can be measured in terms of how long one has been experiencing increased anger episodes, and how long an anger episode lasts. One criterion suggested by DiGiuseppe, Tafrate, Eckhardt, and Robin (1995) and Eckhardt and Deffenbacher (1995) is that one has experienced excessive episodes of anger for a period of 6 months or longer. The normal length of an individual anger episode is usually about 5 to 30 minutes (Kassinove & Sukhodolsky, 1995b). Episodes that last from several hours to an entire day are well beyond the range that most people stay angry. Highly frequent anger episodes are also another measure of anger disturbance. A frequency of once per week would be more than 1 standard deviation above "normal," based on the Kassinove and Sukhodolsky (1995b) research.

Anger appears to be an emotion of the heart. Our clinical experience suggests that most anger is targeted at those we know intimately. This notion was supported by Kassinove and Sukhodolsky (1995b) who found that almost half of all anger episodes occur in the home and 70% of all anger episodes are directed at someone the person knows well or loves. Present theory from social psychology suggests that the activating events for anger and aggression episodes share some common characteristics (Tedeschi & Nesler, 1993). First, they involve a violation of a moral code or rule, and second, there is the attribution that the transgression could have been prevented by the transgressor. The fact that anger is elicited from moral transgressions is again revealed in the words of angry people. One of the most frequently heard phrases they repeat is, "But it is not fair."

REBT theory suggests that the cognitions underlying anger are demands that the activating event be different from reality. The theory distinguishes the *preference* that the activating event not be from the *demand* that it not be. Angry clients reveal this notion in often used phrases such as, "I can't believe that this happened!" or "How could they have done that?" They literally do not register the event as having occurred and spend their energy attempting to argue or wish the event away. This demanding philosophy represents a strong dogmatic and rigid adoption of previously held schemata about the world in the face of evidence to the contrary. From a developmental point of view, one could say that anger results from the process of assimilation. Angry people assimilate the information they receive into their old schemata rather than accommodate the new information and construct a new schema of the world. Rational alternative beliefs acknowledge that the world is not how one likes it, while recognizing the disappointment in having one's preference thwarted.

Ellis proposes that the identification of one's self-angering philosophy may also involve some derivative irrational beliefs that follow from the rigid clinging to old schemata. These thoughts include the belief that one *cannot stand* the "wrong" behaviors of others, and globally damning the personhood of others for acting poorly. Although depressed individuals condemn themselves, angry people use the same total rating of a person but rate the transgressor rather than themselves.

Changing this "angering" philosophy using a variety of REBT techniques will lead to a decrease in the experience and expression of anger and increase one's ability to make more appropriate practical decisions. In working toward a more rational philosophy, the client may experience a rational alternative to anger—annoyance. Experiencing annoyance, rather than anger, may allow the client to deal with the situation more constructively and choose more appropriate solutions—practically, behaviorally, and cognitively (Dryden & Yankura, 1993).

The case illustration that follows will offer an in-depth review of the treatment of a client presenting with anger difficulties. It will describe cognitive-behavioral assessment of the client's anger problem and identification of the client's belief system, and will outline the REBT treatment approaches that were utilized.

CASE ILLUSTRATION

Client Background

Peggy, a 24-year-old Caucasian female, was referred to the Institute for Rational Emotive Therapy's (IRET) outpatient clinic by her employee assistance program at work. She had no preconception as to the nature of the therapy. Peggy had consulted a therapist before for an unspecified reason, for one session, but had discontinued due to general dissatisfaction. She was a college graduate and was employed as a merchandising coordinator for a monthly magazine. She had lived in New York City for approximately 2 years, and had resided with her 35-year-old boyfriend for the previous 8 months in his one-bedroom apartment.

Peggy was raised and attended college in the American South. She reported having a good relationship with her parents and two younger brothers. She did not consider herself religious; however, she refused to tell her father that she lived with a man. Being raised in the American South turned out to be a crucial therapeutic issue. Peggy engaged in certain behaviors that she considered "unbecoming of a lady (*sic*)," which increased her emotional distress. In addition, she restricted discussion of issues concerning her family that she perceived as irrelevant to treatment, since "we don't like to air our dirty laundry."

On a biographical information form completed at IRET, Peggy described herself as "intelligent, pleasant to be with, and a nice person"; however, she perceived these positive traits to be "significantly outweighed" by her "temper and impatience." Her main complaints were "stress and frustration that become manifested in fits of temper, sometimes violent." These problems worsened when she was "tired, and of course" they intensified "when drinking."

Assessment

Peggy completed the IRET biographical information form and several objective measures included in IRET's intake packet. The therapist (M.T.) conducted a thorough clinical interview during the first session. The biographical information form guided the clinical interview and reduced the amount of session time spent gathering information. Specifically, the presence of dysfunctional emotions, behaviors, and cognitions was assessed.

Identifying the ABCs through a clinical interview. The ABC model of REBT structured the clinical interview. Peggy had no difficulty identifying her emotional problem. The only emotional dysfunction she described was her anger. She reported no depression or anxiety. She asserted that her anger was only directed toward her boyfriend, Andrew, and his behaviors. She insisted that she never displayed anger elsewhere. Her expression of anger involved verbal confrontations with Andrew, where she increased the volume and intensity of her voice. Often, these verbal confrontations were motivated by her self-created need to drown-out Andrew and make him listen to her. She would yell and make nasty, sarcastic, and critical comments about him. In addition, she would throw any object at him that was within easy reach. Peggy reported slapping and pushing Andrew approximately once a month. She would often block Andrew's path with her body, so that he would have to listen to her. She frequently paced around the apartment while talking to herself and physically punished herself by hitting the walls with her fists. She perceived this to be a more appropriate target for her anger expression than Andrew. As with many new clients (and with cognitive behavior therapy clients in particular), Peggy was initially unable to identify her faulty patterns of thinking, and she identified her emotions as being caused by Andrew's behavior. The therapist attempted to clarify her activating events—the circumstances that occurred before she felt and expressed her anger. This was done for two reasons. First, it clarified what Peggy defined as the reason for seeking therapy. Second, it supplied the therapist with data that would be used later to develop exposure imagery exercises.

Because Peggy identified Andrew as the "sole cause" of her anger outbursts, specific examples of his egregious behavior that "caused" her anger were requested. Peggy reported that her interactions with Andrew often left her feeling inferior to him. He regularly corrected her syntax and grammar and made her "verbally correct" herself before he would continue to converse with her. He also taunted her about her poor financial management and would remind her when bills were due. Peggy entered the relationship owing approximately $2,000 on her credit cards and was paying approximately 15% interest. Andrew paid off her debts and Peggy made monthly payments to him at a moderate interest rate.

An event that Peggy perceived as particularly upsetting involved Andrew's teaching her to stack boxes appropriately in a storage closet. Andrew, apparently not satisfied with Peggy's skills, took the boxes out of her hands and demanded that she stand and watch as he stored them more efficiently. Peggy felt like "a child" who frequently needed correction from "adults." When Peggy became intensely angry and yelled at Andrew, he attempted to challenge her thinking and scolded her for losing her temper. He said "It's easier for you to change your reactions, than for me to change my actions." Although Andrew thought this statement represented good rational thinking, (which, in fact, it did, insofar as Peggy could only exert control over her emotions and not over Andrew's behavior), it seemed to Peggy to reflect his demanding that she must change her reaction. It meant that Andrew would never change for her.

Peggy described some secondary emotional consequences of her anger. After becoming angry at Andrew, she became increasingly angry at herself for "allowing him to get the best of her." This anger added to her initial upset and led to more disturbed emotional and behavioral reactions on her part, involving intense feelings and expression of anger.

DiGiuseppe, Tafrate, and Eckhardt (1994) propose that angry clients often fail to believe that their anger is a problem and, therefore, underestimate the degree and pervasiveness of their anger reactions. As a result, open-ended questions about the extent of, and eliciting stimuli for a client's anger are unlikely to extract adequate information. They recommend that a comprehensive evaluation of clients' anger be conducted with specific, forced-choice questions about the frequency, duration, and intensity of the anger. These authors have constructed a structured interview for anger that helps to facilitate this goal.[1] This interview includes specific questions on (a) the functional impairments that are the result of one's anger, (b) physiological reactions one experiences when angry, (c) the ways one expresses anger, (d) the activating events that elicit the anger, (e) the beliefs that mediate the anger, and (f) the number of people who have told the client that his or her anger is a problem.

Although Peggy initially reported that her relationship with Andrew was the only area where she displayed anger outbursts, the structured interview revealed a history of anger problems in love relationships. Peggy described other instances where she experienced similar emotions and behaviors in her past. Interestingly, they involved romantic relationships with significantly older men who also "corrected and controlled" her.

After revealing her description of her emotions and behaviors and the condemnable behavior on Andrew's part that "caused" them, Peggy sought some validation from the therapist that her emotions and behaviors were correct and appropriate. She tried to justify her

---

[1] Requests for information on the Structured Interview for Anger Disorders should be sent to Raymond DiGiuseppe, Ph.D., Department of Psychology, St. John's University, 8000 Utopia Parkway, Jamaica, NY 11550.

actions by saying, "he's causing me to behave this way, so he should change," and "people shouldn't treat people they care about the way that he treats me." These were two of the more frequent statements spoken by Peggy early in therapy.

Anger patients often do not elicit empathy from their therapists (DiGiuseppe, Tafrate, & Eckhardt, 1994). Although Andrew's behavior was perceived as pompous and self-righteous by the therapist, Peggy's verbal tirades and projectile attacks sounded more violent and just as disturbed as Andrew's behavior. DiGiuseppe, Tafrate, and Eckhardt (1994) stress the importance of acknowledging the angry client's sense of the significant other's transgression. Failure to do so often results in the client persistently trying to convince the therapist that he or she was justifiably angry. To foster a positive therapeutic relationship, the therapist acknowledged that Andrew's behaviors were quite obnoxious, condescending, and inappropriate. It was acknowledged that it was understandable that Peggy would have some negative feelings about being treated so poorly. However, the nature and degree of her emotional reaction to his obnoxious behavior was controlled by her beliefs about it. This issue would be discussed later as an opportunity to fully explain the B → C connection in the REBT model.

Next, the therapist explored Peggy's secondary emotional dysfunction of anger at herself. The therapist hypothesized that this emotional reaction resulted from her self-downing about her anger expression. To help Peggy explore the exact nature of her irrational self-condemnation, Rational Emotive Imagery (REI) was used (Maultsby & Ellis, 1974). Peggy was asked to use imagery to recall the most recent instance where she experienced the secondary emotional upset of anger at herself after an argument with Andrew. When she was able to report that she was imaginally re-experiencing this feeling, she was instructed to focus on the internal sentences that related to this emotion: "I should be in more control and I shouldn't get angry. And if I do, that shows he is right and I am inadequate." This exercise revealed that Peggy was placing an absolutistic demand upon herself. When she failed to live up to her self-imposed demand, she engaged in negative self-rating.

Next the REI exercise was repeated, but this time Peggy was asked to focus on Andrew's behavior. She was asked to imagine her thoughts when she became angry at him. For Peggy, these internal sentences were demands that Andrew behave differently: "He should not correct me." "He should not treat me like a child and ought to treat me fairly." "He should acknowledge my opinion when I'm correct and should not belittle me when I'm not."

In describing Peggy's irrational beliefs, it appeared that in moments of anger she would experience all three of the irrational demands posited by Ellis: demands about others, about herself, and about the situation (Ellis & Dryden, 1987). Following an anger outburst, Peggy demanded of herself that she not get angry and made global negative ratings of herself, rather than simply rating her negative behaviors. She had strong demands about Andrew's behavior and about her own ability to be able to control her anger. When he "attacked" her or her behaviors, Peggy also made herself angry by interpreting the event as an attack on her self-worth, that she "must defend." This demand on herself to defend her good name trapped her into engaging in verbal arguments.

Peggy exhibited low frustration tolerance (LFT) in two ways. When the attacks were over she continually ruminated to herself, "I can't stand it when Andrew always behaves this way!" In the assessment process, the therapist made note of both the volume and intensity of these self-statements, and the rigidity with which she held on to these irrational beliefs. In addition, Peggy's physiological arousal was noticeable when she vividly created images of Andrew. She would get herself infuriated, turn red, tighten her hands, and make inconsistent, fleeting eye contact with the therapist.

Peggy often made comparisons of her and Andrew's relationship to other couples. She would only make upward comparisons with couples with better or perceived "perfect" relationships. She negatively evaluated their relationship and thought it was "just terrible" that she and Andrew fought the way they did. Peggy's tendency to "awfulize" about both her and Andrew's behaviors appeared driven by her demands. Although rationally she preferred that Andrew not treat her poorly and, if given the choice, she would have preferred to be more in control of her emotions, Peggy made these things more than just preferences and their absence more than just unpleasant. Peggy shouted, both in session and in her head, that these actions must not occur and strongly held on to these beliefs. Attaching this additional idea of terribleness to this existent rational idea led to her emotional upset.

Just prior to therapy Peggy and Andrew made a behavioral contract that they thought would enhance their communication skills and decrease her anger outbursts. The contract entailed three parts. First, each partner would allow the other partner to complete whatever he or she was saying without being cut off. Second, they would both decrease the frequency of completing what the other partner was saying. Finally, they would make a concerted effort to listen to one another.

Although the intent of this contract was good, regrettably the outcome was negative. Andrew's failure to stick to the contract became another activating event about which Peggy infuriated herself. Before the contract, Andrew's finishing her sentences, cutting her off, or failing to listen were "barely tolerable." However, now that they had a "contract" to minimize these behaviors, there were two things to be upset about: the fact that he engaged in them and the fact that he did not keep to the contract. Peggy expressed the belief, "How dare he not work on these things, especially after I was patient and listened to him!" Again, Peggy strongly demanded that Andrew's behavior be different than it was and was going to be. She again perceived that she had a "legitimate" reason to be angry at him.

Objective measures.   All new IRET clients receive a standard intake battery of measures related to various aspects of mental health. Clients are asked to arrive early for the first session to complete these forms and the biographical information form. The measures are computer-scored and are usually available to the therapist by the second session. These instruments are used to help the therapist understand the client's level of emotional disturbance and personality structure, and assist with generating hypotheses about the client's irrational thinking and maladaptive behavioral and emotional consequences. The intake measures also provide a baseline against which to monitor progress. The intake packet includes the Millon Clinical Multi-Axial Inventory II (MCMI-II) (Millon, 1987, 1988), the short form of the Beck Depression Inventory (BDI) (Beck & Beck, 1972), the General Health Questionnaire (Goldberg, 1972), the General Psychological Well-Being Scale (DePue, 1987), the Satisfaction with Life Scale (Diener, Emmons, Larsen, & Griffen, 1985), and the interpreted Attitudes and Beliefs Scale—2 (DiGiuseppe, Leaf, Exner, & Robin, 1988).

Peggy willingly completed these measures and, on returning them, questioned the therapist about the validity of the picture they painted of her. An interpretation of these measures was consistent with her responses in the clinical interview. Her Millon Clinical Multi-Axial Inventory II (MCMI-II) response style indicated some avoidance of self-disclosure. She received a base rate score of 30 on the Disclosure diagnostic scale, suggesting an unwillingness to discuss or share matters of a personal nature. The therapist had to always consider that Peggy would not be forthcoming with information and that he would have to ask more specific questions than he normally would. He planned to respect her desire for privacy and push for information she felt reluctant to reveal only when it seemed especially important. If the therapist believed that important information was being withheld, he attempted to deal with Peggy's embarrassment about revealing it as a clinical issue before pursuing the information.

Peggy's scores on the other MCMI-II scales were close to the interpretable cutting scores but below the clinical cut-off. However, given the Disclosure subscale score mentioned above, it was decided to cautiously interpret them. These scores suggested some Axis II clinical personality disorder problems. Peggy attained high scores on the Histrionic (74), and Passive-Aggressive (72) personality disorder subscales. These scores suggested a tendency to make dramatic attempts to achieve the approval of others, and also that Peggy could be self-defeating, negativistic, and could harbor resentment.

Peggy's responses on the Beck Depression Inventory and the General Health Questionnaire revealed mild levels of depression and disturbance. Additionally, she had an unusually high score for a psychotherapy patient at intake on the Satisfaction with Life Scale. Again, these scores may have reflected Peggy's initial unwillingness to divulge much personal information and did not assist much in the assessment of her anger.

Peggy's responses on the General Psychological Well-Being Scale yielded some interesting results that had potential significance with regard to her anger and hostility. Her overall score on this measure was significantly lower than that for the general population, and her subscale statistics revealed certain aspects of her present functioning that seemed particularly relevant to her anger difficulties. Specifically, she scored more than 2 standard deviations below the general population on perceived self-control, an area in which she had expressed desires to improve during the clinical interview.

Although these instruments offered some insights into Peggy's general patterns of cognitions, emotions, and behaviors, they failed to directly assess her anger, aggression, and hostility. Accordingly, she was administered a new self-report measure of anger (DiGiuseppe, Eckhardt, Robin, & Tafrate, 1993) based on criteria proposed for an anger disorder diagnostic category, and also underwent a structured interview for anger/hostility disorder (Eckhardt, DiGiuseppe, & Tafrate, 1995). The self-report measure has demonstrated excellent internal validity, and the factor structure has confirmed the authors' attempts to construct clinically relevant subscales that can be used in treatment planning. The subscales include cognitive dysfunction or obsessional nature of the anger, physiological reactions, verbal aggression, desire for physical aggression, duration of anger, the use of anger to control others, and holding anger in. A profile analysis on a client's subscales can indicate to the therapist which areas need intervention.[2]

Results yielded by the assessment techniques provided the therapist with more specific information concerning the frequency and intensity of Peggy's anger responses. Peggy reported a general pattern of irritableness and grouchiness over the past 6 months, but would express her anger for a few minutes (20–30 minutes at a time) approximately once a week. The cognitive, affective, and behavioral aspects of Peggy's anger and the situations that elicited her anger reactions were also assessed. Her activating events included (a) others acting unreasonably, and (b) her inability to accomplish what she absolutely *should*. Her ability to identify the frequency and intensity of her physiological reactions when angry proved to be helpful during the cognitive-behavioral relaxation component of therapy. She was able to identify when she was angry by her bodily sensations.

Diagnosis

Diagnosis is always an ongoing process in REBT, as therapists may change their diagnostic impressions as they gather information about a client's thoughts, emotions, and behaviors over the course of treatment. Assigning an official diagnosis from the DSM-IV (American Psychiatric Association, 1994) to a client is necessary for proper record-keeping and for attaining insurance reimbursement for the client. With respect to treatment planning, however, assigning an official diagnosis is not always meaningful. Peggy clearly did not qualify for any of the current available diagnostic categories. The

---

[2] Requests for information on the Anger Disorders Self Report Scale should be sent to Raymond DiGiuseppe, Ph.D., Department of Psychology, St. John's University, 8000 Utopia Parkway, Jamaica, NY 11550.

symptoms she presented did not meet the specific diagnostic criteria of any of the DSM-IV disorders. Her symptoms did have some characteristics similar to other disorders, but failed to meet the requisite number of symptoms for diagnosis. Specifically, she had some of the symptoms for the following DSM-IV categories: (a) Anxiety Disorder Not Otherwise Specified, (b) Impulse-Control Disorder Not Otherwise Specified, (c) Adjustment Disorder Unspecified, or (d) Partner Relational Problem. All of these categories were considered, but none truly captured the nature of Peggy's difficulties.

The failure to have anger-disorder categories appears to be a failure of our present nosology systems. Peggy yelled and threw objects at Andrew regularly. If only she had done it less often she could have met the criteria for Intermittent Explosive Disorder. Peggy also could have met the criteria for Adjustment Disorder with Mixed Emotional and Behavioral Features. However, her reactions had occurred much longer than the 6-month limit stipulated for an adjustment reaction, and she was predominately angry. Thus, the difficulties encountered in assessment of an angry client were also experienced in the diagnosis of one. As noted earlier, it has been proposed that anger disorders be added to the present nosology (DiGiuseppe, Tafrate, & Eckhardt, 1994; DiGiuseppe, Tafrate, Eckhardt, & Robin, 1995; Eckhardt & Deffenbacher, 1995). Based on the suggested categories, Peggy met the criteria for Situational Anger Disorder with Aggression. The disorder is considered situational, because it appears to occur within the context of romantic relationships, and obviously occurs with aggression.

Establishing a Therapeutic Relationship

Assessing a client's expectations of therapy is an important aspect of establishing rapport and building a therapeutic relationship. Peggy had no preconceived notions about therapy, but was initially reluctant to disclose personal information as stated previously. This reluctance could have stemmed from her conservative upbringing, but also seemed related to her fear of being "judged by others." The therapist was aware throughout the sessions that Peggy's fear could prevent her from disclosing information. To combat this fear and to normalize (to some degree) her feelings of annoyance toward Andrew, the therapist self-disclosed some events involving similar individuals in his life and his reaction to them. The self-disclosure was done to offer proper modeling to the client and to also reintroduce the REBT concept of how our thoughts determine our emotions and behaviors. Also, the therapist made a mental note of Peggy's fear of being judged to ensure that he always specifically stated that he was challenging her irrational ideas and not blaming or criticizing her when he disputed her irrational beliefs.

With any client it is important to establish a therapeutic alliance. One core aspect of the therapeutic alliance is agreement on the goals of therapy. Developing this aspect of the therapeutic alliance with an "angry" client may be difficult, because angry clients want to change the people at whom they are angry, not their anger (DiGiuseppe, Tafrate, & Eckhardt, 1994; DiGiuseppe, Tafrate, Eckhardt, & Robin, 1995). Peggy wanted to change Andrew, not Peggy! She was seeking a professional consultation with the therapist in order to learn strategies for improving Andrew's behavior.

One strategy to shift the alliance from changing the transgressor to changing the client's anger is to review the cost of the anger to the client. Angry clients are often unaware of the cost of the anger to them in terms of wasted energy and resources, dysphoria, and missed opportunity. Following Peggy's identification of her reactions to Andrew's behavior, the focus was shifted to how these reactions affected her. The behavioral and affective components of her anger were reviewed. Behaviorally, Peggy reported that she had broken many household items in fits of anger and could no longer afford to replace them. She expressed a strong desire for the relationship with Andrew to work out and lead to marriage. She acknowledged that, when she let her anger guide her behavior, achievement of marriage seemed less likely. She expressed a desire to experience many of the positive emotional components (caring, intimacy, love) of a relationship and realized that she failed to work toward these when she upset herself. She also reported that at times her work performance had deteriorated because of her anger and hostility toward Andrew. Her ruminating demands about him and his behavior "so infuriate me" that it was increasingly difficult for her to focus on her job. We specifically identified the more complex work tasks that she failed to complete because of her self-created cognitive distractions.

In discussing both long-term and short-term goals for anger control, Peggy indicated that she just wanted to be calm and indifferent when Andrew acted in ways that had elicited her anger in the past. This, however, was not a reasonable goal, as a state of indifference would have required Peggy to ignore her preference that Andrew behave differently. From an REBT perspective, a more healthy and helpful goal would be for Peggy to experience an *appropriate* negative emotion (i.e., annoyance) in place of her anger. A description of the distinction between inappropriate and appropriate emotions was discussed using the old television series *Star Trek* as an analogy.

A discourse followed in which Peggy and the therapist examined how Mr. Spock (a nonemotional extraterrestrial of the planet Vulcan) constantly pointed out the irrationality of the behaviors of many of his human crew-mates, who often got over-emotional and failed to think logically. In a humorous counterargument, Peggy stated that the last thing she wanted to become was "a nonfeeling Vulcan" as Mr. Spock also never felt some of "life's true pleasures, like love." The therapist countered by stating, "We're not going to make you into a nonemotional Vulcan, nor an over-emotional, irrational human (sometimes driven by her "libidinal" impulses). Rather, we'll work on having you become someone who can experience more appropriate functional negative emotions without needlessly upsetting yourself so that you can enjoy life more and make better decisions." This helped foster the therapeutic relationship, set a therapeutic goal, and underscored for Peggy that there were numerous ways in which she potentially could respond. Peggy accepted that the goal of therapy was to replace her anger with a more functional but negative emotion that was labeled *annoyance.*

Getting into the specifics of anger control was greatly assisted through the use of the self-report measure of anger (DiGiuseppe, Eckhardt, Robin, & Tafrate, 1993) and the structured interview for anger/hostility disorder (Eckhardt, DiGiuseppe, & Tafrate, 1995). Much like a clinician referring back to previous responses on an objective measure for anxiety or depression, these measures were used periodically to assess the frequency, intensity, and expression of Peggy's anger. The information from these measures helped reinforce the notion that her anger was destructive and that a new emotional reaction was more beneficial.

In addition to anger control, Peggy expressed (as a "goal afterthought"), the desire for better communication between herself and Andrew. This would help her reach her ultimate goal of the progression of the relationship toward marriage. It was agreed that better communication was not necessarily separate from the anger-reduction goal, and that, with practice and effort, both could be worked on using the REBT model. However, in the back of the therapist's mind lurked the suspicion that Peggy subscribed to another overriding belief: "I must make this relationship work and marry Andrew." The therapist was not sure Andrew and Peggy were compatible, even if Peggy did surrender her demanding philosophy. When Peggy was questioned as to whether or not she perceived that she was holding on to this belief, she denied the therapist's hypothesis, but stated that she "would really like this relationship to work out, but it doesn't have to."

Treatment

Teaching the B → C connection.   Peggy's treatment followed a multi-component cognitive-behavioral approach, incorporating relaxation, assertiveness training, and communication skill building, with the classical REBT strategy of disputing her irrational beliefs as the central approach. Upon identifying Peggy's irrational beliefs of demandingness toward Andrew's and her own behavior, the connection between her irrational thinking and her emotional and behavioral disturbance needed to be established. She still blamed his behavior for her emotions. Establishing the B → C connection was the first intervention.

The therapist engaged Peggy in a discussion of various scenarios that demonstrated that other people do not cause our feelings. Using Andrew as an example, Peggy was asked how 100 other women would respond if they had a lover who treated them similarly to how Andrew treated her. Peggy was able to generate numerous alternative emotional consequences that included depression, mild sadness, mild annoyance, and indifference. Peggy was then reminded of her initial explanation that Andrew caused her anger, and confronted with her own evidence that different emotions could potentially be experienced. How could she explain that the same person and the same behavior could elicit so many different emotional reactions? Peggy reported that those hypothetical women just reacted differently. The therapist immediately reinforced Peggy for the insight that people can have different emotional reactions to the same event, and explained that this was because they evaluated the situation differently.

Peggy listened eagerly to the therapist's notion that recognizing how our own individual belief system or philosophy guides our reactions leads to the power to control one's reactions. The therapist suggested that Peggy had an "anger button" that Andrew was quite adept at pushing. However, she could learn to disconnect that button so that he could continue to push without her responding in her characteristic fashion (Walen, DiGiuseppe, & Dryden, 1992). This seemed initially to establish the idea in Peggy's mind that situations and people do not cause our emotions, but, rather, our belief system does. Given Peggy's desire for approval (or, rather, fear of disapproval), the therapist was concerned that Peggy might just be agreeing with the therapist and that she truly hadn't made the B → C connection yet. That is, it was suspected that she didn't fully believe that our thoughts or beliefs are what guide our emotional and behavioral consequences. As such, additional examples involving Peggy's emotional reactiveness were elicited and examined in order to help further establish the B → C connection.

Based on a statement that Peggy had made previously, the therapist used humor to further outline the B → C connection. She had said earlier that, "I feel like a puppet and Andrew's pulling my strings." Upon entering the room for the next session, Peggy was asked "So, who pulled the strings this week?" She responded with a bewildered "excuse me" look. Use of the puppet analogy was suggested by the therapist's supervisor after reviewing the tape of the session in which Peggy had made reference to it. The therapist recounted to Peggy her use of the metaphor previously and suggested to her that Andrew only "pulls the strings" because she allowed him to. She could reclaim the strings, and direct her own emotions and behaviors without blaming him for them.

Challenging irrational beliefs.   The next stage of treatment involved challenging Peggy's irrational beliefs. A major component of an REBT treatment program is to have the client focus on the illogical, anti-empirical, and unhelpful nature of their present irrational beliefs and see that alternative beliefs make more sense, are more reality based, and lead to greater productivity. The therapist first focused on Peggy's secondary emotional problem of self-anger, which she experienced when she lost her temper with Andrew. The idea that it was best not to react in such a fashion was reinforced as a preference. Yet, Peggy was reminded that she was human and had trained herself to act this way. The therapist primarily employed functional disputes for the irrational beliefs that led to her anger at herself (DiGiuseppe, 1991): "How does demanding that you not get angry or condemning yourself for getting angry help you not to get angry at Andrew?" Peggy responded that the opposite happened when she made such demands, because she became more easily upset at Andrew and spent no mental energy thinking about how to avoid getting angry. A functional dispute can be particularly effective when the client ascertains that their current way of thinking may not help them achieve their specific goal(s). For Peggy, this involved assessing that her current way of thinking did not help her attain her goal of anger control with Andrew. Peggy's secondary emotional problem seemed to change quickly (in terms of a decrease in reported self-directed demands about controlling her emotions and a greater sense of self-acceptance) and, as a result, the sessions focused more exclusively on her relationship with Andrew.

Peggy was adamant that Andrew's behavior was obnoxious. Initial attempts to dispute the idea that "He must not act the way he acts" were met with facial grimaces. It was important for Peggy to understand that she wasn't (nor was the therapist) going to challenge her inferences about whether or not Andrew was treating her poorly. Rather, her inferences about his behavior being inconsiderate were assumed to be valid. Instead, Peggy was instructed on how to challenge her rigidly held beliefs that "He must not behave that way and treat me like a child" and "I can't stand it when he treats me poorly." She was currently engaging in all-or-none or black-and-white thinking, and a therapeutic goal was to have her become more adaptive and flexible in her thinking.

Every REBT therapist finds various strategies to effectively teach clients to dispute their irrational beliefs. However, therapists need to be aware that any specific disputing technique may not be effective for a given client, and that it's preferable they be adaptable as a result. DiGiuseppe (1991) has outlined a comprehensive matrix of potential disputes and suggests that therapists try all of them until we have developed sufficient knowledge to predict a priori which disputes will be most effective for which irrational beliefs with which clients. In this case the therapist utilized a large number of disputing interventions targeted at Peggy's demand that Andrew *must* behave in the way she wanted.

For Peggy, some of the more effective strategies for countering her demanding beliefs about Andrew were empirical disputes combined with effective coping statements (DiGiuseppe, 1991). Some empirical disputes were "Why should he behave differently, just because I want him to? He does do many things that I don't want him to do" and "If the evidence holds that he has behaved in this manner consistently in the past, why should he behave any differently now?" She was able to combine these disputes with more effective coping statements, which were more rational beliefs to replace her irrational beliefs: "I would like Andrew to acknowledge my point of view, but I can stand it when he doesn't" and "As much as I'd like to be treated fairly, I can accept that it doesn't always happen." Regarding her demandingness about her own behaviors (anger expression), she worked actively at replacing her irrational beliefs with more rational ones such as "I don't have to be perfect and in control of my emotions—I am a normal, fallible human being, and can accept myself with my faults."

Peggy became able to acknowledge that she could develop other ways of thinking about Andrew's behavior. She reported knowing this on the "cognitive level," and that she had probably known it all along, but had failed to use it. Peggy often pointed to her head and said, "I know it up here, but . . . I don't believe it down here" (pointing to her abdomen). She was holding her new, rational beliefs with light conviction rather than deep conviction. Although this was acknowledged as progress, it failed to sufficiently bring about the kind of behavioral and affective change that had been targeted in developing a treatment plan. She still yelled and hurled objects at Andrew when he corrected her, although she reported a significant decrease in the frequency of these behaviors.

Because the frequency and intensity of Peggy's anger outbursts had decreased only somewhat but not significantly by her and Andrew's reported standards, we planned some between-session homework assignments that involved rehearsal. Although Peggy clearly understood the theory on a "cognitive level," she had not yet rehearsed it enough for it to become a new belief system. Over the next few sessions, we developed a monitoring system that allowed Peggy to chart the situations that elicited her anger and her accompanying thoughts that led to her anger. The assignment involved her actively disputing her thoughts and developing more effective rational thinking that would likely lead to more adaptive alternative emotions. For several sessions we reviewed the specific activating events, the irrational beliefs they triggered, her disputes, and her rational alternative beliefs. These assignments worked and seemed to provide Peggy with the confidence that she could control her anger successfully.

Anger is, in many ways, similar to anxiety, in that it can be a reaction to threat. Anxiety disorders are successfully treated by imaginal and in vivo exposure. DiGiuseppe, Tafrate, and Eckhardt (1994) suggest that the same type of exposure principles are necessary for the successful treatment of anger. Peggy had attempted to avoid anger-provoking situations. That was the purpose of the communications training and the behavioral contract. If only she could talk in a way that did not anger Andrew, or if she could know what Andrew wanted of her, she could avoid anger-provoking activating events. The therapist explained to Peggy that these were good strategies, but even if they were 90% successful, there would still be times when she would have to face the anger-provoking stimuli. Peggy was instructed to intentionally imagine situations about which she would likely make herself angry. Imagery scenes were developed of events that either similarly elicited anger or were similar to such events. Peggy practiced imagining the scenes and rehearsed disputations and new rational coping thoughts. This continued until Peggy gained more confidence that she could control her anger.

The next step was to go from imaginal exposure with coping statements to actually using the rational coping strategy in real situations. Peggy was obsessive in her attempts to correct the things Andrew had criticized about her. She also tried to anticipate Andrew's "needs" and always do what he asked. Because the imaginal homework was going well, the therapist suggested that it was time for her to "forget" to do something Andrew had requested of her. We discussed this and chose something that was not inconsiderate or of any major consequence. Peggy was now afforded the opportunity to prepare for the eventual argument beforehand, something that she had not been able to do previously. For Peggy, this preparation involved using Rational-Emotive Imagery (Maultsby & Ellis, 1974). She was instructed to spend anywhere from 5 to 20 minutes per day, over a period of 4 days, imagining what Andrew's response would be to her mistake of "forgetting" to copy an article for him in this case. In doing so, she was able to create the feelings of anger that she normally would have experienced in the situation, and develop new disputations to argue against her irrational beliefs. As such, she was able to use these disputes and her more effective coping statements in future situations in which she was experiencing anger.

The use of in vivo exposure has always been a crucial component of REBT. Ellis (1973, 1977) has reported using shame-attacking exercises to teach anxious clients that, even if they perform a foolish or silly act, the world will not come to an end (de-awfulizing) and they need not devalue themselves. The plan for Peggy to confront a live anger-eliciting situation was derived from the same principle. Peggy would have made little progress if she avoided all confrontation with Andrew and performed as he wished for fear of confrontation. Facing a confrontational situation would allow Peggy to test the effectiveness of her imagery exercises. If the exercise failed she could still dispute her irrational belief that the consequences of confrontation are unbearably bad.

Peggy confronted Andrew on a minor issue. She used her new rational coping statements to avoid "blowing up" when he began chastising her in the real-life situation. She reported repeating her coping statements to herself while he was arguing with her. One of the specific self-statements that she used was both an example of a functional dispute and of a self-statement or instruction that is reflective of Self-Instructional Training (Rehm & Rokke, 1988): "It doesn't help the situation if I respond with my typical anger. He's not going to change his behaviors just because I'd like him to. It better helps me and the relationship if I don't respond." This exercise succeeded.

To further test her coping resources and her ability to generate disputations and rational coping statements, two techniques were used in alternative weekly sessions: Rational Role Reversal (Kassinove & DiGiuseppe, 1975) and an open-chair technique. In Rational Role Reversal, the therapist role-plays a person who endorses the same irrational beliefs as the client. Peggy was asked to dispute these thoughts and develop more effective ways of thinking. The therapist attempts to convince the client of the irrational beliefs and is as stubborn and persistent as the irrational beliefs that are in the patient's head. The therapist noted that, as therapy progressed, Peggy became more skillful in her ability to come up with a persuasive counter-argument and her disputing style began to match that of the therapist in terms of volume and intensity. The open-chair technique is similar to Rational Role Reversal, but the client role-plays both "Irrational Peggy" and "Rational Peggy." Peggy was instructed that one corner of the office couch was the irrational corner and that the other one was the rational. She was to alternate between the two, actively disputing her irrational beliefs along the way. These techniques were used to help strengthen her conviction in her new beliefs, assess the extent to which she was engaging in her weekly cognitive and behavioral homework, and to prepare for the unpredictable return of her irrational beliefs.

Both of these techniques involve rehearsal of disputation strategies and new rational alternative beliefs. They were chosen because
Peggy reported early in therapy that she understood the logic of her
new rational beliefs but failed to believe them "emotionally." These
rehearsal techniques addressed this issue.

Through regular monitoring of her homework completion and
periodic examination of her anger outbursts using objective measures, it became apparent that Peggy was experiencing fewer fits of
anger. She was becoming more "accepting" of Andrew's behaviors,
although not liking them any better. Peggy was better able to quell
potential arguments before they occurred. After a 9-week period,
where Peggy reported no anger outbursts and was regularly "discon-
necting" her "anger time-bomb," she broached the issue of therapy
termination.

Peggy arrived at the following session crying, with significant
bruises on her arms. She reported that she and Andrew had had a
nasty argument the night before. She had removed herself from the
living room, and had begun punching and hitting the walls in the
bedroom. The argument had been over two issues. Initially it began
over a discussion of finances, and then escalated when Andrew
accused Peggy of becoming angry and not being able to control her
emotions.

Peggy reported that the next morning she attempted to assess
what her thoughts were that led to the anger, and she came up with:
"He should not accuse me of being angry when I'm not" and acknowledged the irrationality of that thought. The therapist hypothesized that her crying behavior and subsequent depressive episode
stemmed from the irrational belief: "Since I've worked on this problem in therapy and haven't had any outbursts in some time, I should
be able to always control my emotions." It was explained to Peggy
that change in her belief system would not occur in a linear fashion,
and that she could expect to suffer occasional setbacks from time to
time. Demanding that she be in control of her emotions at all times
was irrational and would likely lead to further dysfunctional emotional and behavioral consequences. Rather than viewing setbacks in
a nonconstructive manner by telling herself that "I'll always be this
way, and never be able to control my anger," Peggy was encouraged
to work on identifying the situations and thoughts that accompanied
these setbacks and to develop cognitive and behavioral strategies to
handle them in the future. She evaluated this event as a reminder

that she needed to work hard at her thinking, and that, although she would at times fail, she didn't have to condemn herself for such failures. The therapist suspected that Andrew attacked Peggy about getting angry because he was prone to interpret any disagreement with him as arguing.

Peggy's practice at changing her beliefs involved frequent repetition of both the disputes and the effective coping statements. At one point during a therapy session, Peggy became increasingly frustrated with the therapist for "going through the same song-and-dance" that had been gone over so often in recent weeks, and expressed the view that he should "just let her feel angry." This proved to be good grist for the therapy mill. The therapist used Peggy's frustration and anger in the session to help identify her irrational beliefs about the therapeutic process: "Since I understand that I tend to think irrationally when I'm angry, my therapist should not be so persistent in continually rehearsing the disputes and coping statements." When Peggy half-jokingly pointed out to the therapist that he was behaving irrationally in his "demand" that she deepen her conviction in her new rational self-statements, an additional opportunity was created for discussion and delineation of the goals and objectives of therapy.

In discussing her goals for therapy, Peggy initially described occasionally having difficulty focusing on her work when she ruminated over thoughts of Andrew and his behavior. In addition to identifying and disputing her irrational beliefs, a thought-stopping technique (Wolpe, 1958) was introduced as a means of blocking or scattering her anger thoughts and redirecting her thought processes. The visual image of an empty park or field that soon becomes crowded with birds was compared with a mind that soon becomes crowded with anger thoughts. Much like yelling or clapping-of-hands would scatter the birds, yelling "stop" in her head helped Peggy scatter these thoughts and focus on the job at hand.

Oftentimes during therapy, especially in the beginning, the therapist worked on correcting Peggy's semantics while disputing her irrational beliefs. That is, when Peggy made statements such as "Andrew makes me so angry when he patronizes me," the therapist would modify that statement and offer a rejoinder of "You make *yourself* so angry when Andrew behaves in a patronizing manner." Although Peggy understood the importance of this semantic precision, she did not like the therapist correcting her language use (as Andrew had done on numerous occasions) and became motivated to change the frequency of these corrections. As a result, this was an area that Peggy worked hard to modify, and she would regularly correct her language before the therapist had the opportunity to do so. Whether or not this led to deeper conviction in her new-found beliefs was uncertain.

An important aspect of progress in REBT is the assignment and completion of client homework. Initially, Peggy did her homework reluctantly, but later she completed it fairly consistently and her homework assignments covered a wide range of the basic principles of REBT. Bibliotherapy was encouraged and Peggy read 10–12 short articles outlining the basic premises of REBT that had been introduced during the first few sessions. Specifically regarding her anger, Peggy was assigned and reportedly completed *Anger: How to Live With and Without It* (Ellis, 1993) and *Overcoming Frustration and Anger* (Hauck, 1974). At first, Peggy described some embarrassment about reading these books on the train and would hide them in her desk at the office. She identified her own self-downing thoughts about others knowing that she had an anger-control problem, and worked on this, to the point that by the second book she reported no more embarrassment, would leave the book lying around, and even went so far as to recommend it to others.

Written assignments were also an important part of the homework component of Peggy's treatment plan. Initially she began keeping an anger log book, in which she would keep track of specific situations in which she had difficulty controlling her anger or situations in which she may have previously had difficulty but was able to successfully control it. Either way, this was useful for Peggy, in that she was able to compile a data bank of "anger situations" that she could call on during her imagery exercises and actively work on disputing her irrational beliefs and developing more effective, productive ways of thinking. The anger log book soon gave way to Peggy filling out an REBT self-help form that helped monitor the "A-B-C-D-E" aspects of her thinking and was used to further strengthen her conviction in her rational beliefs. This form also allowed the therapist to ascertain if the client really understood the ABC's of REBT.

Peggy agreed to practice Rational Emotive Imagery for homework, but she did not complete it consistently at the outset. Her excuses focused on not understanding the assignment (a pardonable offense) or on not having the time to do the imagery (also pardonable but easily remedied). To further engage her in the REI process, it was pointed out that not using the imagery exercises was not going to help her achieve the goals outlined. Using the analogy of exercising to strengthen a specific part of the body, the REI was considered to be a mental exercise that would help strengthen her new-found philosophy. To further engage her commitment to using REI, a behavioral component was added, with Peggy using positive reinforcers and penalties if she didn't do this "mental exercise" for 10–20 minutes a day, 4 days a week.

Given that the experience of anger has a cognitive, behavioral, and physiological component, Peggy was also instructed in how to do relaxation exercises and to incorporate them into her homework assignments. In doing the in-session, imagery exercises and role-playing, Peggy became more in-tune with her physiological arousal (increased heart rate, muscular tension, shortness of breath) and would use these signs as a "red flag" that she was experiencing anger and would look to identify her thoughts and work on managing her anger physiologically. Specifically, Peggy was taught a progressive muscle relaxation (PMR) technique described by Bernstein and Borkovec (1973), that is a shortened version of Jacobson's (1938) procedure. PMR training consisted of sequentially learning to tense and relax the major muscle groups of the body. In so doing, the client realizes that it is possible physiologically to create and uncreate the symptoms of tension and, when used in conjunction with strong disputing statements, achieve fewer periods of intense anger. The goal of this technique was to combat stress and anger, by producing a physiological response that was incompatible with the symptoms of stress.

One of Peggy's initial goals was more effective communication skills. The therapist used both didactic and rehearsal strategies to help her achieve these. Watzlawick, Beavin, and Jackson (1960) suggest that we communicate on two levels—verbal and nonverbal. Peggy was taught this distinction. Nonverbally, body motions and gestures can convey general messages and Peggy was encouraged to present with an "open" body posture, to decrease her frequent need to keep her hands busy while talking (whether twirling her hair or tapping her fingers) and to face Andrew squarely, demonstrating a welcoming of communication.

The pitch, loudness, and tone of her voice when she was angry were demonstrated to Peggy by replaying an audiotape of her role-playing exercises. Peggy was able to discern the difference between her vocal qualities at the beginning of therapy during a friendly conversation, and the voice qualities she expressed while "being angry" in session. Peggy rehearsed on audio tape in session a specific phrase ("I'd really rather you didn't do that") with various emotional intonations attached to it. In hypothesizing how others might respond to the various voice intonations, Peggy comprehended that it's "not only what you say, but how you say it" and agreed to work on stating her preferences without giving them the intonation of a demand.

Therapeutic work on the verbal elements of communication skills involved helping Peggy to change her attributional statements and develop several active communication skills (Norvell & Belles, 1990). Peggy was instructed to rehearse the use of "I-statements" as a way to reclaim and own her own feelings. One of Peggy's frequent statements to Andrew would be of the nature "You make me so angry." In making such statements, Peggy denied any responsibility for her own feelings. By developing the use of "I-statements" (e.g., "I feel angry because I don't like being criticized and you criticized me again"), she could reduce the likelihood of arousing defensiveness in the other person.

Norvell and Belles (1990) outlined three active communication skills that were developed during therapy with Peggy. She focused on developing her ability to listen carefully and reflect back to Andrew what was being said and, in particular, what he was feeling. Paraphrasing what was being said by Andrew involved not just parroting him, but also summarizing what he was saying so as to reduce misunderstandings in communication. Another useful communication tool was that of pinpointing the source of stress, which involved Peggy requesting Andrew to elaborate on an unclear point. For example, when Andrew did not like Peggy's new reaction of not responding to some of his requests he would immediately express a vague "displeasure" with Peggy. Peggy would then request further elaboration. This enabled Peggy to evaluate the specifics of his request and decide (without any extra emotional baggage) whether or not it was a request with which she was willing to comply. Assertiveness training was also done to develop new behaviors to request things, rather than relying on irrational demands. Peggy first acknowledged that she had the right to be assertive. When acting assertively, clients are better served by not "demanding" that, because they have behaved assertively, they should always get what they want, and by not catastrophizing the consequences of an unfavorable outcome. In essence, acting assertively does not mean that you will necessarily get what you want.

Initially, Peggy reported that when Andrew acted poorly she did not see herself as having a selection of available solutions (both cognitively and behaviorally) as alternatives to anger. Problem-solving skills training (D'Zurilla & Goldfried, 1971) was used with Peggy to identify effective alternative behaviors to anger outbursts. REBT was used in conjunction with the generation of alternative solutions and improved decisions to lessen the emotional component that played a substantial role in Peggy's decision-making.

A benefit for Peggy in being able to control her emotional responsiveness and not letting Andrew push her buttons was that she was able to make better decisions about the relationship. She could look at the relationship without her anger-colored glasses and determine if Andrew was the type of person with whom she wanted to maintain a relationship.

With individual therapy coming to a close, Peggy began looking for a place of her own to live, where she could have "time to herself." An important component to preparing her for moving out involved identifying and disputing the awfulness of the termination of the relationship. In addition to beliefs about leaving, Peggy generated a list of activities that she could do individually and with friends to distract her from the negative evaluative thoughts about no longer being in the relationship.

At the Institute for Rational-Emotive Therapy, outcome measures are used at 3–4 week intervals to assess client progress during therapy. By termination of individual therapy, Peggy achieved normal scores on all measures, with no reported depression or anxiety and a high score on the Satisfaction with Life scale. However, it should be noted that the measures used did not contain validity measures to detect subjects attempting to present themselves in a favorable light. Given Peggy's beliefs about being perceived poorly by others, perhaps her unwillingness to disclose weaknesses (as discussed with reference to the initial MCMI-II) manifested itself here as well. The possibility of Peggy attempting to present herself in a more positive light was considered by the therapist and discussed with her during a review of the positive changes she had made. Following this discussion, it was the therapist's impression that Peggy had indeed made significant progress in changing her dysfunctional cognitions and resulting emotional and behavioral consequences; however, it seemed likely that she embellished the level of change she had attained.

Peggy's performance on the self-report measure of anger (DiGiuseppe, Eckhardt, Robin, & Tafrate, 1993) at termination of individual therapy indicated significant reduction in her anger. To prepare Peggy for termination of individual therapy, the therapist showed her her initial responses on this measure and compared them with her present responses. Peggy was asked to identify in which areas she expected to experience trouble so she could continue to work on these herself.

Teaching Peggy some self-analysis skills (with which she would examine her "self-talk") helped prepare her for "becoming her own therapist" with the idea that therapy and the acquisition of a new philosophy is best served if worked on regularly. During the final three weeks of therapy, Peggy "scheduled" sessions with herself to work independently on her healthy "self-talk', practice her imagery and disputing exercises, and assign herself both behavioral and cognitive homework assignments similar to those discussed in therapy. The nonlinear aspect of progress in approaching her goals was examined, and Peggy worked on thwarting her perfectionistic tendencies about controlling her anger. Peggy also listed activities that she had previously enjoyed, but had not done lately. She used these enjoyable behaviors as reinforcers for sticking to her homework assignments and scheduling and keeping her regular "appointments" with herself.

Although Peggy completed her homework assignments to correct her anger, she failed to see the positive changes in her relationship with Andrew that she desired. Even with a decrease in her anger outbursts, Andrew was still not perceived as compassionate and understanding. In Peggy's view, he continually tried to "push my buttons." REBT makes the distinction between emotional and practical problems (Dryden & DiGiuseppe, 1990). The theory states that it is advisable to work on the emotional problem first, in order to not become overly upset about not having your way. It is perfectly acceptable and healthy to try to get what you want. As such, Peggy continually requested that Andrew attend therapy so that the therapist could outline the specific gains she had made in therapy and work on changing their relationship. Andrew did attend three couples sessions with Peggy's individual therapist toward the end of individual therapy. It seemed to the therapist that while Peggy was less angry, she was still trying to improve her relationship with Andrew. At the conclusion of Peggy's individual therapy Peggy and Andrew entered couples therapy with another therapist (J.N.). This was done to eliminate any concerns that Andrew may have had about the therapist having a bias toward Peggy, and also to offer Andrew and Peggy a fresh perspective from a new therapist.

Couples Therapy with Peggy and Andrew

Assessment.   When Peggy entered couples therapy with Andrew, her partner of a year-and-a-half, it was clear that she had developed adequate anger-control skills. Andrew reported that Peggy had successfully learned to limit "temper tantrums" to two or three times per week. Progress was also evident in that Peggy now took emotional responsibility for her anger and wanted to avoid the negative consequences associated with it. She worked hard at limiting her anger outbursts, by vigorously disputing her irrational beliefs and by practicing relaxation exercises daily. Both Peggy and Andrew agreed that she was better able to manage her anger in terms of frequency and intensity; however, Andrew still had tremendous difficulty dealing with the remaining anger episodes, in which Peggy screamed at him, scratched him, and often stormed out of their one-bedroom apartment.

Thorough assessment revealed that Peggy was adept at calming herself down; however, she lacked more effective, alternative assertive and conflict resolution skills to replace her "tantrum behaviors." She reported feelings of "helplessness" and depression. Specifically, she did not know what to do when she felt frustrated and, as a result, she was crying on a daily basis. Peggy stated that she was motivated to give up her anger and to improve her relationship with Andrew and was quite interested in pursuing assertiveness and communications-skills training.

Andrew completed the IRET biographical information form and the same objective measures that Peggy had completed at the initiation of her individual therapy. His MCMI-II response pattern revealed Axis I clinical problems. He achieved high scores on the Anxiety (102), Dysthymic (106), and Alcohol Dependence (100) clinical syndrome subscales. These results suggested that Andrew suffered from feelings of anxiety and depression and that he tended to turn to alcohol in order to cope with strong negative emotions.

His responses on the General Health Questionnaire and the Beck Depression Inventory indicated severe levels of disturbance and moderate levels of depression. He had an extremely low score for a psychotherapy patient at intake on the Satisfaction with Life Scale. On the MCMI-II he reported that his main problems consisted of "girlfriend\roommate difficulties" and "poor business." Yet despite Andrew's willingness to divulge relevant information on the objective intake measures, on the Biographical Information Form he reported that he had no past complaints and that he was unaware of the conditions that exacerbated or alleviated his symptoms.

Andrew presented as quite "rational" in the clinical interview. He maintained that he "wanted Peggy to change so that their relationship could improve." Andrew reported feeling "disappointed" or "surprised" when Peggy became enraged and lashed out at him. He denied any feelings of anxiety, anger, and depression. He reluctantly admitted to staying up "until all hours of the night and consuming one or two bottles of wine" when things "didn't go his way," only after Peggy voiced her concern about this behavior. Peggy believed that this was a major contributor to her anger difficulties. She stated that when they drank "everything got out of control."

It became apparent to the therapist that Andrew did experience intense anger when Peggy expressed any emotion or divulged "personal information" in session. For example, when Peggy described Andrew's excessive alcohol consumption he glared at her, tightened his jaw muscles, and his face reddened. When the therapist inquired about his thoughts and feelings, he stated that he was "just surprised" at what Peggy was saying. He continued to deny any other thoughts and feelings, despite persistent efforts by the therapist to elicit information. Even when confronted with the discrepancy between his verbal and nonverbal behavior he maintained his "reasonable" response.

It was clear that Andrew viewed any expression of negative emotion as inappropriate, and demanded that Peggy conform to his perception of "a nice Southern girl." This view significantly contributed to Peggy's anger episodes. Whenever Peggy was annoyed at Andrew he tended to accuse her of being angry in order to deflect criticism because, as he endorsed on the Attitudes and Beliefs Scale-2, he strongly believed that "it was terribly painful to be criticized or to lose the approval of special people." Once falsely accused of being angry, Peggy would lose her temper and respond violently.

After thorough assessment, we agreed that a combination of couples and individual sessions would be most helpful so that

Andrew could "catch up" with Peggy in terms of psychological mindedness. Specifically, it was important for Andrew to acknowledge the fact that it was normal for humans to experience negative emotions so that he could then learn how to identify, label, and express his thoughts and feelings in a more adaptive way. However, because this chapter is concerned with the treatment of anger and hostility, the focus will be on individual-couples sessions with Peggy.

Individual-couples sessions with Peggy.   Individual-couples sessions were undertaken with Peggy to help reduce the frequency and intensity of remaining anger outbursts and to determine her agenda for coming to premarital therapy. The individual-couples sessions were facilitated by the couple's therapist, who provided repetition of concepts that were covered with her individual therapist. In addition, communication skills and assertiveness training were conducted. Initially, the couple's therapist began to identify the nonconstructive communication practices that Peggy utilized. The following patterns in Peggy's communication with Andrew were discovered: overgeneralization, name-calling, digging up the past, becoming overwhelmed by anger and despair, the "accusatory you," and failing to bring up anything positive. Next, Peggy was taught that functional couples communicate effectively by powerfully and directly stating their positions. They are able to (a) explicitly define the problem and share responsibility for it; (b) remain focused on the issue; and (c) listen, recognize, and try to understand their partner's position. Couples that communicate effectively tend to see conflicts as challenges that can lead to growth and mutual benefit (Wolfe, 1992).

Because Peggy had already learned to minimize her anger, only 10 minutes each session were devoted to reviewing cognitive strategies for managing her emotions. Coping statements that were particularity effective were (a) I create my own anger; (b) no matter how Andrew acts I do not have to upset myself; (c) when I get angry I am acting out of weakness, not strength; (d) I can judge his behaviors without judging him; and (e) I am giving up my power and draining my energy when I become enraged.

The next step was to teach Peggy the difference between assertive, nonassertive, and aggressive modes of communication and the thoughts, feelings, and behaviors associated with each. The therapist explained that assertive behavior involves a direct, non-hostile statement of thoughts, feelings, and preferences or a request for change in another person. In contrast, nonassertive behavior involves indirect or passive communication or a failure to communicate one's desires at all. Finally, aggressive behavior involves hostile demands and is often intended to punish others (Bernard & Wolfe, 1993; Walen, DiGiuseppe, & Dryden, 1992).

A great deal of time was spent on teaching these distinctions. Although this material was reportedly new to Peggy, she recognized that she frequently vacillated between nonassertive and aggressive modes of communication. The therapist thoroughly reviewed basic rules to follow when behaving assertively: (a) use "I" statements, (b) begin by stating your feelings briefly, (c) comment only on the specific behavior and avoid personal attacks, (d) offer a concrete suggestion for behavioral change, and (e) use nonverbal communication that is consistent with assertive behavior (e.g., direct eye contact, body gestures that denote strength, etc.) (Lange & Jakubowski, 1976; Walen et al., 1992; Wolfe, 1992).

Utilizing the DESC model, a four-step communication system found in the self-help literature (Walen et al., 1992), Peggy and the therapist role-played hypothetical difficult situations typically encountered with Andrew. Peggy was taught to (a) **D**escribe the event as briefly and objectively as possible, (b) simply state the **E**motion she experienced using "I" language, (c) **S**pecify clearly and concretely what she wanted, and (d) present the positive **C**onsequences that would result if her request were granted.

Through much didactic skills training and subsequent behavioral rehearsal Peggy seemed competent enough to complete the behavioral homework assignment of asserting herself three times with Andrew. However, after three unsuccessful attempts, the therapist decided to assess the beliefs that blocked Peggy from behaving assertively (Ellis, 1979). It quickly became apparent that the following irrational beliefs were preventing her from expressing her desires and feelings directly: (a) I must never upset Andrew, (b) I couldn't stand his disapproval, (c) I must get what I want quickly and easily, (d) It is too hard to stand the conflict and continue asserting myself, and (e) I would be a bad person if I lost Andrew's approval by asserting myself. Once these self-defeating beliefs were identified, therapeutic work turned toward getting Peggy to persistently challenge them. New coping statements were developed that helped Peggy successfully risk enacting assertive behaviors with Andrew, both in and out of session. Disputation of these core beliefs proved to be pivotal in establishing alternative behavioral responses that were incompatible with previous "angry" behaviors.

Once Peggy began to believe more strongly that she had the right to express her feelings and state her preferences and that she could stand Andrew's disapproval, she decided to end their relationship. In an individual session she had disclosed that she had wanted to end the relationship months ago; she blocked herself, however, by perpetuating her nonassertive belief system. Ending the relationship would be the ultimate test of Peggy's self-control and new assertiveness skills.

Peggy ended their relationship in their next couples session in a nonangry, assertive fashion and remained strong in her conviction despite Andrew's attempts to sway her. While she experienced much sadness and regret about the outcome, Peggy reported a great sense of relief and was hopeful about her future. Two final individual sessions were scheduled with Peggy to work on maintenance of gains, relapse prevention, and setting future goals. By the end of therapy she was no longer depressed or angry, and crying on a daily basis and anger outbursts were eliminated.

Follow-Up

One month after termination the couple's therapist received a letter from Peggy stating that her "first single month had gone extremely well." She stated that she had maintained her gains and expressed gratitude for the assertiveness skills that helped her to experience "a true sense of independence for the first time in my life."

Andrew became more depressed after Peggy ended their relationship. He rigidly held onto his demand that Peggy "give it another try." He remained in individual therapy with the couple's therapist to help him reduce his depression and experience more adaptive negative feelings such as sadness and disappointment. He agreed to attend individual sessions, because he admitted that it was time for him to "learn more effective ways to cope with his feelings" and to "figure out how to avoid making similar mistakes in future relationships."

CONCLUSION

Peggy and Andrew never reconciled; however, they did go out on a few dates after Peggy terminated the relationship. Reportedly, they decided not to continue dating each other because it was "too painful for both of them." Instead, Peggy and Andrew remained on amicable terms so that socializing with mutual friends would be more tolerable. Peggy still retained some feelings of annoyance toward Andrew for all of the negative things he had said and done during their relationship. However, this emotional reaction was not dysfunctional. It did not dominate her thinking and interfere with her other activities.

Peggy communicated her enjoyment of the "fun and freedom associated with the single life" to both therapists via follow-up letters. As noted above, Andrew remained in individual therapy with the couple's therapist and began working on identifying and challenging irrational beliefs that led to self-defeating emotions and behaviors that interfered with his interpersonal relationships. During the course of therapy he began dating and is currently enjoying his new behavioral homework assignments. Specifically, he entered into an agreement with the therapist that he would date at least three women simultaneously. The purpose of this exercise was to help Andrew avoid repeating old patterns of entering intimate relationships too quickly. Instead, Andrew is learning to get to know his prospective partners in relation to other women, so that he can make more informed, rational decisions when establishing intimate relationships.

The therapists consider this case illustration to be a strong example of the effectiveness of using REBT with clients who have anger problems. We would note, however, that there is work to be done for the REBT clinician/researcher. As Tafrate (1995) stated, "There are currently no controlled outcome studies that directly examine the effectiveness of REBT for clients with anger problems." Research needs to be conducted to assess the applicability of REBT to anger treatment and specifically to identify the components of REBT that are most efficacious in eliciting change. While there are many sources for the reader outlining REBT's application to anger, additional outcome studies will help specify which REBT "tools" can be used effectively with clients with anger and hostility difficulties.

REFERENCES

American Psychiatric Association. (1994). *Diagnostic and statistical manual of mental disorders* (4th ed.). Washington, DC: Author.

Beck, A., & Beck, R. W. (1972). Screening depressed patients in family practice: A rapid technique. *Post Graduate Medicine, 52*, 81–85.

Bernard, M. E., & Wolfe, J. L. (Eds.). (1993). *The RET resource book for practitioners.* New York: Institute for Rational Emotive Therapy.

Bernstein, D. A., & Borkovec, T. D. (1973). *Progressive relaxation training: A manual for the helping professions.* Champaign, IL: Research.

DePue, P. (1987). The General Psychological Well-Being Scale. In I. McDowell & C. Newell (Eds.), *Measuring health: A guide to rating scales.* New York: Oxford University Press.

Diener, E., Emmons, R., Larsen, R., & Griffen, S. (1985). The satisfaction with life scale. *Journal of Personality Assessment, 49*, 71–75.

DiGiuseppe, R. (1991). Comprehensive cognitive disputing in rational-emotive therapy. In M. E. Bernard (Ed.), *Using rational-emotive therapy effectively: A practitioner's guide* (pp. 173–195). New York: Plenum.

DiGiuseppe, R., Eckhardt, C., Robin, M., & Tafrate, R. (1993, August). *The development of an anger measure.* Paper presented at the annual meeting of the American Psychological Association, Toronto.

DiGiuseppe, R., Leaf, R., Exner, T., & Robin, M. (1988, September). *The development of a measure of irrational/rational thinking.* Poster session presented at the World Congress of Behavior Therapy, Edinburgh, Scotland.

DiGiuseppe, R., Tafrate, R., & Eckhardt, C. (1994). Critical issues in the treatment of anger. *Cognitive and Behavioral Practice, 1*, 111–132.

DiGiuseppe, R., Tafrate, R., Eckhardt, C., & Robin, M. (1995). The diagnosis, assessment, and treatment of anger in a cross cultural context. *Journal of Social Distress and the Homeless, 3*, 229–262.

Dryden, W., & DiGiuseppe, R. (1990). *A primer on rational-emotive therapy.* Champaign, IL: Research Press.

Dryden, W., & Yankura, J. (1993). *Counselling individuals: A rational-emotive handbook* (2nd ed.). London: Whurr.

D'Zurilla, T. J., & Goldfried, M. R. (1971). Problem solving and behavior modification. *Journal of Abnormal Psychology, 78*, 107–126.

Eckhardt, C., & Deffenbacher, J. (1995). Diagnosis of anger disorders. In H. Kassinove (Ed.). *Anger disorders: Definition, diagnosis and treatment.* Washington, DC: Taylor & Francis.

Eckhardt, C., DiGiuseppe, R., & Tafrate, R. (1995, August). *Initial validation of a structured interview for anger disorders.* Paper presented at the annual meeting of the American Psychological Association, New York.

Ellis, A. (Speaker). (1973). *How to stubbornly refuse to be ashamed of anything* (cassette recording). New York: Institute for Rational-Emotive Therapy.

Ellis, A. (1977). The basic clinical theory of rational-emotive therapy. In A. Ellis & R. Grieger (Eds.), *Handbook of rational-emotive therapy* (pp. 3–34). New York: Springer Publishing Co.

Ellis, A. (1979). *The intelligent woman's guide to dating and mating.* New York: Lyle Stuart.

Ellis, A. (1993). *Anger: How to live with and without it.* New York: Carol.

Ellis, A., & Dryden, W. (1987). *The practice of rational-emotive therapy.* New York: Springer Publishing Co.

Goldberg, D. (1972). *The detection of psychiatric illness by questionnaire: A technique for the identification and assessment of non-psychotic psychiatric illness.* London: Oxford University Press.

Hauck, P. A. (1974). *Overcoming frustration and anger.* Philadelphia: Westminister.

Jacobson, E. (1938). *Progressive relaxation.* Chicago: University of Chicago Press.

Kassinove, H., & DiGiuseppe, R. (1975). Rational role reversal. *Rational Living, 10*(1), 44–45.

Kassinove, H., & Sukhodolsky, D. G. (1995a). Anger disorders: Basic science and practice issues. In H. Kassinove (Ed.), *Anger disorders: Definition, diagnosis, and treatment* (pp. 1–26). Washington, DC: Taylor & Francis.

Kassinove, H., & Sukhodolsky, D. G. (1995b, August). *The experience of anger.* Paper presented at the annual convention of the American Psychological Association, New York.

Lange, A. J., & Jakubowski, P. (1976). *Responsible assertive behavior: Cognitive/behavioral procedures for trainers.* Champaign, IL: Research.

Maultsby, M., and Ellis, A. (1974). *Techniques for using rational-emotive imagery.* New York: Institute for Rational Living.

Millon, T. (1987). *Millon clinical multi-axial inventory* (2nd ed.). Minneapolis: National Computer Systems.

Millon, T. (1988). *Millon clinical multi-axial inventory-II: Manual.* Minneapolis: National Computer Systems.

Norvell, N., & Belles, D. R. (1990). *Stress management training: A group leader's guide* (pp. 34–44). Sarasota, FL: Professional Resource Exchange.

Rehm, L. P., & Rokke, P. (1988). Self-management therapies. In K. Dobson (Ed.), *Handbook of cognitive behavioral therapies* (pp. 136–166). New York: Guilford.

Tafrate, R. C. (1995). Evaluation of treatment strategies for adult anger disorders. In H. Kassinove (Ed.), *Anger disorders: Definition, diagnosis, and treatment* (pp. 109–128). Washington, DC: Taylor & Francis.

Tavris, C. (1989). *Anger: The misunderstood emotion (revised edition).* New York: Simon & Schuster.

Tedeschi, J., & Nesler, M. (1993). Grievances: Development and reactions. In R. Felson & J. Tedeschi (Eds.), *Aggression and violence: Social interactionist perspectives* (pp. 13–46). Washinton, DC: American Psychological Association.

Torrey, E. F. (1992). *Freudian fraud: The malignant effect of Freud's theory on American thought and culture.* New York: HarperCollins.

Walen, S. R., DiGiuseppe, R., & Dryden, W. (1992). *A practitioner's guide to rational-emotive therapy* (2nd ed.). New York: Oxford University Press.

Watzlawick, P., Beavin, J. H., & Jackson, D. D. (1960). *Pragmatics of human communication.* New York: Norton.

Wolfe, J. (1992). *Creating renewed desire in your man: What to do when he has a headache.* New York: Hyperion.

Wolpe, J. (1958). *Psychotherapy by reciprocal inhibition.* Stanford, CA: Stanford University Press.

CHAPTER 7

REBT with Obsessive-Compulsive Disorder

Albert Ellis

I FRANKLY used to be wrong about obsessive-compulsive disorder (OCD), because I considered it to be an extreme neurotic anxiety disorder, largely caused by afflicted people's unrealistic and illogical demands for certainty. I mistakenly thought that because they strongly thought and felt, "I *absolutely must* be safe under *all* conditions at *all* times!" OCD sufferers kept compulsively locking their homes many times or checking their pilot lights to *make sure* that nothing "terrible" happened to them. Also, because they demanded *absolute certainty* that they be clean and lovable, they washed their hands 20 times after defecating or kept calling their love partners to *make sure* that they were approved (Ellis, 1962b).

I still think that the need for certainty drives some people into nauseatingly repetitive, useless, and self-defeating rituals, countings, obsessions, and other common aspects of OCD. Probably all of us humans have some of these foolish tendencies; and our *dire need* for certainty, safety, and approval may well drive us to act on them—especially when, for example, we are passionately in love with someone and have doubts about our feelings for him or her being strongly reciprocated. This kind of obsessive-compulsive behavior is somewhat "normal"—and often temporary. Once we are no longer madly in love, we may give it up (Ellis, 1962a).

Real OCD is different. It takes many forms and guises—and seems to be rarely about one thing. It usually begins in childhood or adolescence and lasts a lifetime. But it may also accompany serious neurological disorders, including Huntington's disease, Sydenham's chorea, Pick's Disease, Postencephalic Parkinsonism, and Tourette's Syndrome.

Recent neuroimaging studies tend to show that dysfunction of the frontal lobes of the brain and the frontal-caudate circuit are associated with idiopathic OCD (Foa & Wilson, 1991; Steketee, 1993). Successful treatment of OCD with clomipramine (Anafranil), fluoxetine (Prozac), and other serotonic agents tends to show that deficiencies in the neurotransmitter, serotonin, is often involved in OCD.

The need for certainty, which I previously mentioned, may well be a factor in creating OCD, but it is not clear whether biological deficiencies create this "need" and/or they block obsessive-compulsive individuals from interrupting and giving up this "need" when they see that it is doing them little good. Quite likely, both!

People with OCD, including practically all that I have seen over the years, also frequently have other related personality disorders. Thus, they often have severe panic states and serious depressive disorders. They also may be addicted to alcohol, drugs, nicotine, overeating, or gambling. Some of these afflictions may be reactions to the difficulties that ensue from their obsessive-compulsive behavior, but some of them may go along with their biological deficits.

The rational emotive behavior therapy (REBT) theory of causation of severe personality disorders, including those that may accompany OCD, holds that afflicted individuals usually have cognitive, emotive, and behavioral deficits; and that they then have cognitive distortions about having these deficits and the difficulties of living that accompany them (Ellis, 1994a, 1994b, 1994c). Thus, cognitively, individuals with OCD probably have more aspects of learning disability and focusing (or overfocusing) handicaps than what I call "nice, normal neurotics." Emotively, they tend to be overactive. Behaviorally, they are prone to disorganization, procrastination, and compulsivity. Such deficits, again, can partly be reactions to their OCD. But it is highly likely that they are also, at least in part, real biological deficits (Cloninger, Svrakic, & Przybek, 1994).

Cognitive distortions, or what I have often called irrational Beliefs (iBs) seem to be the human condition. All "neurotics" have them fairly frequently, and virtually all humans are in some degree neurotic. Those with OCD, like people with personality disorders, and like psychotics, not only have the usual kinds of iB's, but they may (for biological reasons, again) hold them more rigidly and strongly, than "nice, normal neurotics" do (Ellis, 1989, 1994b).

Moreover, because neurotic cognitive distortions are about life's adversities and handicaps (e.g., "I hate failing and *therefore* I must not fail!), and because OCD itself *is* a handicap, obsessive-compulsive individuals usually have a serious neurosis *about* their condition—and that consequently aggravates their OCD and their other life problems.

The sequence often goes somewhat as follows:

1.   The person with OCD is usually born and reared with several cognitive, emotive, and behavioral deficits, including the strong tendency to overfocus on a particular problem and to compulsively perform ritualistic and/or other habits (such as compulsively checking, handwashing, and locking doors). He or she also has great difficulty in stopping the obsessive-compulsive behavior, no matter how foolish and destructive it is acknowledged to be.

2.   People with OCD, because of their somewhat bizarre behavior, engender many more frustrations and criticisms than the rest of us "nice neurotics" do. They therefore *easily* develop great low frustration tolerance (LFT) by irrationally believing, "*I absolutely should not, must not* be so severely frustrated by my OCD and the disadvantages to which it leads. Such *great* frustration and such *severe* handicaps *must not* afflict me! It's *awful* [*completely* or *more than* bad] when they do. *I can't stand* it and will *never* be able to conquer it. How horrible!"

3.   At the same time, because of social disapproval of their dysfunctional behavior, and of themselves for having it, those afflicted with OCD frequently put themselves down, depress themselves, and make themselves anxious about other failures and disapproval. This self-denigration and its accompanying feelings of worthlessness stem from irrational Beliefs (iB's), such as "I *must* not be as disapproved as I am being! I'm *no good* for bringing on this disapproval! If I can't function better than I do function, I'm a *worthless person.*"

4.   People with OCD, like normal neurotics, often then construct secondary disturbances about their cognitive distortions and about the poor emotional and behavioral results which accompany such irrational Beliefs. Thus, they may think, "I *must not* be anxious about my OCD! I must not *demand* that I be free of OCD! I must not have low frustration tolerance about my OCD!" In this manner they can easily create self-downing about their self-downing and LFT about their LFT—all related to their OCD.

5. In addition, OCD-afflicted people can have *regular* self-denigration and *regular* LFT about other aspects of their lives. Thus, they can put themselves down for *any* hassles, mild or serious. Their tendency to castigate themselves for their "poor" performances and their tendency to make "utter horrors" out of normal hassles may, once again, be partly innate. I suspect this but have no hard evidence to back it up. An alternate hypothesis is that they have so many and so profound difficulties and failures because of their OCD, that they easily develop self-downing and LFT when non-OCD-related problems are added to their OCD-related difficulties.

6. Clients with OCD then, frequently have ego anxiety and depression (self-downing) and discomfort anxiety and depression (LFT) about (a) their OCD difficulties, (b) their other regular life problems, and (c) their self-downing and their LFT that often— probably, usually!—accompany their OCD and their non-OCD difficulties. Quite a series of interrelated personality disorders and neuroses!

GENERAL CBT AND REBT METHODS
OF TREATMENT

The treatment of OCD itself has been fairly intensively studied by a number of practitioners of behavior therapy (BT) and cognitive behavior therapy (CBT). Nearly all these BT and CBT practitioners emphasize in vivo desensitization or exposure and activity-oriented homework assignments designed to significantly cut down, if not entirely eliminate, the interminable ruminations and wasteful compulsions to which victims of OCD are prone. Because REBT has always favored in vivo desensitization and activity homework assignments, I have used these methods with OCD-afflicted clients for more than 30 years and find that they usually work—*if* my clients consistently and steadily work at effecting them.

But, of course, they often don't do this steady work. Instead, they find it most difficult to cut down their incessant checking, ritualizing, and ruminating; and when they finally do so, they easily fall back to their former pernicious habits. Moreover, when they give up or minimize one set of compulsions they frequently begin to establish a set of different ones. They then often convince themselves that they *can't* change and *can't* stay free of obsessions and compulsions; and then, because of these convictions, they "really" can't.

Nonetheless, even before the advent of medications like Anafranil and Prozac, I have had some startling successes. Thus, a man of 40 years, who all his life had got out of his bed at least 15 times every night to make absolutely sure that the "dangerous" pilot light in his kitchen stove was extinguished, cut down his checking compulsion to no more than one or two checkings a night, and maintained that schedule for the next 5 years. A woman who took from 1 to 4 hours to shower every morning—and who couldn't hold any regular jobs because of the time she consumed showering—cut down her time in the shower to at most 15 minutes a day and began to hold a regular 9-to-5 job.

So OCD-afflicted clients can change with the persistent use of REBT and CBT methods. But often they don't—or they make very limited gains. Why? For a number of reasons, including the fact that some clients with severe OCD seem to be so basically disorganized and so obsessed with repetitive behaviors that they find it almost impossible to follow the cognitive, emotive, and behavioral methods of REBT (and of other forms of therapy) and therefore fail to do so. So they are not merely DCs (difficult customers) for therapy. Many of them are VDCs (*very* difficult customers)!

A number of clients with OCD, however, not only can significantly improve but some of them work hard and actually do cut down their obsessive-compulsiveness. With these clients, the use of regular REBT and CBT methods can be quite helpful, especially when combined with proper medication, such as Anafranil and Prozac. These clients tend to have relatively high frustration tolerance and less self-denigation than other clients with OCD; and by using REBT they raise their tolerance for frustration and their self-acceptance even more.

Regular REBT and CBT procedures have been quite adequately presented by several authorities in this field, including Baer (1991), Enright (1991), Fals-Stewart and Lucente (1994), Foa and Wilson (1991), Greist (1992), Perce (1988), Rapoport (1989), Steketee (1993), and Zetin and Kramer (1992).

Let me summarize these techniques as follows, as particularly noted by Foa and Wilson (1991) and as combined with some methods of regular REBT:

1. Show clients with OCD that they have a specific anxiety (or panic) disorder that usually (not always) involves: (a) negative, continual obsessions, thoughts, images, and/or impulses; (b) severe feelings of anxiety, panic, disgust, and/or shame; (c) compulsions that exist in their own right or are attempts to relieve their anxiety and panic (compulsions may include repetitious thoughts, images, urges, and/or actions); (d) temporary relief from anxiety and panic when a client constructs and follows compulsive rituals to interrupt and halt his or her anxiety.

2. Show people with OCD that they can reduce their afflictions by working with a therapist, and/or with self-help procedures, but that this work usually has to be consistent, persistent, and forceful.

3. Have clients explore and check to see which symptoms they have and how severely they have them. Thus, they can determine how often and how strongly they check and repeat, wash and clean, compulsively hoard, compulsively order, engage in thinking rituals, and obsessively worry.

4. Show clients that when they desperately resist having a thought or a ritual—and demand that they *absolutely must* not have it—they make themselves obsess more about it and frequently repeat it more.

5. Show clients with OCD that mild or brief obsessions and compulsions—like looking three times to "make sure" that one has her or his keys before leaving home—are innocuous and tolerable but that severe and prolonged rituals are destructive and had better be minimized or stopped.

6. Teach them that severe OCD may well have a strong biological or innate tendency that is difficult to change and may never be completely overcome. Let them know that people like themselves may well have innate tendencies to denigrate themselves for their foolish behaviors and to have low frustration tolerance about life's difficulties and about their OCD.

7. Encourage them to make a list of situations that frequently and intensively help them to feel anxiety, panic, or the impulse to act impulsively and undertake repeated rituals.

8. If they have repetitious thoughts, feelings, or urges that lead to serious anxiety and panic, let them list what these are and how distressful they are.

9. They can also make a list of the "horrible" consequences they fear will result if they stop their compulsions and their rituals and how much they believe these "horrors" will actually occur.

10.   They can list their worst compulsions and how much time they spend indulging in them each day.

11.   You, as a therapist, can help them to be strongly determined to minimize their obsessions and compulsions.

12.   Show them that the anxieties that underlie their OCD behaviors are irrational—that is, unrealistic, illogical, and self-defeating. Show them how to Dispute their irrational Beliefs (iBs) that spark these anxieties.

13.   Show them that reducing their anxieties by OCD rituals will only work temporarily and in the long run exacerbate them; and that they can use much better cognitive, emotive, and behavioral ways of reducing them.

14.   Particularly show clients that they can see their obsessions and compulsions as "bad," "handicapping," and "undesirable" but never put *themselves* down for having them and never think that their OC behaviors are *so* bad that they absolutely *must* not exist. Teach them to undesperately work to reduce their obsessions. Persuade them to accept their OCD manifestations as only undesirable and not *horrible.*

15.   Show them how to schedule their obsessions and compulsions only at certain specified and limited times—e.g., at 7:00 P.M. for 15 minutes—and to think and do other things at other times.

16.   Convince them—and help them convince themselves—that they can practically always keep postponing indulging in their obsessions and compulsions—and can keep postponing their indulgence in them more and more.

17.   Teach them how to use distraction methods—such as Jacobson's (1938) progressive relaxation technique, Yoga, meditation, breathing, and biofeedback methods—to interrupt and postpone their OCD behaviors. They can also use other behaviors—such as exercise, writing, and playing music—to interrupt their obsessions and compulsions.

18.   Show clients how to make a tape of their obsessive thoughts and compulsive urges and to desensitize themselves to them and to their "horrors" by listening to the tape a half hour or more every day. This tape may be arranged so that it plays in a loop and keeps repeating itself.

19.   Instruct your OCD clients how to change some aspects of their rituals—to change their specific thoughts or actions or the number or the times they ritualize.

SPECIAL REBT METHODS OF TREATMENT

It is often best to assume, as I noted previously, that clients with OCD have a strong biological tendency to think and act in the ways that they do, that they will make less gains than most other clients, and that they will have to work harder than these others to achieve improvement. Consequently, they frequently put themselves down for having severe OCD, and Believe—at point B in the ABC's of REBT, "I *absolutely must not* be so handicapped! Because I *am* more handicapped as I *must not* be, I am an *inadequate person* and probably *don't deserve* to do better than I have done in the past and am still badly doing!"

Using REBT, you, as a therapist, can show these clients that they frequently have OCD as their primary symptom but they also may well have self-denigration as a secondary symptom. Thus, Activating Event$_1$ (A$_1$) is a "dangerous" situation, irrational Belief$_1$ (iB$_1$) is "I must check this danger twenty times!" and the Consequence$_1$ (C$_1$) is their OCD symptom. Then Activating Event$_2$ (A$_2$) is their OCD symptom, irrational Belief$_2$ (iB$_2$) is a self-downing Belief such as those mentioned in the previous paragraph, and Consequence$_2$ (C$_2$) is their feelings of inadequacy or worthlessness.

After helping your clients to fully acknowledge their self-deprecation (C$_2$), you unconditionally accept them *with* their OCD and *with* feelings of worthlessness and then you use a variety of REBT cognitive, emotive, and behavioral methods to help them Dispute (D) their anxiety, depression, self-hatred, and other disturbed feelings that constitute their neurosis *about* their having OCD and *about* their having one hell of a time ameliorating it.

In addition, for reasons explained in the beginning of this chapter, clients with OCD frequently have low frustration tolerance (LFT) or discomfort disturbance about their affliction. Thus, they may believe (at point B), "I *shouldn't* be so afflicted! It's too unfair! And I *must* not have to work so hard to reduce my OCD! It's *awful* that so much work is required!"

Using REBT, therapists usually show these clients that they probably do have secondary problems of self-downing and LFT about their handicaps. Once they acknowledge either or both these secondary disturbances, they are helped to overcome them. First, they are helped to acquire unconditional self-acceptance (USA). This method is an REBT specialty that is used with practically all seriously disturbed individuals (including psychotics, organically defective, and personality disordered people), a large percentage of whom often make themselves feel worthless for having these deficiencies and therefore had better alleviate this secondary neurosis about their primary emotional problems.

These seriously disturbed individuals, moreover, frequently have self-downing as a primary issue—because, like regular neurotics, and perhaps more so, they denigrate themselves for other "deficiencies" and "inadequacies." Thus a large number of clients with OCD are perfectionistic and demand that they *absolutely must* do many things, including their rituals, counting, and checking, exactly and perfectly right; and their "natural" or "biological" tendency may be perfectionistic.

In any event, the achieving of USA is a prime REBT recipe for helping people with OCD on both the primary and secondary level of disturbance. To this end, they are, as previously noted, unconditionally accepted, in manner as well as word, by their REBT therapist. But they are also specifically taught that they do not *need* his or her approval in order to fully accept themselves (Ellis, 1972, 1973, 1976, 1985, 1994d; Ellis & Harper, 1961, 1975; Franklin, 1993; Hauck, 1992; Mills, 1993).

Instead, they are taught the two main REBT solutions to achieving unconditional self-acceptance (USA). One: The practical, if somewhat inelegant, solution: That they can choose to fully accept themselves, *whether or not* they perform well and *whether or not* they are approved by significant others, *just* because they are alive and human, *just* because they choose to do so. This pragmatic solution to achieving unconditional self-worth is practically guaranteed to work until they are dead—and then they won't have to worry about self-acceptance very much! Clients just have to strongly *believe* that they are okay because they are alive and human. This belief practically assures their having USA.

Two: Unfortunately this practical solution to self-worth is philosophically flawed, because anyone could raise the following objection to a person who uses it: "Well, yes. I acknowledge that you are alive and human, but I personally think that you are worthless. In fact, I think you're a real worm, a terribly rotten person! All humans are no good and deserve to die. Especially you!"

Now if this sharp disagreement occurs, who is right about your client's being a "good person?" The client with OCD, or his or her detractor?

Using REBT with your client, you can say the following: "Actually, neither of you is right. You're both entitled to your opinion, but neither of you can prove—or disprove—the other's view. You are claiming—by your own *definition*—that you *are* okay; and your opponent is claiming—by his or her—*definition* that you are not okay. Impasse.

"So REBT has dreamed up a more 'elegant' solution to this problem of human intrinsic worth. Using this 'elegant' solution, you stubbornly refuse to rate, evaluate, or measure your *self*, your *being*, your *essence*, or your *person*hood at all. You merely establish (and/or take from your culture) goals, values, and preferences such as: 'I want to remain alive and achieve success in (a) my schooling, (b) my career, and (c) my interpersonal relationships. Why? Because those are the goals I desire to fulfill, and I think I will live longer, better, and happier if I achieve them.' You pick whatever goals and values that you desire. Fine. You decide, 'My main ones are (a), (b), and (c).' "

"Once you set these goals and aims—which, of course, you may change later—you rate or measure as 'good' or 'valuable' any of your (and other people's) thoughts, feelings, and actions that seem to aid or further these goals; and you rate as 'bad' or 'disadvantageous' the behaviors that you find are impeding or sabotaging your chosen values. You never, however—yes, never—globally rate *you*, your *self*, or *personhood* at all. You *only* measure what you *do*, not what you (supposedly) *are*. Then, of course, you can never be a *good person* nor a *bad person*. Only a person who often acts 'badly' and a person who often acts 'well.' "

REBT offers both these "elegant" and "inelegant" concepts of self-acceptance to all its clients, including—especially—those with OCD. It does its best to help all handicapped individuals—actually, the human race!—to unconditionally accept themselves *whatever* they think, feel, or do. Not again, to accept as "good" their "foolish," "rotten," or "immoral" behaviors, but themselves, the doers of these "vile" deeds.

This includes teaching clients to accept themselves unconditionally with their (frequent) abysmal LFT. Because they have more than their share of frustrations, often from childhood onward, those with OCD frequently have considerable LFT. They therefore may not push themselves to control their OCD, to work at using REBT methods, nor even to strive for USA. No matter. Their REBT therapists still unconditionally accept them and try to persuade them to have

USA for themselves. I and other REBT practitioners hardly always succeed in this endeavor. But, damn it, we try!

While doing so, we usually try to help clients ameliorate and raise their LFT. For unless they persist in curbing their obsessive-compulsive tendencies and acts, they will *temporarily* feel good about indulging in them—and a little later probably feel much worse. In the long run, indulgence in OCD behaviors will frustrate and hinder them more—and thereby often encourage them to have *lower* frustration tolerance!

Therapists, however, had better unmask and persuade clients with OCD to ameliorate their LFT with caution—because it is not easy to define exactly what it is, how it arises, and what can effectively be done to reduce it. Let me give a fascinating example.

Mary, a 40-year-old attorney, had OCD in the form of continually checking on her pension if she retired from her firm at the age of 45, 50, or 55, and spent hours doing so, even though she knew that her rumination didn't affect the amount of her pension one whit and that it was a complete waste of time. She also procrastinated on her briefs for her court presentations because, first, she was afraid to do an imperfect case and, second, she hated some of the onerous activity involved in getting her briefs together. She agreed that she had LFT about cutting down the time she spent obsessing and that she also had LFT about buckling down, doing her briefs, and getting them out of the way before she and her partners tried a case. So I kept after her to work on her LFT by convincing herself that the immediate "gratification" she received from indulging in her obsessive checking on the amount of her pension and that the relief she felt when putting off finishing her briefs until the last minute weren't worth the short-term gains she received and were irrational and self-defeating. She "intellectually" agreed with me, but still refused to work to ameliorate her LFT.

After weeks of this kind of "resistance," Mary and I figured out that she was really very depressed and lacking in energy and that was why it was "easier" to indulge in her checking obsessions, and to procrastinate on her briefs—and to indulge in other forms of "LFT," such as eating too much, not exercising, and smoking. We were both treating her as if she were a "normal neurotic" instead of a severe endogenous depressive and a biologically inclined client with OCD. She felt—and somewhat rightly—that I was blaming her LFT behavior and also blaming *her* for having it. She finally admitted that I was only doing the former (that is, I *was* trying to get her to assume responsibility for her indulgences, and that I was not blaming her as a person).

We both agreed, however, that people like Mary who are also severely depressed—and have panic states as well—are not really as self-indulgent as the rest of us "nice neurotics" may be. She, like many other individuals with OCD, had several "good" or "legitimate" reasons for her "goofing off." Thus: (a) She had innate and very strong OCD tendencies. (b) She was often naturally and innately depressed. (c) When in a state of panic—which she also was prone to experience—she was "naturally" sidetracked from working to reduce her so-called LFT. (d) She had more frustrations, because of her disturbances, than the great majority of other people—and therefore *was* unfairly put upon. (e) She may well have been born with strong biological tendencies to avoid frustrations, even sensible ones like those involved in exercising. (f) Like a majority of clients with OCD, she also was a strong self-damner, and by castigating herself for her handicaps she tended to exacerbate them, sidetrack herself from working against them, and waste time and energy that could have been much better spent in trying to ameliorate these handicaps.

Working with this client, and several others somewhat like her, showed me how unfair life really *is* to those afflicted with OCD and how I (and other therapists) can also be unfair to them by giving them too much responsibility for their handicaps and ignoring their natural resistance to improving themselves. With this particular client, Mary, I showed her how natural and expectable was her resistance to change, and I simultaneously induced her to give herself unconditional self-acceptance (USA) even if she had been "goofing" neurotically, instead of as a more direct result of her innate handicaps. When she started to experience USA, Mary worked harder than ever to overcome her resistance to change and did to some degree alleviate it.

REBT, then, tries to fully acknowledge the unusual difficulties that clients with OCD encounter in trying to stop their obsessive-compulsive behavior and tries to help them resist defaming themselves for engaging in it. It greatly emphasizes showing them that they usually have a biologically based disorder and that they may also have a neurosis about this disorder—including serious self-downing and low frustration tolerance. It tries to help them to stop damning themselves for *anything*, including their basic disturbances *about* their disturbances. As this treatment process proceeds, it also uses the regular REBT and CBT methods previously described to help clients reduce and minimize, but rarely entirely eliminate, their OCD behaviors.

OTHER SPECIAL REBT TREATMENTS OF OCD

In addition to the general and special REBT methods of treating individuals afflicted with OCD, I consistently use a number of common REBT methods to help them cope with their disorder and with their neurosis about this disorder. These methods have been described in detail in a number of my writings (Ellis, 1973, 1977, 1985, 1988, 1991a, 1991b, 1994d; Ellis & Abrahms, 1978; Ellis & Abrams, 1994; Ellis, Abrams & Dengelegi, 1992; Ellis & Dryden, 1987; Ellis & Grieger, 1977, 1986; Ellis & Harper, 1961, 1975; Ellis & Lange, 1994; Ellis & Velten, 1992). They have also been described in several articles and books by other REBT professionals, including Bernard (1991, 1993), Bernard and Wolfe (1993), Dryden (1994), Dryden and DiGiuseppe (1990), Dryden and Hill (1993), Walen, DiGiuseppe, and Dryden (1992), and Wessler and Wessler (1980).

Let me briefly describe some of these methods, as I often use them with clients afflicted with OCD. I shall take the case of John, a 32-year-old teacher, who had several serious obsessive-compulsive behaviors that stopped him from succeeding at his work, at forming a good relationship with a woman, and at completing his Ph.D. in history. For example: (a) He had to go over his students' papers at least three times and average each of three separate marks he gave them before he could come up with a final mark. (b) He had to gather every possible bit of information he could find about every woman he dated before he could allow himself to have a first date with them. (c) He compulsively told every new woman about his past relationship failures, so that she would accept him with his screwups and he would then feel it was safe to keep seeing her. (d) He locked the door to his apartment at least twelve times before he found it to be *really* locked, so that he could feel secure about going to sleep.

Cognitive REBT Techniques

I first used a number of cognitive REBT techniques with John to help him reduce his obsessive-compulsiveness:

Disputing Irrational Beliefs (iBs). John strongly believed, to create one of his OCD symptoms, "I must be absolutely safe about going with the right woman, who will never reject me even though she learns about the worst things I have done in my past relationships." So I actively Disputed this dysfunctional Belief with him:

AE: Why *must* you be absolutely safe about going with the right woman?

JOHN: Because I must not be rejected.

AE: Where is it written that you *absolutely must not* be rejected?

JOHN: I hate rejection!

AE: Why must you always avoid what you hate—especially, rejection?

JOHN: It'll prove that I'm no good, worthless, if I keep getting rejected.

AE: It will prove that *it's* not good, because you strongly want acceptance. But how does *it's* not being good prove that you, a total person, are worthless—and that you presumably *never* will be worthy of winning a suitable woman?

JOHN: But didn't I *create* the rejection? Aren't I *responsible* for it?

AE: Maybe. But you could do everything right with a woman and still get rejected by her.

JOHN: Yes, but let's suppose that I acted badly with her.

AE: Well, let's suppose you did. You acted quite badly and so you "made" this woman reject you. How does that still prove that you're no good at anything?—that you're *completely* unlovable?

JOHN: Hmmm. Maybe it really doesn't.

AE: Damned right it doesn't! Your *behavior* with this woman, we are assuming, may be bad. But can that one bit of behavior make you, a total *person*, bad?

JOHN: Well, no. I guess not.

AE: You *guess* not?

JOHN: Well no, it really can't make *me* bad. It's *one* set of my behaviors, and *one* real rejection. But that doesn't show that I, totally, am a rejectable, unlovable individual.

AE: Right! It shows nothing of the sort!

Referenting. I showed John how to make a list of the real disadvantages of his obsessive-compulsive actions. And I also showed him how to list the disadvantages of putting himself down *for* his OCD characteristics. By going over these disadvantages ten times a day, he was able to consciously see how self-defeating some of his compulsions were, and to therefore persist at cutting them down.

Rational coping statements. By using Disputing of their irrational Beliefs people with OCD are taught how to come up with Effective New Philosophies (E's), to write them down, and to rehearse them several times a day. In John's case, he was able to come up with rational coping statements such as, "I *can* decrease the frequency of my compulsions, even though it's very hard for me to do so and though I usually resist cutting them down." "If I keep locking my door before I go to sleep at least twelve times, the door won't be locked any better and I won't be any safer. In fact, in the process I might well finally leave the door unlocked!" "Even if I never find out all possible information about a new woman I date, I can still safely date her without taking any great risks. And even if she turns out to be the wrong person for me, it'll only be inconvenient, and not the end of the world, and I *can* stand it and lead a fairly happy existence."

Teaching others REBT. I encouraged John to use REBT with his friends and relatives and, by showing them how to use it and to ameliorate their anxieties and compulsions, to help himself ameliorate his own. Thus, he showed a friend of his, who compulsively went only with "safe" men, just as John compulsively tried to go only with "safe" women, that if she picked a "wrong" man to go with nothing terrible would happen and she would merely waste some of her time and energy. This helped him to take some chances himself with "unsafe" women.

Modeling. I placed John in one of my regular REBT therapy groups, where most of the members had problems of anxiety and depression but were not too obsessive-compulsive. By modeling himself after some of these noncompulsive group members, he acquired more courage in trying to be noncompulsive himself. He also read accounts of highly obsessive-compulsive people who overcame their problems and was able to use them as good models to help himself ameliorate some of his OCD behaviors.

Psychoeducational materials. John was encouraged to read some REBT psychoeducational materials, such as *A New Guide to Rational Living* (Ellis & Harper, 1975) and *How to Stubbornly Refuse to Make Yourself Miserable About Anything—Yes, Anything!* (Ellis, 1988). Because OCD overlaps with and includes other compulsive behaviors, such as addiction to alcohol, drugs, and gambling, John was led to use REBT materials on addiction, such as *The Small Book* (Trimpey, 1989), *When AA Doesn't Work For You: Rational Steps to Quitting Alcohol* (Ellis & Velten, 1992), and *The Art and Science of Rational Eating* (Ellis, Abrams, & Dengelegi, 1992). To help him achieve unconditional self-acceptance (USA), he was urged, by myself and by his therapy group, to use materials describing USA and how to achieve it, especially those by Ellis (1972, 1973, 1976), Franklin (1993), Hauck (1992), and Mills (1993).

Cognitive homework. John agreed with me and with his group members to do regular homework on the ABCDE's of REBT, including his using the *REBT Self-Help Form* that the Institute for Rational-Emotive Therapy publishes (Sichel & Ellis, 1984).

REBT Emotive Methods

REBT assumes that severely disturbed individuals, such as people with OCD, often hold their irrational Beliefs (iB's) strongly and powerfully and that they therefore had better forcefully, vigorously, and emotively Dispute and act against them (Bernard, 1991, 1993; Dryden, 1994; Ellis, 1969, 1985, 1988, 1993, 1994b, 1994d; Walen, DiGiuseppe, & Dryden, 1992). Some of the regular REBT emotive-evocative methods that I used with John included these:

Relationship procedures. Like Carl Rogers (1961), REBT practitioners go out of their way to give all their clients, especially those with OCD, *un*conditional acceptance. I gave this to John by consistently showing him that, no matter how foolishly he kept thinking, feeling, and behaving, I fully accepted *him*, as a person, even though I didn't approve of many of his *actions*, and kept trying to help him change them. Unlike Rogerian therapists, I did not try to help him accept himself unconditionally because *I* accepted him—for that would lead him to highly *conditional* self-acceptance. I instead taught him how to achieve *un*conditional self-acceptance, as I have previously noted in this chapter (Ellis, 1972, 1973, 1976, 1988; Franklin, 1993; Hauck, 1992; Mills, 1993).

Forceful coping statements.   I often helped my clients with OCD to use forceful coping statements. With John, I helped him to tell himself vigorously and powerfully, sometimes aloud and sometimes in front of a mirror or in the presence of his friends and intimates, "I DON'T have to carry out my repetitive and compulsive marking of my students' papers! I CAN mark them only once and CAN give them this single mark, even though it may not be perfectly fair or accurate!" "I will ONLY, ONLY allow myself to lock my door at night only, at most, twice and no more, NO, NEVER MORE than twice. And if I get robbed or killed in my sleep, that's TOO DAMNED BAD BUT NOT AWFUL!" "My OCD behaviors are stupid and wasteful. But they NEVER, NEVER make me a stupid PERSON! NEVER!"

Rational emotive imagery.   Maxie Maultsby, Jr., a psychiatrist who studied with me in 1968, created Rational Emotive Imagery (REI) in the 1970s. This is a useful method of REBT and I have made it even more emotive and behavioral than Maxie's original version and have used it widely (Ellis, 1993; Maultsby, 1971). In my version, as used with John, it goes as follows: "Close your eyes and imagine one of the worst things that could happen to you—such as remaining hooked on compulsively locking your door many times each night. While imagining this 'terrible' event, let yourself feel as badly as you would naturally feel when you actually give in to this compulsion. Now, how *do* you actually feel?" John would usually say, "As low as I can feel. Like a worm! An idiot!" "Good," I would say. "Now feel that keenly. Let yourself feel very low, very wormy!" "Oh, I really do!" "Fine! Get in touch with that low feeling. Feel it, feel it, feel it!" "I really do." "Great. Now, keep the same vivid image, that you keep locking the door many times each night, and can't unhook yourself from locking it. Now make yourself feel, instead of low and wormy, sorry and disappointed about what you are doing, only sorry and disappointed, but not low and wormy. Change your feeling to this healthy, though still negative one. You can change it. Make yourself feel only, only sorry and disappointed, not low and wormy."

John would then change his feeling, as I had instructed him to do; and then I would ask, "How did you change it? What did you do to change it?" Usually, he would reply with a rational coping statement, such as, "I told myself, 'Well, it's certainly stupid and wrong for me to do this but that doesn't make me a complete idiot, only a person who's acting stupidly this time, and who can surely act better next time. Very idiotic and stupid behavior; but that never makes me an idiot!' " "Good," I would then say. "Now repeat this on your own every day for ten, twenty, or thirty days. First, let yourself feel very upset, low, wormy about your vividly imagining you're still very compulsive. Then change your feeling the way you just did, and with other rational coping statements that will occur to you—until, at the end of a number of days, you will tend to feel automatically sorry and disappointed, and not wormy, when you think of doing so or even when you actually do so."

John would follow these instructions as daily homework and would thus train himself to feel healthfully, appropriately sorry and regretful instead of unhealthily self-downing about his silly compulsiveness. Then, accepting himself with his poor behavior, he would be much more able to work at changing this behavior.

Shame-attacking exercises.   Because people with OCD are often foolishly out of control, know that they are, but still feel unable to give up their obsessive-compulsive behavior, they are often, like John, quite ashamed of their affliction. So I often give them my famous shame-attacking exercise, which I created in 1968, as an emotive technique of REBT (Ellis, 1969, 1985, 1988, 1994d; Ellis & Abrams, 1994; Ellis & Velten, 1992). To do this exercise, John would pick something that he considered very shameful and would be embarrassed to do in public; would deliberately do this "shameful" act; and would simultaneously work on his NOT feeling ashamed, embarrassed, or humiliated for doing it.

Thus, he would tell some of his friends and relatives how obsessive-compulsive he was, and let them know the worst about himself, while showing himself that his behavior was ridiculous but that he was *not* a ridiculous fool for indulging in it. And at times he would deliberately force himself NOT to do one of his compulsive rituals (like locking his door at least twelve times), let himself feel anxious about not doing it, and then shamelessly accept himself with his anxiety, and not at all put himself down for feeling it. After doing several of these shame-attacking exercises, John was able to accept himself better than he had ever done before, and to have more time and energy to work on ameliorating his compulsions.

Forceful disputing.   I often encourage my clients with OCD to state one of their irrational Beliefs and to vigorously Dispute it on a cassette tape. Thus, John would state on a cassette, "I must keep locking my door at least twelve times every night before I go to bed, so that I can be absolutely certain, with no doubt whatever, that no one will break in and harm me while I am sleeping." He would then Dispute this iB several times and give a very strong answer to it. For example: "Why the hell do I have to make absolutely sure that my door is locked before I go to bed? Answer: I DON'T have to make sure. The chances are 99 out of a hundred that it is okay, even if I lock it only once. And even if it is unlocked once in a great while, no one will know that it is and therefore will not break in. But even if, in one out of a million chances, someone does break in, I can handle it. They WON'T be interested in killing me, but probably only in stealing something. So it is NOT that dangerous. And if they DO kill me, I won't know about it for long, anyway! So I DON'T have to be absolutely sure that the door is locked. I Absolutely DON'T have to be absolutely sure! I HOPE that it is locked. But it never, never HAS to be!"

By doing this kind of vigorous Disputing on tape, and letting his friends and the members of his therapy group listen to it to see *how* convincing it was, John was able to tone down the obsessive-compulsive idea that he absolutely HAD TO be certain that his door was locked every night.

Role-playing.   REBT uses role-playing with clients having OCD to help them get over their dire needs for others' approval, such as their needs to conceal their obsessive-compulsive behavior from others who would think them foolish for indulging in it. In John's case, he was asked about which of his OCD characteristics he would be most ashamed to reveal, and he replied that he wouldn't want anyone to know that he was afraid to go on a first date with a woman without compulsively investigating her whole history and background. So I took the role of a friend of his to whom he would reveal this "horribly stupid" behavior and John roleplayed himself in the course of a few of his group therapy sessions. He rehearsed telling me, in the role of his friend, about his "idiotic" compulsion, got behavior rehearsal in doing this kind of shame-attacking exercise, and was critiqued by me and the other group members, so that he soon improved his performance. Also, when he became anxious and flustered during the roleplay, we interrupted it for awhile to ask him what he was telling himself to make himself anxious. Thus, he was telling himself, "I really AM stupid for having this compulsion and now for letting my friend see that I have it. He must think that I'm a complete numbskull! I can't let him think that of me!" We got him to Dispute this irrational Belief right then and there, and to see that even though his compulsion was silly, his friend might well forgive him for having it, and that even if his friend saw him as a completely stupid person, he didn't have to see himself in that overgeneralized light. After doing this kind of roleplay several times, John lost his anxiety about revealing his compulsion to his friend and also became much smoother and more adept at revealing it.

Reverse role-playing.   I used REBT reverse role-playing with John by taking his dysfunctional Belief, "I have to compulsively tell every new woman I meet all about my past relationships that didn't work out, so that she'll be sure to accept me with my screwups," and rigidly held on to it myself, as he tried to talk me out of it. In other words, I played his role and he played the role of the therapist trying to talk me—that is, himself—out of this self-defeating idea. I deliberately held on to the idea and refused to give it up, so that he had some great practice in trying to talk me out of it—and thereby trying to talk himself out of his own foolish notion.

REBT Behavioral Methods

As is invariably the case in using REBT, I used several of its behavioral methods in trying to help John overcome his obsessive-compulsive disorder. Here are some of the behavioral techniques that I employed with him.

In vivo desensitization.   I persuaded John to force himself to reduce his obsessive-compulsive door-locking by giving him the in vivo assignment of starting with his usual routine of locking it twelve times, and then every week cutting it down by one time. Thus, the first week he allowed himself to do it twelve times every night; the second week eleven times; the third week ten times, etc. At the end of ten weeks he was locking the door only, at most, twice each night, and was able to keep that up, with a few relapses, indefinitely.

Remaining in "bad" situations. REBT often encourages clients to remain in a "bad" situation—such as with a very negative boss or a critical mate—until they overcome their horror about this situation, and then decide whether or not it is worth leaving it. When I saw John, he was going with a womanfriend who pushed him to spend large sums of money on her and who sometimes actually encouraged him to be even more compulsive than he usually was. He wanted to leave her and to get a womanfriend who would be more suitable. But I encouraged him to stay with the "bad" one for awhile, to get over his rage at her, and to stop giving in to some of the compulsions that she helped him to continue. Then, when he was no longer enraged at her and when he was able to resist her urging to be more compulsive, he was encouraged to break up the relationship with her.

Use of reinforcements. REBT frequently uses reinforcements and penalties to help individuals with obsessive-compulsive behaviors cut down on these actions. Often, reinforcements are not effective because people with OCD suffer so much (at least temporarily) from stopping their compulsions and feel so greatly relieved after indulging in them that reinforcements like eating good food, enjoying entertainment, having sex, or engaging in other pleasures after curbing their rituals and obsessions won't consistently work. However, if the reinforcers they use are things that they very *strongly* desire, reinforcement will sometimes be effective.

Thus I saw Jill, a 28-year-old graduate student, who agreed to allow herself to register for her next term at school only *after* she had cut down her handwashing to no more than three times after she urinated or defecated. When she first came to see me, she was obsessively compulsively washing her hands at least 20 times, and sometimes 30 or more times, whenever she went to the bathroom.

Again, I saw Harry, a 42-year-old investment banker who obsessively compulsively had to put everything in his office in perfect order before he started to work everyday, and consequently was at least 20 minutes late. But when he forced himself, with my help, to make dates with Joanne, with whom he was madly in love, only *after* he cut his office-ordering time to no more than 7 (lucky number!)

minutes every day, he was able to keep his compulsive ordering under control.

In John's case, getting him to use pleasurable reinforcements only after he had cut down his compulsive door-locking at first didn't work. But when he agreed to allow himself the great pleasure of masturbating while watching an adult video only *after* he cut down the number of times he locked the door each night, that reinforcement technique worked somewhat better. But still not perfectly!

Use of penalties.   Again, as is often true with serious addicts, I have found that if clients with OCD will make sure that they enact what they consider (and not what *I* consider) a stiff penalty every time they fail to cut down on their OCD patterns of behavior, they will sometimes—but hardly always!—minimize their compulsions. One of my clients, Sid, said that he absolutely could not stop putting reams of toilet paper on every toilet seat that he used when out of town, and often when he used his own toilet seat at home, where he lived with his wife and three children. He insisted that only by doing so could he ward off all venereal disease, including AIDS. When he agreed to burn a $100 bill (one of REBT's favorite penalties) every time he used more than a few sheets of toilet paper, and when his wife, who was helping monitor him, actually burned a hundred dollars on three different occasions, he began to considerably moderate his compulsive use of "protective" toilet paper. As he accomplished this, he also stopped his avoidance of going on out-of-town trips and to local parties in other people's houses.

In John's case, when reinforcement procedures did not work very well to help him cut down his compulsive door-locking, he agreed that he would give himself the penalty of having at least three dates with an obnoxious and unattractive woman every time he locked his apartment door more than five times each night. Knowing that he would make himself enact this penalty, he quickly did cut down his door-locking; and, as noted above, with the use of this and other REBT methods, he was able to finally keep it to a maximum of two lockings each night.

CONCLUSION

Severe manifestations of OCD usually have both biological and learned causes and are difficult to minimize or to stop. The use of medication is often helpful but rarely works too well without simultaneous use of behavior therapy, cognitive behavior therapy, or rational emotive behavior therapy.

REBT specializes in helping clients to give themselves unconditional self-acceptance about their being afflicted with OCD, as well as to minimize their low frustration tolerance about their affliction. While helping them to ameliorate their self-downing and their LFT (their secondary symptoms) about OCD it also shows them how to use a number of its cognitive, emotive, and behavioral methods to cut down its primary symptoms of self-defeating countings, checkings, repeatings, orderings, hoardings, and other obsessive-compulsive rituals.

In some instances, especially when clients with OCD are helped to fully accept themselves with and to stop awfulizing about their ritualizing, they can quickly and dramatically improve. Usually, however, they strongly resist change, make only moderate gains, and are still prone to obsessive-compulsive and other disturbed behavior. If, however, their rational emotive behavior therapists themselves achieve unconditional self-acceptance and high frustration tolerance, they can find working with OCD clients rewarding and growth-enhancing. Try it and see!

REFERENCES

Baer, L. (1991). *Getting control: Overcoming your obsessions and compulsions.* Boston: Little, Brown.

Bernard, M. E. (Ed.). (1991). *Using rational-emotive therapy effectively: A practitioner's guide.* New York: Plenum.

Bernard, M. E. (1993). *Staying rational in an irrational world.* New York: Carol.

Bernard, M. E., & Wolfe, J. L. (Eds.). (1993). *The RET resource book for practitioners.* New York: Institute for Rational-Emotive Therapy.

Cloninger, C. R., Svrakic, D. N., & Przybek, T. R. (1994). A psychobiological model of temperament and character. *Archives of General Psychiatry, 50,* 975–990.

Dryden, W. (1994). *Progress in rational emotive behavior therapy.* London: Whurr.

Dryden, W., & DiGiuseppe, R. (1990). *A primer on rational-emotive therapy.* Champaign, IL: Research Press.

Dryden, W., & Hill, L. K. (Eds.). (1993). *Innovations in rational-emotive therapy.* Newbury Park, CA: Sage.

Ellis, A. (1962a). *The American sexual tragedy* (rev. ed.). New York: Lyle Stuart and Grove Press.

Ellis, A. (1962b). *Reason and emotion in psychotherapy.* Secaucus, NJ: Citadel.

Ellis, A. (1969). A weekend of rational encounter. *Rational Living, 4*(2), 1–8. *Reprinted in* A. Ellis & W. Dryden, *The practice of rational-emotive therapy* (pp. 180–191). New York: Springer Publishing Co., 1987.

Ellis, A. (1972). *Psychotherapy and the value of a human being.* New York: Institute for Rational-Emotive Therapy. *Reprinted in* A. Ellis & W. Dryden, *The essential Albert Ellis.* New York: Springer Publishing Co., 1990.

Ellis, A. (1973). *Humanistic psychotherapy: The rational-emotive approach.* New York: McGraw-Hill.

Ellis, A. (1976). RET abolishes most of the human ego. *Psychotherapy Theory, Research, and Practice, 13*, 343–348. Reprinted: New York: Institute for Rational-Emotive Therapy (rev. ed.), 1991.

Ellis, A. (1977). *Anger—how to live with and without it.* Secaucus, NJ: Citadel.

Ellis, A. (1985). *Overcoming resistance: Rational-emotive therapy with difficult clients.* New York: Springer Publishing Co.

Ellis, A. (1988). *How to stubbornly refuse to make yourself miserable about anything—yes, anything!* Secaucus, NJ: Lyle Stuart.

Ellis, A. (1989). *The treatment of psychotic and borderline individuals with RET.* (Orig. publication, 1965). New York: Institute for Rational-Emotive Therapy.

Ellis, A. (1991a). The revised ABCs of rational-emotive therapy. In J. Zeig (Ed.), *The evolution of psychotherapy: The second conference* (pp. 79–99). New York: Brunner/Mazel. Expanded version: *Journal of Rational-Emotive and Cognitive-Behavior Therapy, 9*, 139–172.

Ellis, A. (1991b). Using RET effectively: Reflections and interview. In M. E. Bernard (Ed.), *Using rational-emotive therapy effectively* (pp. 1–33). New York: Plenum.

Ellis, A. (1993). Vigorous RET disputing. In M. E. Bernard & J. L. Wolfe (Eds.), *The RET resource book for practitioners* (pp. II–7). New York: Institute for Rational-Emotive Therapy.

Ellis, A. (1994a). Post-traumatic stress disorder (PTSD) in rape victims: A rational emotive behavioral theory. *Journal of Rational-Emotive and Cognitive-BehaviorTherapy, 12*, 3–25.

Ellis, A. (1994b). *Reason and emotion in psychotherapy revised.* New York: Carol.

Ellis, A. (1994c). The treatment of borderline personalities with rational emotive behavior therapy. In C. R. Cloninger (Ed.), *The treatment of personality disorders.* Washington, DC: Psychiatric Press.

Ellis, A. (1994d). Rational emotive behavior therapy. In R. Corsini & D. Wedding (Eds.), *Current Psychotherapies.* Itasca, IL: Peacock.

Ellis, A., & Abrahms, E. (1978). *Brief psychotherapy in medical and health practice.* New York: Springer Publishing Co.

Ellis, A., & Abrams, M. (1994). *How to cope with a fatal disease.* New York: Barricade.

Ellis, A., Abrams, M., & Dengelegi, L. (1992). *The art and science of rational eating.* New York: Barricade.

Ellis, A., & Dryden, W. (1987). *The practice of rational-emotive therapy.* New York: Springer Publishing Co.

Ellis, A., & Grieger, R. (Eds.). (1977). *Handbook of rational-emotive therapy. Vol. 1.* New York: Springer Publishing Co.

Ellis, A., & Grieger, R. (Eds.). (1986). *Handbook of rational-emotive therapy. Vol. 2.* New York: Springer Publishing Co.

Ellis, A., & Harper, R. A. (1961). *A guide to successful marriage.* North Hollywood, CA: Wilshire.

Ellis, A., & Harper, R. A. (1975). *A new guide to rational living.* North Hollywood, CA: Wilshire.

Ellis, A., & Lange, A. (1994). *How to stop people from pushing your buttons.* New York: Carol.

Ellis, A., & Velten, E. (1992). *When AA doesn't work: Rational steps for quitting alcohol.* New York: Barricade.

Enright, S. J. (1991). Group treatment for obsessive-compulsive disorder: An evaluation. *Behavioral Psychotherapy, 19,* 189–192.

Fals-Stewart, W., & Lucente, S. (1994). Behavioral group therapy with obsessive-compulsives: An overview. *International Journal of Group Psychotherapy, 44,* 35–51.

Foa, E. B., & Wilson, R. (1991). *Stop obsessing: How to overcome your obsessions and compulsions.* New York: Bantam.

Franklin, R. (1993). *Overcoming the myth of self-worth.* Appleton, WI: Focus.

Greist, J. H. (1992). *Obsessive compulsive disorder: A guide.* Madison, WI: Obsessive-Compulsive Information Center.

Hauck, P. A. (1992). *Overcoming the rating game: Beyond self-love—beyond self-esteem.* Louisville, KY: Westminster/John Knox.

Jacobson, E. (1938). *You must relax.* New York: McGraw-Hill.

Maultsby, M. C., Jr. (1971). Systematic written homework in psychotherapy. *Psychotherapy: Theory, Research and Practice, 8,* 195–198.

Mills, D. (1993). *Overcoming self-esteem.* New York: Institute for Rational-Emotive Therapy.

Perce, J. L. (1988). Obsessive-compulsive disorder: A treatment review. *Journal of Clinical Psychiatry, 42,* 48–55.

Rapoport, J. L. (1989). *The boy who couldn't stop washing.* New York: Dutton.

Rogers, C. R. (1961). *On becoming a person.* Boston: Houghton-Mifflin.

Sichel, J., & Ellis, A. (1984). *RET self-help form.* New York: Institute for Rational-Emotive Therapy.

Steketee, G. S. (1993). *Treatment of obsessive compulsive disorder.* New York: Guilford.

Trimpey, J. (1989). *Rational recovery from alcoholism: The small book.* New York: Delacorte.

Walen, S., DiGiuseppe, R., & Dryden, W. (1992). *A practitioner's guide to rational-emotive therapy.* New York: Oxford University Press.

Wessler, R. A., & Wessler, R. L. (1980). *The principles and practice of rational-emotive therapy.* San Francisco: Jossey-Bass.

Wolpe, J. (1990). *The practice of behavior therapy* (4th ed.). Needham Heights, MA: Allyn & Bacon.

Zetin, M., & Kramer, M. (1992). Obsessive-compulsive disorder. *Hospital and Community Psychiatry, 43,* 689–699.

CHAPTER 8

Conclusion

Joseph Yankura and Windy Dryden

A CROSS THE LAST SIX CHAPTERS, this book has illustrated rational emotive behavior therapy's (REBT) effective application to a cross-section of common clinical problems. The reader should not, however, come away from this volume thinking that it represents a complete survey of REBT's clinical applications. A recent review of REBT treatment outcome research reported that this approach's effectiveness has been studied with reference to a broad range of problems, including sexual dysfunction, hypochondriasis, alcoholism, obesity, and shoplifting (Silverman, McCarthy, & McGovern, 1992).

Certain alternative therapeutic approaches can be melded with REBT to produce a highly effective hybrid therapy. For example, the chapters by Warren and Yankura (both of which deal with anxiety disorders) illustrate how REBT can readily incorporate a number of elements and techniques of general cognitive-behavior therapy. In the second casebook volume, *Special Application of REBT*, Charles Huber shows how REBT can be effectively combined with the family systems approach to treatment.

It is important, however, to underscore the fact that REBT contains a number of elements and emphases which make it distinct from other cognitive-behavioral approaches. In particular, these features include the following:

A focus on profound philosophic change. Whereas general CBT usually first focuses on helping clients to identify and correct their negatively distorted inferences, REBT quite often places an emphasis upon helping clients to achieve a profound and lasting philosophic change. It does this by:

1. Quickly moving to show clients the "musturbatory" philosophies (i.e., absolutistic demands) that underpin their emotional problems;
2. Also showing clients the absolutistic negative evaluations (e.g., awfulizing, negative person-rating, and I-can't-stand-it-itis) that derive from their musturbatory philosophies;
3. Swiftly showing clients (through a variety of means, including didactic teaching and the Socratic method) how their musts and associated derivatives are unhelpful, illogical, and unrealistic, and teaching them how these cognitions are implicated in their emotional problems;
4. Showing clients how their musturbatory philosophies (and associated derivatives) may be implicated in emotional and behavioral problems other than the ones that led them to seek treatment;
5. Quickly teaching clients how to begin independently identifying and challenging their musturbatory philosophies and absolutistic evaluations;
6. Showing clients how to apply their disputing skills to worst-case scenarios, such that they ultimately become able to minimize their upsets about very negative events that may occur in the future, as well as negative circumstances with which they are faced in the present.

A focus on secondary problems. To a greater extent than general CBT approaches, REBT emphasizes identifying and treating clients' secondary emotional problems. A secondary emotional problem constitutes "disturbance about disturbance." Thus, clients may make themselves depressed about their anxiety, ashamed about their depression, guilty about their anger, and so forth. REBT views treatment of secondary emotional problems as being quite important to the course of therapy, since their existence may make it more difficult for clients to face and overcome their primary emotional problems.

A focus on discomfort disturbance. REBT is unique in the central role it accords discomfort disturbance in the genesis and maintenance of psychological problems (Ellis, 1979a, 1980). It is noted that discomfort disturbance can effectively block clients from working hard to change within therapy (Ellis, 1986), as it is associated with low tolerance for frustration and discomfort. As such, REBT therapists are particularly focused on remediating it when it is part of the clinical picture. Some REBT therapists, in fact, have designed disputations that specifically target clients' LFT about completing difficult homework assignments (see, e.g., "The Terrorist Dispute" in Dryden & Yankura, 1992).

A preference for behavioral flooding assignments. General CBT approaches often advocate helping clients to try out new behaviors in a gradual fashion (Dryden, 1991a). REBT, on the other hand, encourages clients to swiftly and directly face the negative A's that they disturb themselves about. Such exposure provides clients with the opportunity to work at disputing their upset-producing irrational beliefs (which presumably would be triggered by the particular negative A to which they've exposed themselves), and is viewed as a means for making therapy both more efficient and effective. In addition, behavioral flooding assignments (as opposed to the graded assignments typically used in general CBT) will not inadvertently reinforce a client's philosophy of low frustration tolerance (Ellis, 1983).

A focus on fostering self-acceptance. Moreso than most CBT approaches, REBT places a distinct and specific emphasis upon helping clients to accept themselves despite the fact that they have problems, flaws, and weaknesses. Whereas many other therapies would uncritically accept and promote "increased self-esteem" as a worthwhile therapeutic goal for clients, REBT views this goal as problematic when it requires clients to develop global positive ratings of themselves. According to Dryden (1991b), a good number of therapeutic procedures "based on self-esteem notions encourage [clients] to define themselves as worthwhile or competent so long as they gain approval or succeed at valued tasks" (p. 275). Such procedures convey the implicit message that it is possible and perhaps even desirable to apply global ratings to human beings. REBT, however, takes the position that human beings defy global ratings because (a) they are amazingly complex and comprised of countless behaviors, traits, and characteristics, and (b) they are ongoing and ever-changing entities. Therefore, any global rating will fail to capture the complexity of a human being and will also neglect to account for the fact that a human being is capable of changing both positive and negative characteristics. REBT attempts to teach clients, whenever possible, how to refrain from global self-rating while still realistically evaluating their particular traits and behaviors. Clients who are able to approach the therapeutic goal of self-acceptance may be less vulnerable to future psychological disturbance after their formal therapy has ended.

An emphasis on force and vigor in effecting cognitive change. Stemming from its view that human beings are biologically predisposed to create and perpetuate disturbance-producing irrational beliefs (Ellis, 1976), REBT emphasizes the importance of applying force and vigor in the service of effecting cognitive change. This is because biologically-based tendencies will often be quite difficult to modify. Unlike most other forms of CBT, REBT contains within its therapeutic armamentarium a number of specific procedures for helping clients to challenge their irrational thinking in particularly forceful and vigorous ways. Such procedures include the use of forceful tape-recorded disputing (Ellis, 1985), rational role reversal (Kassinove & DiGiuseppe, 1975), and the judicious use of flamboyant therapist behaviors within therapy sessions (Dryden, 1991c).

It is important to note that while REBT therapists tend to favor deployment of the above approaches and emphases, they are not absolutistic about using them in their actual work with clients. On the contrary, REBT therapists attempt to make flexibility an operating principle with respect to their therapeutic endeavors. When particular clients refuse to try or fail to benefit from particular rational-emotive methods, REBT therapists will attempt to strike therapeutic compromises. Dryden (1987), for example, has noted that when attempts to help a client achieve philosophical change have been unsuccessful, REBT therapists are free to try and help the client to effect change on other levels. Thus, REBT therapists may work with their clients to help them (a) change negative activating events (such as leaving a job with a critical boss for a job where the boss is more patient and tolerant), (b) effect inferentially based change (e.g., assisting a given client to reinterpret her inference that others will stare at her if she dances at social functions), and (c) effect behaviorally based change (e.g., assisting a client fearful of rejection to develop improved conversational skills). In addition, REBT therapists will sometimes choose to engineer compromises with clients who refuse to carry out behavioral flooding homework assignments. Employing the principle of "challenging but not overwhelming" (described in Chapter 5 on Panic Disorder with Agoraphobia; see also Dryden, 1987), they will invite these clients to identify and undertake homework assignments which are not experienced as "overwhelming" (such that enactment of the assignment is avoided), but that are sufficiently challenging to discourage reinforcement of LFT philosophies.

At this point in time, numerous experimental studies have been published which support REBT's effectiveness with a variety of psychological problems.[1] Still, within the larger psychotherapeutic community, REBT currently is not regarded as the treatment of choice for any particular clinical disorders. In this sense, it lags behind the work of cognitive-behavior therapists such as Beck (see Beck, Rush, Shaw, & Emery, 1979) and Barlow (see Craske, Barlow, & O'Leary, 1992; Barlow & Craske, 1994), who have respectively developed highly regarded research programs and treatment protocols for depression and several of the anxiety disorders. To date, REBT treatment outcome research has not systematically studied REBT's application to any particular diagnostic category. In addition, the treatment outcome literature that does exist has been variously criticized for (a) employing subjects (such as college students) with subclinical problems, (b) utilizing flawed outcome measures, (c) inadequate long term follow-up on treatment effects, and (d) a lack of standard treatment protocols that would help to ensure that subjects are indeed receiving preferential (as opposed to general) REBT (Ellis, 1979b).

If REBT is to gain more recognition as an important and effective treatment for the various clinical diagnoses described in the *Diagnostic and Statistical Manual of Mental Disorders* (4th ed.) (DSM-IV; American Psychiatric Association, 1994), its numerous proponents and practitioners will have to (in a non-absolutistic sense!) make efforts at designing and implementing high-quality treatment outcome research. Such research will need to employ subjects with clinical level disorders, utilize appropriate and psychometrically sound outcome measures, include meaningful efforts at long-term follow-up on treatment effects, and employ standardized treatment protocols which will encourage treatment uniformity and allow for meaningful comparisons within and between studies.

---

[1] To date, a number of reviews of treatment outcome studies involving REBT have been published. These include DiGiuseppe and Miller (1977), McGovern and Silverman (1984), and Silverman, McCarthy, and McGovern (1992).

This last issue is of particular interest to the editors of the present volume. Currently, two excellent general REBT treatment manuals are in print. *Rational-Emotive Counselling in Action* (Dryden, 1990) describes a rather specific thirteen-step sequence for implementing REBT. *A Practitioner's Guide to Rational-Emotive Therapy* (Walen, DiGiuseppe, & Dryden, 1992), now in its second edition, more broadly describes deployment of REBT's essential elements. We advocate, however, that experienced REBT practitioners and researchers make efforts at designing comprehensive disorder-specific treatment manuals. These manuals could then serve as a basis for generating REBT treatment protocols for use in treatment outcome research. Given the variety of clinical disorders discussed in the present book, it seems quite possible that disorder-specific treatment manuals could be created for depression, obsessive-compulsive disorder, panic disorder with agoraphobia, generalized anxiety disorder, and so on. Based upon our shared clinical experience, we believe that such manuals could also be readily produced for problems such as social phobia, substance-related disorders, impulse-control disorders, adjustment disorders, and the array of personality disorders.

With respect to essential content for disorder-specific REBT treatment manuals, we recommend that the following points be covered by way of introductory material:

1. Diagnostic criteria for the particular clinical disorder that is the focus of the treatment manual, as per DSM-IV (American Psychiatric Association, 1994). Any nuances or complexities involved in the diagnosis of the disorder could be discussed in this section, as well as established diagnostic measures that may prove helpful.
2. What is currently known about the disorder, based upon review of the empirical literature.
3. Discussion of the REBT conceptualization of the disorder.
4. Brief description of alternative cognitive-behavioral approaches, with discussion of how the REBT approach differs and why. This section would especially emphasize differences between inferential disputing and REBT-style philosophical disputing.

Material detailing the application of REBT to the particular disorder would follow the sections containing introductory material. In terms of organizing material pertinent to actual disorder-specific deployment of REBT, we believe that Dryden's (1990) 13-step counseling sequence offers a useful framework. This sequence (which is described in detail in other sources) places an emphasis upon (a) defining the client's target problem; (b) working with the client to set goals in line with the problem as defined; (c) accurately assessing the A's, B's, and C's of the client's problem; (d) assessing for the presence of a secondary emotional problem; (e) teaching the B → C connection to the client; (f) disputing the client's operative irrational beliefs; (g) helping clients to construct and deepen their conviction in more helpful rational beliefs; (h) designing and following up on homework assignments of relevance to the client's problem; (i) helping the client to facilitate the "working-through" process.[2] In the sections that follow, we describe how these elements of Dryden's stepwise sequence can be combined with treatment methods distinct to REBT to structure an REBT treatment manual for a fairly common clinical problem, social phobia. According to DSM-IV (American Psychiatric Association, 1994), individuals with social phobia fear and avoid social or performance situations in which they may be subjected to negative evaluations by others.

Defining the client's target problem. Initially, the therapist will want to obtain enough information from the client to be able to make an accurate clinical diagnosis. Once the diagnosis of social phobia is made, the therapist may opt to share this information with the client. More importantly, however, the therapist would work with the client to define the target problem in terms of emotional and behavioral C's. For the client with social phobia, anxiety and avoidance behavior (with respect to particular social or performance situations) would be identified as primary target problems at C.

At this early point in therapy, it would also be highly important for the therapist to ensure that the client is focused on changing C, not A. Here, it is noted that some clients with social phobia may enter therapy with the goal of minimizing the possibility that they will be negatively evaluated by other persons. Thus, they may believe that their therapy should be primarily focused upon enhancement of their social skills. While skills training (such as assertiveness training

---

[2] For the sake of brevity, some of the 13 steps of Dryden's (1990) REBT treatment sequence have been omitted or grouped together. Step 1 ("Ask for a Problem") has been omitted, while steps 3, 4, and 7 ("Assess C," "Assess A," and "Assess iB") have been grouped together.

or training in conversational skills) can readily be integrated within REBT, the socially phobic client may need to be presented with a strong and explicit rationale for working to modify dysfunctional C's.

Setting goals in line with the problem as defined. Clients with social phobia may enter therapy with a variety of goals related to their problems with social and performance situations. Some may want to improve their ability to function in evaluative situations, such that they can facilitate their progress toward desired goals at work or at school (e.g., receive a promotion or a diploma). Others may want to become partnered, and thus may wish to remove obstacles to meeting, interacting with, and being accepted by potential mates. In any scenario, it is important for the therapist to make clear to the client the relationship between anxiety and impaired social performance. Once the client is able to see this relationship, therapist and client can collaboratively agree to work on changing the client's anxiety about social situations.

Deciding to work on changing the client's anxiety about social situations is not, however, specific enough to constitute an REBT-style therapeutic goal. Setting a meaningful therapeutic goal in REBT involves specifying the appropriate negative emotion that will ultimately replace the inappropriate negative emotion which the client currently experiences. For the client with social phobia, the therapist would attempt to obtain agreement to work on replacing *anxiety* with *rational concern* about the possibility of being negatively evaluated by others. In setting such an emotional goal, the therapist would explain to the client the distinctions between appropriate and inappropriate negative emotions, and why a feeling of rational concern is preferable to a feeling of complete calm in evaluative situations. Concern will motivate one to perform to the best of one's ability without undue emotional interference, while a state of complete calm connotes that one simply doesn't care about the quality of one's performance.

Assessing the A's, B's, and C's of the client's problem. Accurate assessment of these components of a client's problem is quite important, as the information gathered at this point in therapy will greatly influence the directions that treatment will take. In working with a socially phobic client, the REBT therapist will want to determine the specific A's that tend to trigger the particular client's irrational beliefs. Typically, for the individual with social phobia, these A's will take the form of negative inferences such as the following: "I am performing (or will perform) poorly in [a particular social or performance situation], and others are judging (or will judge) me negatively for it." In addition to assessing that this sort of negative inference is implicated in the client's problems, the REBT therapist will also work to identify the particular social or performance situations in which the inference comes into play. Common situations within which socially phobic clients may experience anxiety include making conversation at social gatherings, dancing at social functions such as weddings, eating in public, waiting in line in stores, and public speaking situations. An REBT treatment manual for social phobia could usefully provide a "catalogue" of the sorts of situations that socially phobic individuals often make themselves anxious about, as well as providing a review of common variations on the inferential theme outlined above.

In alternative approaches to cognitive-behavior therapy, the therapist would likely focus initial cognitive-restructuring interventions on showing the client how the negative inference described above involves cognitive errors such as "mind-reading" and "fortune-telling" (Burns, 1980). The REBT therapist, however, would refrain from challenging the client's negative inferences in favor of assessing (and later disputing) the client's operative irrational beliefs. It is, in fact, standard practice for REBT therapists to accept (at least temporarily) clients' descriptions of A as if these descriptions were accurate portrayals of reality (Dryden, 1990).

Given the nature of the socially phobic client's problems, the REBT therapist would be able to rather quickly begin forming hypotheses about the nature of the client's operative irrational beliefs. The REBT therapist assumes, a priori, that the client's anxiety stems from absolutistic demands and evaluations that the client brings to bear upon various social and performance situations. The therapist can choose from a variety of assessment procedures (including imagery techniques and the skillful use of questions) to determine the specific form of the client's irrational beliefs. Within a treatment manual for social phobia, these assessment procedures would be fully described and irrational beliefs common to social phobia could be listed.

With respect to identifying the client's relevant C's, the therapist already knows (given the client's DSM-IV diagnosis) that anxiety specific to various social situations is a prominent emotional C. Therefore, the therapist will want to devote time to specifying the client's behavioral C's. For socially phobic clients, these behavioral

C's will often take the form of avoidance or "warding off" behaviors. Avoidance behavior consists of a variety of strategies which the client utilizes to completely avoid or minimize exposure to particular situations in which negative evaluations by others are a possibility. Some avoidance strategies can be quite subtle in nature and will not always be immediately obvious to the therapist (as in the case of the client who consistently arrives five minutes late for sessions in order to avoid sitting in the clinic's waiting area with other people); as such, a treatment manual would contain information on how to effectively assess for the presence of such subtle strategies. "Warding off" behaviors refer to client attempts to minimize the likelihood of being judged negatively by others, as with clients who compulsively over-prepare for a public speaking situation or who "rehearse" in advance the conversational topics they will speak about at an upcoming party. Information gathered by the therapist about the client's A's and C's will ultimately be used in the design of homework activities for helping the client to challenge and change operative irrational beliefs.

Assessing for a secondary emotional problem. As noted above in the previous discussion on REBT's unique aspects, REBT places an emphasis upon identifying and remediating clients' secondary emotional problems. With respect to secondary problems, individuals with social phobia may be especially prone to experience shame about their social anxiety. The REBT therapist would be alert to this possibility, as feelings of shame may interfere significantly with the therapeutic process. If, for example, the client is ashamed of having social phobia, he or she may be less likely to be fully disclosing with the therapist within therapy sessions. In addition, the client who feels ashamed may avoid homework assignments that involve exposure to social situations within which other people may "see" that they're anxious.

A REBT manual for treating social phobia would provide details on the particular types of secondary emotional problems that socially phobic clients may tend to experience, and would outline procedures for dealing with such problems. General procedures for dealing with clients' secondary problems have been outlined in a number of REBT sources currently in print (see, e.g., Dryden, 1990; Dryden & Yankura, 1993; and Walen, DiGiuseppe, & Dryden, 1992). We would note that it is also quite possible for a client with social phobia to develop a *tertiary* emotional problem about the fact that they are ashamed of their anxiety. This third level of emotional disturbance would result when clients subscribe to the following sort of irrational belief: "I shouldn't be so ashamed of the fact that I experience social anxiety; the fact that I am only proves what an emotionally weak and helpless person I really am!"

Teaching the B → C connection. Before the therapist proceeds to disputing the client's irrational beliefs, it is quite important to be sure that the client understands the B → C connection. If the therapist begins disputing interventions without teaching this connection, the client may experience confusion and believe that the therapist is being argumentative and nonsupportive.

The B → C connection can be taught directly with reference to the particular client's emotional and behavioral problems; it can be also be conveyed via a variety of specially designed metaphors and analogies. Ellis, for example, often uses his famous "Money in Your Pocket" metaphor for showing clients the relationship between beliefs and feelings (see Yankura & Dryden, 1990, for a description of this metaphor). Techniques and teaching devices of particular relevance for socially anxious clients could be included in an REBT treatment manual for social phobia.

Disputing irrational beliefs. Once the therapist has assessed operative irrational beliefs and has explained the B → C connection to the client, it can be appropriate to begin disputing interventions. Initially, the goal of such interventions is to help the client see, at least on an intellectual level, that his or her irrational beliefs are illogical, unhelpful, and inconsistent with reality (Dryden, 1990). A treatment manual for social phobia would include information on deploying disputes that have demonstrated (through clinical experience) effectiveness in helping clients to surrender the irrational beliefs that underpin their social anxiety.

Because socially phobic clients will usually have irrational beliefs centered around the possibility of being judged negatively by other people, effective disputes will target these sorts of beliefs in a specific and vivid manner. As an example of a dispute that may have particular relevance for a socially phobic client who fears negative evaluations by others, the therapist may bring in to the session a reproduction of a painting by a famous artist. Ideally, this painting would be of the sort that has tended to elicit widely varying reactions from art critics. The therapist describes the various reviews, both positive and negative, that the painting has received, and uses it as a vehicle for demonstrating the points that (a) people's opinions are influenced by their own prejudices, and are not absolute judgments as to whether the object of criticism (even if the "object" is another human being) is "worthwhile" or "worthless," and (b) the object of criticism (particularly when the object is a human being) is too complex to be assigned a simplistic "good" or "bad" rating. This type of disputing intervention may help some clients to de-awfulize about the prospect of being negatively evaluated, and may help them to see that they can keep the opinions of others in a reasonable perspective.

Helping clients to construct and develop conviction in more rational beliefs. DiGiuseppe (1991) has pointed out that it is advisable to take explicit steps to help clients construct rational beliefs with which to replace their unhelpful, irrational ones. This view is based on the observation that people will tend to cling to old ways of thinking (even if those ways are contributing to dysfunctional consequences) if a plausible, alternative way of thinking is unavailable to them. The process of helping the client to construct alternative rational beliefs can often be initiated with a well-timed question: "If it is indeed unhelpful and unrealistic for you to think that being rejected by another person is absolutely awful, how then could you think about rejection experiences that would be both more realistic and helpful to you?"

After working with a client to construct a set of more rational beliefs, the therapist would next want to point out to the client that mere *knowledge* of these beliefs (sometimes referred to as *intellectual insight*) is insufficient to produce meaningful and lasting therapeutic change. At this point, the therapist would emphasize to the client that increased conviction in rational beliefs will come about through regular practice in (a) disputing irrational beliefs, and (b) replacing irrational beliefs with rational beliefs in the face of negative activating events. The stage is now set for the therapist to describe to the client the critical role that homework assignments play in the change process. Since relevant homework assignments for a socially phobic client will involve exposure to social and evaluative situations that are typically avoided, the therapist will want to be sure to provide the client with a cogent rationale for such assignments. Here, it would also be helpful for the therapist to stress that meaningful change will usually entail some degree of discomfort on the client's part. For some clients, a useful metaphor is to compare the process of enacting difficult homework assignments to the process of improving one's physique through weight-training: the operating principle is "no pain, no gain."

Designing and checking on homework assignments. Information gained through prior thorough assessment of the client's A's, B's and C's will prove very helpful in the design of relevant homework assignments for the client with social phobia. Often, such assignments will include the following basic components: (a) identification of a social or evaluative situation that is typically avoided; (b) specifying the manner in which the client will expose him or herself to this situation (i.e., determining when and for how long the exposure will occur); (c) instructions to resist engaging in avoidance or escape behavior with reference to the targeted social situation; (d) instructions concerning the manner in which the client is to dispute operative irrational beliefs and work at replacing them with more rational ones. It is important for therapists to adopt a collaborative stance when designing homework assignments with clients, as this will help to ensure that a homework assignment is identified that the client (a) sees the sense in doing, and (b) believes he or she can carry out.

When therapeutically appropriate, REBT therapists will encourage their clients to take on behavioral flooding assignments. As discussed above, such assignments (when compared with assignments involving more gradual exposure) are viewed as helping to make therapy more efficient. Behavioral flooding assignments are of particular relevance for socially phobic clients, as it is likely that they will make swifter progress in overcoming their social anxiety when they engage in full and prolonged exposure to the situations they typically avoid. Some socially phobic clients, however, will resist the notion of directly exposing themselves to these situations. Often, this is because they subscribe to the following sort of irrational belief: "I must avoid situations in which I experience anxiety, because I absolutely can't tolerate feeling such emotional discomfort!" Under such circumstances, it is usually advisable for the REBT therapist to work collaboratively with the client and target this unhelpful belief for change. In some instances, this intervention will result in the client becoming more willing to undertake a behavioral flooding assignment. If, however, this does not occur, the therapist has the option of encouraging the client to undertake an assignment that is "challenging but not overwhelming" (Dryden, 1987). This involves taking a somewhat more gradual approach to exposure activities; however, the client is still prompted to choose an assignment that is to some extent challenging insofar as it entails some degree of emotional discomfort. For clients who refuse to attempt any type of *in vivo* exposure activity, the therapist can use imagery techniques wherein the client disputes operative irrational beliefs while vividly imagining an anxiety-provoking social situation. It is sometimes the case that clients will become amenable to taking on more difficult exposure assignments after experiencing success with "lower-level" exposure activities.

It is, of course, quite important for therapists to follow up on clients' progress with homework assignments. By following up on homework assignments, therapists are able to (a) communicate to clients that these assignments are indeed an integral part of therapy, (b) determine if clients are experiencing any success in changing their irrational beliefs, (c) identify any obstacles to homework completion and engage in collaborative troubleshooting with the client, and (d) reinforce clients for any meaningful attempts to complete a given homework activity. With clients who have social phobia, therapists will want to be alert to the possibility of their completing exposure assignments in potentially unhelpful ways (e.g., the client who enables himself to eat in public by engaging in cognitive distraction rather than by disputing his irrational beliefs). Careful questioning can help the therapist to determine if the client actually faced a negative A while concurrently challenging his or her irrational beliefs.

Facilitating the working-through process. If clients are to attain lasting therapeutic change, they need to continually and vigorously work at challenging and replacing their irrational beliefs while facing their negative activating events. Such efforts help clients to continue weakening their conviction in their irrational beliefs while strengthening their conviction in their rational beliefs. This is called the working-through process, the goal of which is to have clients integrate their rational beliefs within their emotional and behavioral repertoires. When such integration is accomplished, clients are more easily and naturally able to think rationally about negative activating events that previously triggered their irrational beliefs. According to Dryden (1990), REBT therapists can facilitate the working-through process with their clients by (a) suggesting different homework assignments to change the same irrational belief; (b) teaching about the non-linear model of change, such that clients are prepared in advance to deal with backsliding; and (c) encouraging them to become their own therapists. This last component of the working-through process requires clients to take on an increasing amount of responsibility for designing and implementing homework assignments for modifying their unhelpful belief system. Clients who achieve this will be better able to function independently without the assistance of their therapist after formal therapy has ended.

For clients with social phobia, the working-through process will focus to a large extent on constructing homework assignments that will assist them in challenging their basic musts about anxiety, approval, and rejection in a variety of contexts. Thus, if earlier phases of therapy have focused primarily on helping a given client to minimize her anxiety about receiving performance evaluations on her job and engaging in conversation at social gatherings, the later part of therapy can be focused on teaching her (a) to recognize other situations in which her anxiety-producing irrational beliefs come into play, and (b) how to design homework activities that will help her to change her irrational beliefs with reference to these additional situations. At this point in therapy, the REBT therapist would gradually reduce his or her level of directive activity during sessions, and would make greater use of questions intended to prompt the client to engage in independent thinking. If the client appeared to experience anxiety about the prospect of functioning as her own therapist, efforts would be made to uncover and challenge the irrational beliefs behind this anxiety.

The design and publication of disorder-specific REBT treatment manuals may well represent an important step in facilitating and improving the quality of REBT treatment outcome research. In addition, for the general practitioner of REBT, such manuals would eliminate much of the "guesswork" involved in treating particular disorders. The more broadly based REBT manuals currently in print are quite excellent for teaching therapists the fundamental principles and techniques of this approach to therapy; they do not, however, provide much information on how to deal (as per the REBT model) with the nuances and complexities of specific clinical problems. This knowledge is certainly available within the neuronal pathways of many experienced rational emotive behavior therapists—we hope that some of them are intrigued by the challenge of codifying and disseminating the clinical lore they have accumulated!

REFERENCES

American Psychiatric Association. (1994). *Diagnostic and statistical manual of mental disorders* (4th ed.). Washington, DC: Author.

Barlow, D. H., & Craske, M. G. (1994). *Mastery of your anxiety and panic II.* Albany, NY: Graywind.

Beck, A. T., Rush, A., Shaw, B. F., & Emery, G. (1979). *Cognitive therapy of depression,* New York: Guilford.

Burns, D. D. (1980). *Feeling good: The new mood therapy.* New York: William Morrow.

Craske, M. G., Barlow, D. H., & O'Leary, T. (1992). *Mastery of your anxiety and worry.* Albany, NY: Graywind.

DiGiuseppe, R. (1991). Comprehensive cognitive disputing in RET. In M. E. Bernard (Ed.), *Using rational-emotive therapy effectively: A practitioner's guide* (pp. 173–195). New York: Plenum.

DiGiuseppe, R., & Miller, N. J. (1977). A review of outcome studies on rational-emotive therapy. In A. Ellis & R. Grieger (Eds.), *Handbook of rational-emotive therapy* (pp. 72–95). New York: Springer Publishing Co.

Dryden, W. (1987). Compromises in rational-emotive therapy. In W. Dryden (Ed.), *Current issues in rational-emotive therapy* (pp. 72–87). London: Croom Helm.

Dryden, W. (1990). *Rational-emotive counselling in action.* London: Sage.

Dryden, W. (1991a). Rational-emotive therapy and cognitive therapy: A critical comparison. In W. Dryden (Ed.), *Reason and therapeutic change* (pp. 246–259). London: Whurr.

Dryden, W. (1991b). Rational-emotive therapy and eclecticism. In W. Dryden (Ed.), *Reason and therapeutic change* (pp. 272–279). London: Whurr.

Dryden, W. (1991c). Vivid methods in rational-emotive therapy. In W. Dryden (Ed.), *Reason and therapeutic change* (pp. 153–177). London: Whurr.

Dryden, W., & Yankura, J. (1992). *Daring to be myself: A case study in rational-emotive therapy.* Buckingham: Open University Press.

Dryden, W., & Yankura, J. (1993). *Counselling individuals: A rational-emotive handbook* (2nd ed.). London: Whurr.

Ellis, A. (1976). The biological basis of human irrationality. *Journal of Individual Psychology, 32,* 145–168.

Ellis, A. (1979a). Discomfort anxiety: A new cognitive-behavioral construct. Part 1. *Rational Living, 14*(2), 3–8.

Ellis, A. (1979b). Rejoinder: Elegant and inelegant RET. In A. Ellis & J. M. Whiteley (Eds.), *Theoretical and empirical foundations of rational-emotive therapy* (pp. 240–267). Monterey, CA: Brooks/Cole.

Ellis, A. (1980). Discomfort anxiety: A new cognitive-behavioral construct. Part 2. *Rational Living, 15*(1), 25–30.

Ellis, A. (1983). The philosophic implications and dangers of some popular behavior therapy techniques. In M. Rosenbaum, C. M. Franks, & Y. Jaffe (Eds.), *Perspectives on behavior therapy in the eighties* (pp. 138–151). New York: Springer Publishing Co.

Ellis, A. (1985). *Overcoming resistance: Rational-emotive therapy with difficult clients.* New York: Springer Publishing Co.

Ellis, A. (1986). Rational-emotive therapy approaches to overcoming resistance. In A. Ellis & R. M. Grieger (Eds.), *Handbook of rational-emotive therapy, Vol. 2* (pp. 221–245). New York: Springer Publishing Co.

Kassinove, H., & DiGiuseppe, R. (1975). *Rational role reversal. Rational Living, 10*(1), 44–45.

McGovern, T., & Silverman, M. (1984). A review of outcome studies on rational-emotive therapy. *Journal of Rational-Emotive Therapy, 2,* 7–18.

Silverman, M. S., McCarthy, M., & McGovern, T. (1992). A review of outcome studies of rational-emotive therapy from 1982–1989. *Journal of Rational-Emotive and Cognitive-Behavior Therapy, 10*(3), 111–186.

Walen, S. R., DiGiuseppe, R., & Dryden, W. (1992). *A practitioner's guide to rational-emotive therapy* (2nd ed.). New York: Oxford University Press.

Yankura, J., & Dryden, W. (1990). *Doing RET: Albert Ellis in action.* New York: Springer Publishing Co.

Index

Index

The Practice of
Rational Emotive Behavior Therapy
Second Edition
Albert Ellis, PhD, and Windy Dryden, PhD

This volume systematically reviews the practice of Rational Emotive Behavior Therapy and shows how it can be used by therapists in a variety of clinical settings. The book begins with an explanation of REBT as a general treatment model. It then addresses different treatment modalities, including individual, couple, family, and sex therapy.

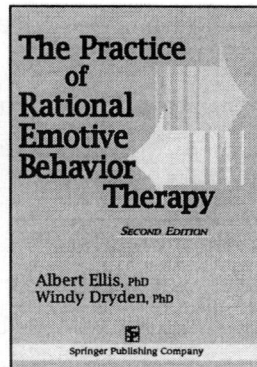

The Practice
of
Rational
Emotive
Behavior
Therapy
SECOND EDITION

Albert Ellis, PhD
Windy Dryden, PhD

Springer Publishing Company

The new edition modernizes the pioneering theories of Albert Ellis and contains a complete updating of references over the past ten years. The authors have added new information on teaching the principles of unconditional self-acceptance in a structured, group setting. With extensive use of actual case examples to illustrate each of the different settings, this volume will appeal to clinical and counseling psychologists as well as any other helping professionals involved in therapy.

Contents:

1997   280pp   0-8261-5471-9   hardcover

536 Broadway, New York, NY 10012-3955 • (212) 431-4370 • Fax (212) 941-7842

⑤ *Springer Publishing Company*

Brief But Comprehensive Psychotherapy
The Multimodal Way

Arnold A. Lazarus, PhD, ABPP

The current healthcare environment has created a need for short-term, time-limited, cost-effective and brief forms of psychotherapy, emphasizing efficiency and efficacy. The central message is "don't waste time." But how can one be brief and also comprehensive?

In his latest addition to the psychotherapy literature, the prestigious Arnold Lazarus modernizes his eclectic and goal-oriented approach to psychotherapy. Dr. Lazarus employs and transcends customary methods of diagnosis and treatment by providing several distinctive assessment procedures and therapeutic recommendations.

Using his traditional acronym — BASIC ID — he stresses the assessment of seven dimensions of a client's personality: behavior, affect, sensation, imagery, cognition, interpersonal relationships, and the need for drugs. This volume contains many ideas that will augment and enhance the skills and clinical repertoires of every therapist.

Contents:

Let's Cut to the Chase? • Elucidating the Main Rationale • What is the Multimodal Way? • Theories and Techniques • Assessment Procedures Employed Only by Multimodal Therapists (Part One: Bridging and Tracking) • Assessment Procedures Employed Only by Multimodal Therapists (Part Two: Second-Order Basic ID and Structural Profiles) • Some Elements of Effective Brevity • Activity and Serendipity • Two Specific Applications: Problems of Sexual Desire and the Treatment of Dysthymia • Couples Therapy • Some Common Time Wasters

Springer Series on Behavior Therapy and Behavioral Medicine
1997   196 pp   0-8261-9640-3   hardcover

536 Broadway, New York, NY 10012-3955 • (212) 431-4370 • Fax (212) 941-7842

$P *Springer Publishing Company*

Stress Counseling
A Rational Emotive Behavior Approach

Albert Ellis, Jack Gordon, Michael Neenan, and **Stephen Palmer**

This book is a comprehensive study of the theory and practice of the Rational Emotive Behavior Therapy approach applied to counseling and psychotherapy with patients coping with stress. The distinguished authors provide case studies and client examples and client exercises to assist clinicians in both individual and group therapy.

Recognizing that their clearly laid out programs may need to be altered for specific clients, further information is provided on occupational stress, crisis intervention, brief psychotherapy situations, and difficult clients. With extensive appendices and resource lists, and material on techniques such as skills training, relaxation methods, hypnosis and biofeedback, this book is appropriate for practitioners, educators and trainees in clinical and occupational settings.

Contents:
- Stress: A REBT Perspective
- Assessment in REBT
- The Beginning Stage of Stress Counseling
- The Middle Stage of Stress Counseling
- The Ending Stage of Stress Counseling
- Additional Techniques for Stress Counseling With REBT
- Brief Psychotherapy with Crisis Intervention in REBT
- How to Deal With Difficult Clients
- Occupational Stress and Group Work
- Afterword: Training in REBT

1997   200pp   0-8261-1163-7   softcover

536 Broadway, New York, NY 10012-3955 • (212) 431-4370 • Fax (212) 941-7842

$ Springer Publishing Company

The Essential Albert Ellis
Seminal Writings on Psychotherapy
Windy Dryden, PhD, Editor

This insightful new book gathers a selection of Ellis' most important writings in one concise resource. The text includes an introduction providing a brief review of the development of Ellis' thought, and serves to place the successive articles in context. The Essential Albert Ellis is therefore both a convenient reference for knowledgeable professionals and a helpful guide for students.

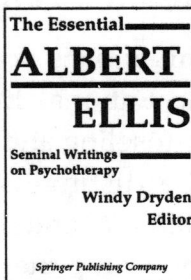

The Essential
**ALBERT
ELLIS**
Seminal Writings
on Psychotherapy
Windy Dryden
Editor

Springer Publishing Company

Partial Contents:

- The General Theory of Rational-Emotive Therapy (RET)
- Toward a Theory of Personality
- The Biological Basis of Human Irrationality
- Psychotherapy and the Value of a Human Being
- Discomfort Anxiety:
  A New Cognitive-Behavioral Construct
- Is RET "Rationalist" of "Constructivist"
- The Basic Practice of RET
- Intimacy in RET
- The Use of Rational Humorous Songs in Psychotherapy
- The Issue of Force and Energy in Behavioral Change
- The Value of Efficiency in Psychotherapy
- Failures in Rational-Emotive Therapy
- Rational-Emotive Therapy Approaches to
  Overcoming Resistance
- How to Deal with Your Most Difficult Client —You

1990   336pp   0-8261-6940-6   hardcover

536 Broadway, New York, NY 10012-3955 • (212) 431-4370 • Fax (212) 941-7842